EDUCATION
AND THE CITY

EDUCATION AND THE CITY
Theory, history and contemporary practice

Edited by
Gerald Grace

Routledge & Kegan Paul
London, Boston, Melbourne and Henley

*First published in 1984
by Routledge & Kegan Paul plc*
39 Store Street, London WC1E 7DD, England
9 Park Street, Boston, Mass. 02108, USA
*464 St Kilda Road, Melbourne,
Victoria 3004, Australia and*
*Broadway House, Newtown Road
Henley-on-Thames, Oxon RG9 1EN, England*

*Set in Press Roman
by Cambrian Typesetters, Aldershot
and printed in Great Britain
by The Thetford Press Ltd
Thetford, Norfolk*

© *Routledge & Kegan Paul 1984*

*No part of this book may be reproduced in
any form without permission from the publisher,
except for the quotation of brief passages
in criticism*

Library of Congress Cataloging in Publication Data
Education and the city.
Includes bibliographies and index.
1. Education, Urban—Addresses, essays, lectures.
2. Educational sociology—Addresses, essays, lectures.
3. Education, Urban—History—Addresses, essays, lectures.
4. Education, Urban—Great Britain—Addresses, essays,
lectures. 5. Education, Urban—United States—Addresses,
essays, lectures. I. Grace, Gerald Rupert.
LC5115.E38   1984   370.19'348   83-22983
British Library CIP data available
ISBN 0-7100-9918-5

Contents

Notes on contributors vii
Foreword
  A.H. Halsey ix
Preface xi
Acknowledgments xiv

Part I: The study of the urban

1 Urban education: policy science or critical scholarship?
   Gerald Grace /3
2 Urban education and the current crisis
   Rachel Sharp /60
3 Theorising the urban: some approaches for students of education
   Gerald Grace /94

Part II: Historical location

4 Reconstructing the history of urban education in America
   Sol Cohen /115
5 The university settlements, class relations and the city
   Tony Evans /139
6 The urban, the domestic and education for girls
   Mica Nava /159

Part III: Contemporary policy and practice

7 Policy for schools in inner London
  Frances Morrell / 195
8 Education in New York City: public schools for whom?
  Dale Mann / 210
9 Contradictions and constraints in an inner city infant school
  Jan Lee / 234
10 Teachers for the inner city: change and continuity
  Christopher Cook / 269

Index of names 292
Index of subjects 298

Notes on contributors

A.H. Halsey is Professor of Social and Administrative Studies in the University of Oxford and Fellow of Nuffield College.
Gerald Grace is Lecturer in Education in the University of Cambridge and Fellow of Wolfson College.
Rachel Sharp is Lecturer in Education in the School of Education, Macquarie University, New South Wales.
Sol Cohen is Professor of Education in the Graduate School of Education, University of California, Los Angeles.
Tony Evans is Coordinator for the Greenwich and Lewisham Catholic Schools Consortium (ILEA).
Mica Nava teaches sociology of education at Homerton College, Cambridge.
Frances Morrell is the Leader of the Inner London Education Authority.
Dale Mann is Professor and Chairman of the Department of Educational Administration, Teachers College, Columbia University.
Jan Lee is Research Officer at the Centre for Educational Research and Development, University of Lancaster.
Christopher Cook is Senior Lecturer in the Department of Teaching Studies, Polytechnic of North London.

Foreword

The commonplace that the city, citizens and civilisation have literally a common root often seems ironic to those who teach in inner city schools. Yet both human evolution out of barbarism and the harsh struggle against the return to it are integral to the challenge and the explanation of urban education. To understand the nature of urban schooling is as urgent and difficult now as it ever was. Dr Grace in this book makes a further contribution to answering the challenge and supplying the explanation.

In one sense the British teachers and would-be teachers who will read this collection may initially ask, why 'education and the city', with the implication that the vast majority of schools are urban because Britain is virtually totally urbanised. True, of course: but true, too, that the problems of the city school are the major ones and the emergent problems of schools in general. The point and focus of this collection of essays is to show on the one hand that understanding the contemporary urban school requires appreciation of its history, and on the other hand that complete understanding ultimately requires us to put the school and its history in the context of a theory of society.

Dr Grace himself argues these twin themes in his Introduction and in Chapter 3. He sets out, in other words, an ambitious programme for students of education which, fully realised, would transform both the theory and the practice of modern education. The other chapters are chosen to illustrate the themes by essays on the theory and the history of urban education in Britain and America.

However, they can only begin to do so, not only because of the limitations of a single volume (and a second is promised) but because this field of study is still surprisingly undeveloped. There are, of course, classical sources, for example in Max Weber's *The City*, or Emile Durkheim's *Evolution Pédagogique en France*, or in the Chicago School of urban sociology. But more recently the most vigorous thrust towards a general theory of society applied or readily applicable to urban education has unquestionably come from Marxism. Dr Grace relies heavily on the writings of Harvey and Castells. In doing so he reflects the state of the literature.

Nevertheless, the theoretical problems raised and the empirical study invited by Dr Grace take us beyond, as well as question, the validity of the strong claims on the field made by recent Marxist writing. For example, their interpretation of social control in the urban schools of Western Europe and America as contradictions of capitalism cannot be adequately judged without comparative study of urbanisation and schooling in communist countries and in the Third World.

This volume, then, is more an invitation to further work than a conclusive sociology of urban education. Meanwhile, however, it offers much insight into the sociology of the city school in Western capitalist countries. And it does so through a determination to analyse the present in the context of seriously researched history and through an equal determination to set the school in the context of the wider social structure of class, ethnicity, bureaucracy, and the state. The definition is surely correct even though it makes embarrassingly clear the shortcomings of current educational theory and empirical study. The need for further work is imperative. What is ultimately at stake is civil society.

A.H. Halsey
Oxford
May 1983

Preface

When Kay-Shuttleworth asked in 1862 whether the preparation of elementary schoolteachers in Britain would render them 'capable of contending with the greater difficulties of town schools', he was making an early statement of the urban education problem. That town schools presented greater difficulties than those in other locations was a commonplace to the providers of mass schooling both in Britain and America. Why this was so and what might be done about it were founding preoccupations both for social inquiry and for educational policy and practice.

The literature of urban education as a field of study represents the institutionalised forms in which contemporary engagement with such questions continues. These institutionalised forms are however failing to develop a coherent and integrated approach to the issues of urban schooling. Among the reasons for this it is clear that strong internal classification of knowledge and sectional or ideological response to other theoretical positions are central. Some writers, following Bernstein's[1] premise that 'alive in the context, contents and institutional embodiment of education is the distribution of power and the principles of social control', have directed their analysis towards the social, economic and political structures which shape the difficulties of urban schooling. Where such work has penetrated the internal boundaries of urban education study it has often been accused of being 'negative'; of undermining the morale of teachers; of being political rather than professional and of indulging itself in unhelpful grand theory. Other writers, who have scrutinised the origins and historical development of mass urban schooling both in Britain and America in the belief that such activity will illuminate principles of change and continuity in contemporary urban schooling, have been charged with academic irrelevance in the face of pressing current problems. On the other hand, those who have engaged with the close detail of policy and practice in urban education abstracted from wider issues have laid themselves open to the charge of producing naive school-centred solutions with no sense of the structural, the political and the historical as constraints.

As in the sociology of education, so in urban education these internal boundaries and their associated ideological struggles mark a stage in the growth towards critical scholarship. Critical scholarship attempts to bring these various elements into some sort of intellectual relation or at least dialogue. This is not mere eclecticism. It is the recognition that it is unhelpful for understanding (of say the problems of urban schooling) if urban historians talk only to other historians; if urban structuralists talk only to other structuralists; if urban policy makers talk only to other policy makers and if those engaged in empirical research in urban contexts talk only to other researchers. Critical scholarship requires, among other things, that the formulations of the structuralists should be interrogated by the work of historians and empirical researchers. On the other hand it also requires that empirical researchers and policy makers should be challenged by the work of structuralist analysts.

The problem is, how is this to be done? It is here that collections of original papers have an important role to play. Ideally, contributors representing a range of theoretical and ideological positions would have an opportunity to read each other's papers in advance and thus be encouraged to enter into the dialogue described. In practice, constraints of production and time make this difficult to achieve and therefore collections often have to stand as the beginning of a dialogue rather than as a realisation of it. It has to be admitted that this is the case here. While all the contributors share a concern about understanding the difficulties of urban schooling, their perspectives illuminate different features of this understanding and there has not been much opportunity for internal dialogue within the text. The text however begins the process both among the contributors themselves and among those who read it. It is hoped that teachers, students, practitioners and policy makers in urban education will find here in the contributions from theory, from history and from contemporary practice at least a basis for the development of critical scholarship and critical insight.

Note

1 B. Bernstein (1977), *Class, Codes and Control: Towards a Theory of Educational Transmissions*, London, Routledge & Kegan Paul (second edition), page 160.

Acknowledgments

This project was conceived while I was Tutor to the MA (Urban Education) course at King's College, University of London. Its appearance is the result of encouragement and support for the idea which I received from June Grace, from students on the course and from Professor A.H. Halsey as its chief examiner. Without their support it would not have appeared.

My own intellectual debts will be obvious to the reader. Chapter 1 owes much to the writings of C. Wright Mills and to the fruitful mediations and extensions of Mills's work provided by Michael F.D. Young. Chapter 3 has been significantly influenced by the writings of David Harvey and of Manuel Castells.

Valuable assistance has come from Basil Bernstein who has given me once again the benefit of his critical insights, and from Professor Paul Hirst who in a reading of an early draft helped me to clarify what I wanted to say.

Discussion with my colleagues John Furlong, John Ahier, Michael Flude and Jan Hardy on various approaches to urban education study has greatly assisted the work, without any of them necessarily approving what has been written here.

In thanking all the contributors (most of whom met the deadline!), I am particularly grateful to Frances Morrell who accepted an invitation to write at a late stage and was able to carry this through in the face of pressing political commitments.

Anne Ketteridge has patiently typed endless drafts and author's amendments and in thanking her I am uncomfortably aware that exploitation is not only a phenomenon of the inner city.

Part I

The study of the urban

1
Urban education: policy science or critical scholarship?
Gerald Grace

If the argument of the urban sociologist Ray Pahl (1975) is accepted, that metropolitan cities in all societies provide a crucial arena for the making visible of fundamental social, economic, cultural and political relations and conflicts, then the potential value of a field of study concerned with urban education would appear to be high. Urban education, conceived of as the investigation of such relations and conflicts as they impinge upon and are exemplified in metropolitan education systems, could be intellectually and practically fruitful. On the other hand, if urban education continues to justify Raynor's description of it (in Raynor and Barnes 1978: p. 3) as 'a loose collection of disparate topics gathered under one heading, lacking in definition and therefore susceptible to whim, current concern or the crisis of the moment', then it will be a mystification and a diversion.

It is in the hope of advancing the former cause and of resisting the latter that this paper is written. It has two purposes. The first is to provide some epistemological location for the existing field of urban education by placing it in its theoretical and historical context. The intention here is to trace the origins of urban education study in the USA in the 1960s, to examine the nature of the researches and publications developed subsequently in this field and to consider the ways in which such researches and publications have influenced the development of urban education study in Britain from the early 1970s. The second purpose is to offer a critique of the study of urban education as it currently exists and to suggest a possible reformulation of its theory and its practice.

Urban education studies in America

Urban education as a 'topic of inquiry'[1] or as a discrete area of study began to take significant institutional form in the USA in the 1960s and early 1970s. Among the first courses were those directed by Robert J. Havighurst at Chicago University in 1960. Havighurst, originally a science educator, then psychologist and sociologist of education, became one of the founding fathers of the subject.[2] Commissioned by the Chicago Board of Education to make an appraisal of the problems confronting the city's schools, his reputation was first established by the subsequent report *The Public Schools of Chicago* (1964). By 1965, he was Director of the new Center for the Study of Metropolitan Problems in Education at the University of Missouri and in 1967 occupied the new chair in urban education at Fordham University in New York City. His publications, *Education in Metropolitan Areas* (1966) and *Metropolitanism: Its Challenge to Education* (1968) provided an important focus for the growing interest in urban affairs among educationists and policy makers.[3]

At the same time, other developments were taking place. At Teachers College, Columbia University, New York, a co-ordinating committee for work in urban education had been established in 1966 under the chairmanship of A.H. Passow. Teachers College and Teachers College Press played an important part in the early institutionalisation and dissemination of urban education study. In 1962, supported by a grant from the Ford Foundation, a Work Conference on Curriculum and Teaching in Depressed Urban Areas had been organised at the college. This resulted in the publication of a reader, *Education in Depressed Areas* (1963), which became a widely used text. Further annual conferences and published collections of papers consolidated the field with texts such as *Education of the Disadvantaged* (1967), *Developing Programs for the Educationally Disadvantaged* (1968) and *Reaching the Disadvantaged Learner* (1970). The appearance of specialist journals in the form of *Urban Education* (1964) and *Education and Urban Society* (1968) marked a further stage in the institutionalisation process, as did the appearance of social foundations courses in urban education in many teacher colleges and universities.[4] By this time, interest in education and the urban question was widely shared among educationists, administrators, policy makers and government departments in America. In 1969 the Secretary of the Department of Health, Education and Welfare announced the formation of a

Urban education: policy science or critical scholarship? / 5

number of task forces to assist him in long-range planning, budgeting and legislative process. An Urban Education Task Force was established to assist in 'finding solutions for the educational crisis in the urban areas of the nation' and to produce 'recommendations for steps that could be taken by the Administration to deal effectively with the crisis', (Riles 1970: p. 351). The Urban Education Task Force Report was published in 1970, and this substantial document with its analysis of the 'urban education problem' and its suggestions for action and policy became a focus for academic and political discussion and debate. By 1972 it was possible for the editors of a collection of papers in honour of R.J. Havighurst to remark that it was becoming difficult for an educationist to keep up with the amount and range of disciplinary work in urban education.[5]

Urban studies and urban education

The phenomenon of the rise of urban education in the 1960s can be seen to be a part of the general expansion of urban studies which took place at this time both in the USA and in Europe. In treating urban education as a field of academic and policy concern it is important to reflect upon the social and political context in which all forms of urban study flourished and it is important also to examine the theoretical roots of urban studies in general. Writing of this period in America, Cohen (1977: p. 120) refers to the 'alienation and rebelliousness throughout America ... the war in Vietnam, the oppression of the black population, the blighting of cities, the lawlessness of politics, the corruptibility and impersonality of institutions'. Castells (1977: p. 405) points to the riots of blacks in Harlem in 1964 and in Watts in 1965 as constituting 'a most significant factor in the breakdown of social order in the cities during the sixties'. The National Advisory Commission on Civil Disorders (1968, p. 410) (Kerner Report) had warned Americans that 'none of us can escape the consequences of the continuing economic and social decay of the central city.' It is no random coincidence that urban studies should begin to flourish at this time with contributions coming from urban economics, geography and environmental studies, urban planning, design and administration, locational studies and political science. It would seem to be clear that the rise of urban studies as a general field was facilitated by the expectation that academics and researchers would be able to provide some strategies for policy makers faced with increasingly volatile urban situations. During the 1960s and early 1970s journals were founded, courses established and research projects launched to examine the causes of the 'urban crisis'. Whilst this phenomenon was most visible in America it had its parallels in Europe. Pickvance (1976) has interestingly pointed out the way in which the French government provided funds for urban research in universities and independent research institutions following the 'events' of May 1968 in Paris.[6]

What might be seen as a crisis in legitimation in social, economic, race and political relations, particularly in America, was being interpreted in this period as a problem of the cities. Since the most dramatic manifestations of economic decay, social deprivation, race conflict and political resistance found their expression in the metropolitan cities it was possible for such an interpretation to command a prima facie credibility. Urban studies arose therefore in conditions of crisis (understood in these terms) and their fundamental mandate was to find solutions for the crisis.

The Chicago School

The theoretical roots of urban studies may be discerned at two levels, a level which drew upon the theoretical and methodological legacy of the Chicago School of urban sociology and a level which drew upon a wider range of disciplines loosely organised around the notion of an 'urban system'. The Chicago School as the only systematic school of urban sociology provided crucial and influential inputs into the field of urban studies. Park's (Park, Burgess and McKenzie 1925) view of the city as an organised unit in space 'produced by laws of its own' offered a paradigmatic framework to be elaborated or contested. A preoccupation with the moral and social order of the city and its relationships with social solidarity at local levels in 'natural areas' or 'communities' fitted well with contemporary concern over just such questions. The concentric zone theory of urban growth associated with Burgess (ibid.) and the work on human ecology of McKenzie (ibid.), Hawley (1950) and Duncan et al. (1960) provided models for further empirical inquiry into the interaction of environment, population, technology and social organisation. Wirth's theories (1938, 1964) of city forms of social life made 'urbanism' a distinct phenomenon for investigation.[7] The Chicago School provided not only the first corpus of systematic urban study but also the models, the procedures and the parameters for future study. The work of Park, McKenzie,

Urban education: policy science or critical scholarship? / 7

Burgess and Wirth generated a type of 'urban imagination' which was compelling because it caught something of the dramatic structural changes and cosmopolitan cultural variety of a great city. The forms of urban ecological and spatial modelling which emanated from this school, the brilliance of its urban ethnography and community studies and its insistence upon direct empirical engagement with the social life of cities all help to explain its considerable influence.[8] But perhaps the most important theoretical function of the Chicago School was to provide a legitimation for the developing field of Urban Studies. By making available a sociological definition of the city constituted in terms of its own laws and characterised by new forms of social relations (urbanism) related to dimension, density and heterogeneity of population, the Chicago School assisted crucially in the construction of an urban problematic.

Policy science

While Chicago School urban sociology legitimated the field and provided important theoretical and methodological models for use or criticism, the particular conditions of the urban crisis in America in the 1960s and early 1970s were seen to require a more wide-ranging and modern treatment. This was to be found in notions of inter-disciplinary inquiry which took as their major focus the structure, operation and functioning of 'urban systems'. In essence, urban systems were taken to represent complex divisions of labour located in space and involving a dense and heterogeneous population, an intricate pattern of exchange, consumption, distribution and movement all held in a delicate state of equilibrium but constantly in danger of crisis because of technical, economic, social or political dysfunctions. The investigation of urban systems provided an appropriately scientific and policy-related focus for a new field which required both research funding and political and institutional recognition. The 1960s saw the rise of concepts of the urban system and of issues of planning, management and control associated with such systems; thus 'the urban research industry was mobilised towards an understanding of the urban system so that "planners" could intervene to push the system in the chosen direction' (Pahl 1975: p. 294). Castells (1976: p. 63) observes that the Chicago School's initial concern with integration in the city had by the 1960s been extended to other questions, 'problems of management of the system as a whole ... public sector intervention to organise the consumption of collective goods, attempts to manage the social tensions produced by the spatial expression of processes of ethnic and social segregation'. The policy science[9] features of the urban studies of this period are epitomised in publications such as *Urban Research and Policy Planning* (1967), *The Urban Challenge to Government* (1969), *Financing the Metropolis* (1970), *Urban Economics: Processes and Problems* (1972), *Urban Management and Social Change* (1974). While it is impossible to put a precise location upon the emergence of this technicist phase of urban studies, the founding of the *Urban Affairs Quarterly* (1965) designed 'to facilitate interchange ... between those engaged in basic or applied research and those responsible for making or implementing policy and programs' provides at least a significant marker of this development.

It is within the American social and political context which has been described and against a background of wider developments in urban studies that the emergence of urban education has to be appreciated and understood. James Conant in his classic study *Slums and Suburbs: A Commentary on Schools in Metropolitan Areas* had warned the American public that 'social dynamite is building up in our large cities in the form of unemployed, out-of-school youth especially in the Negro slums' (Conant 1961: p. 146). By the 1970s his predictions of the coming crisis had been realised but there had been at the same time a considerable response to his call that 'our large city educational problems be analysed in far more detail than in the past'. Urban education had emerged as a response both to the crisis and to the call.

The professional ideology of urban educationists

What are the characteristics of the sort of urban education studies which were generated in such conditions? Perhaps the most productive way of answering that question is to follow the example of C. Wright Mills in his essay in the sociology of knowledge, 'The professional ideology of social pathologists' (1943). In that paper, Mills scrutinised American textbooks current in the study of social disorganisation or social pathology in order to clarify the selecting and organising principles which they used to present contents and the 'thought style' which they exhibited in interpretation and analysis. Young (1971) has suggested the fruitfulness of applying Mills's technique more widely in the sociology of knowledge. The intention here is to follow such advice and to apply Mills's technique to a study of urban education texts, monographs, reports and journals in America in the 1960s and 1970s. Given the range of literature to be surveyed, it is only possible to follow Mills's example and seek to illuminate 'typical perspectives and key concepts' which characterised the field in this period. The general strategy adopted is to try to locate dominant emphases in the analysis and study of the urban education problem and to clarify the nature of the policies and action recommended.

The founding fathers

For Conant (1961), the urban problem and its educational repercussions were constituted fundamentally by the existence of large numbers of unemployed black youths in inner city areas. The existence of such groups in such locations not only threatened the credibility of the theory of equality of educational opportunity but more seriously posed a direct social and political threat to the stability of the American nation. Thus Conant wrote,

> these young people are my chief concern especially when they are pocketed together in large numbers within the confines of the big city slums. What can words like 'freedom', 'liberty' or 'equality of educational opportunity' mean to these young people? With what kind of zeal and dedication can we expect them to withstand the relentless pressures of communism? . . . I am deeply disturbed by the implications that widespread unemployment among the youth of our big cities has for the future of our society (Conant 1961: p. 34).

While Conant's work had a sense of urgency and contained a set of policy recommendations, its analysis of the underlying causes of the urban problem as such was relatively uncomplicated:

> the slum areas of certain big Northern cities are today largely inhabited by Negroes who have recently moved from the South hoping to improve their lot. The economic changes in the South which have forced this migration are too well known to require elaboration. The Negro is being displaced as a farm laborer and being unable, because of discrimination, to obtain other employment in the section where he was born, he becomes a migrant headed North (Conant 1961: p. 7).

The contemporary urban problem arose in Conant's view because of discrimination against blacks in the northern labour markets compounded by their inappropriate socialisation in slum backgrounds and their educational deficiencies arising from an inadequate and inappropriate public school system.

In the writings of Havighurst (1963–1970) a variant of this analysis appeared in the concept of 'metropolitanism' and its consequences. Using the US Census definition of a standard metropolitan statistical area (SMSA) as any city with a population of fifty thousand or more, together with its surrounding county and such other counties as were tied to the central city by economic and cultural ties, Havighurst argued that 'metropolitan developments have produced or intensified many social problems, most of which have had repercussions in education' (Havighurst 1963: p. 24). Metropolitanism had caused or intensified the economic and ethnic polarisation between the central city and the suburban area: 'it has led to increased segregation on the basis of income and race. This segregation is a threat to democratic unity and educational opportunity, for slums and gray areas of the central cities breed political and social divisiveness and discontent' (Havighurst 1967: p. 20). Metropolitan developments had also caused a major disparity in the levels of expenditure on central city schools when compared with suburban schools. Presenting research data for Chicago, Havighurst was able to show that 'the suburban schools as a whole have a significant financial advantage over the Chicago city schools' (Havighurst 1970: p. 159). Mediating the work of Havighurst to students of urban education, Miller and Woock explained the fiscal problem as

> the disparity in local financial resources available for schooling as affluent members of the area moved to the suburbs, taking with them a major source of tax revenue for schools and . . . the growing numbers of educationally disadvantaged children concentrated in the central city requiring greater than average educational efforts that central city governments do not have the tax resources to finance (Miller and Woock 1970: p. 113).

Although an overall critique of urban education writings in America will be attempted later, some interim comment on the work of these influential writers seems appropriate at this stage. Both saw the urban education problem as constituting a threat to the credibility of equality of educational opportunity at one level but at a more serious level to the social and political stability of American society. For Conant, the problem crystallised upon the existence of unemployed black youths in inner city areas and for him the causes were a compound of discrimination and the deficiencies of negro upbringing and schooling. For Havighurst, metropolitanism and its segregating and dysfunctional consequences were a prime concern. Both of these writers provided dramatic and detailed descriptions of the urban education problem (in a style not unlike that of the Chicago School urban sociologists), but neither of them engaged in any profound analysis of the underlying historical, structural or ideological causes of that problem. While it is true that Conant recognised a process involving 'the transformation of the status of the Negro from that of a slave into that of a member of a lower, quite separate caste' (Conant 1961: p. 12), no serious examination of the ideology and mechanisms of racism was attempted in his work. Racial discrimination was a 'legacy' to be overcome.

In Havighurst's writing, metropolitanism substitutes for a fundamental cause. It is metropolitanism which 'causes' or intensifies the problems of the city and of its schools. No explanation for metropolitanism is given other than as a stage in the evolution of American cities. The parallels with Chicago School biological and evolutionary models of the city and of urban growth are here very clear. Metropolitanism was something which happened 'naturally', but which had unnatural or unhealthy consequences.

Contextual rhetoric and cultural disadvantage

If the work of Conant and of Havighurst provided the initial stimulus for the development of urban education study, the Work Conferences on Urban Education held at Teachers College, Columbia University annually from 1962, under the direction of A.H. Passow, generated a considerable corpus of readings published in the period 1963–1972. In the introduction to the initial volume, *Education in Depressed Areas* (1963), the urban education problem was described in all its complexity[10] and drama:

> Statistics do not depict the physical and economic deterioration of the central city gray areas, the movement of the middle class to the suburbs, the transiency and instability of the in-immigrant families, the concentration and intensification of social problems

in depressed areas . . . . Ethnic, racial and socio-economic groups have coalesced in areas of the city, creating de facto segregation in the schools even where laws imply non-segregation. School buildings in the depressed urban areas seem to house the greatest array of educational problems. It is in the depressed urban areas that the web of social problems is thickest; crime, alcoholism, drug addiction, poverty, illiteracy, disease, unemployment and broken families are found in city slums in massively greater degree than in society as a whole. . . . The ethnic and racial composition tends to be primarily from the so-called minority groups — southern Negro, Puerto Rican, Appalachian white, American Indian, Mexican and most recently Cuban (Passow 1963: p. 1).

The collections of readings in Urban Education published in the 1960s and early 1970s were generally characterised by descriptions of this type, of what Mills (1943: p. 171) called 'the liberal multiple factor view'. Almost every element in the situation was touched upon in a global and portmanteau fashion often in a preface or introduction. This impression of a breadth and comprehensiveness in the examination of the urban education problem was further reinforced by a procedure which utilised work conferences (of educationists, administrators, psychologists, sociologists and those 'charged with leadership responsibility for educational programs in disadvantaged areas') and the publication of papers from these different perspectives. Thus the urban education problem was depicted as having multiple causation which required the application of inter-disciplinary perspectives for its proper understanding. However it is argued here that this impression of multiple causation and of inter-disciplinary breadth in the study of the urban education problem is, so far as the Passow readings are concerned, largely illusory. In fact a close scrutiny of them reveals a comparatively narrow focus upon the concept of 'disadvantage' and upon theoretical and policy discussion around the notion of 'compensatory education'.

It is important in analysing these texts to make a distinction between *contextual rhetoric* and *'substantive emphasis'*. Contextual rhetoric rehearses the elements of the wider framework in which a particular problem is located but does not develop these elements in any significant detail. Substantive emphasis points the reader to what is seen to be at the heart of the particular problem under examination and elaborates discussion around this. The contextual

Urban education: policy science or critical scholarship? / 13

rhetoric of the writings of this period continually referred to an interlocking network of variables which constituted the urban education problem. Thus Passow concluded the 1963 readings with the observation that 'the importance of looking at the problem in terms of its educational, sociological, psychological, economic, political, health, welfare and housing dimensions is increasingly clear' (Passow 1963: p. 350). Despite such assertions the substantive emphasis of the readings (1967, 1968, 1970, 1972) was focused upon notions of 'disadvantage', 'cultural deprivation', 'compensatory education' and 'instructional programs'. To all intents and purposes the study of urban education, in so far as these readings defined the field, became another name for an extended debate about the cultural deficiencies of urban blacks and other ethnic minorities. Such debate might extend to the cultural and organisational deficiencies of inner city schools and to the pedagogic and personal deficiencies of inner city teachers but it remained firmly within a 'culture' problematic. The wider structural, economic and political issues referred to remained at the level of contextual rhetoric rather than being elaborated in any detail.

Riessman (1962: p. 1) had introduced the proposition that the 'culturally deprived child' was 'clearly one of the most pressing problems facing the urban school'. While the Passow readings used the apparently broader frame of reference signalled by the term 'disadvantage', the substantive emphasis of the term was not economic and political disadvantage (or powerlessness) but cultural disadvantage (or deprivation).[11] Influential articles by the psychologists, Ausubel, Deutsch, Goldberg, and Hess and Shipman sharpened the focus upon the cultural, intellectual and socialisation deficiencies of urban blacks and other ethnic groups[12] and in the light of such diagnoses elaborated the policies of compensation and intervention which seemed educationally necessary. Although a thin strand of critical writing co-existed with such formulations,[13] the overwhelming emphasis of the literature was upon the notion of cultural disadvantage.[14] By effectively separating the study of cultural and institutional problems in urban education from their economic and structural base, by marginalising questions of power and by neglecting historical context, the Passow readings put severe limitations on the explanatory potential of urban education as a field of study.

The ethnography of inner city schools

These limitations were only partially modified by a whole genre of studies of urban schools and teachers which appeared in the 1960s and which were written from interpretive, interactionist and anthropological perspectives. Such studies were generally informed by an intention to show that the urban education problem was not caused primarily by the cultural deficiencies of urban blacks and others but rather by the alienating or dysfunctional features of inner city schooling. The intention of studies such as R.D. Strom (ed.), *The Inner City Classroom: Teacher Behaviours* (1966), J. Kozol, *Death at an Early Age* (1967), H. Kohl, *36 Children* (1967), G. Moore, *Realities of the Urban Classroom* (1967), L. Smith and W. Geoffrey, *Complexities of an Urban Classroom* (1968), E. Fuchs, *Teachers Talk: A View from Within the Inner City Schools* (1968), and E. Leacock, *Teaching and Learning in City Schools* (1969) was to expose the 'realities' of urban schools and classrooms as an important part of the problem. The rich ethnographic description which such studies generated and an accessible style of writing resulted in the integration of this material in urban education texts and courses. Such work, which continued into the early 1970s with texts like Ray Rist's *The Urban School: Factory for Failure* (1973) placed the deficiencies of urban schools and teachers high on the agenda of urban education inquiry. The schools were seen to be too 'bureaucratic', 'authoritarian', 'custodial' and 'hierarchical'. The curriculum was 'fossilised' and a prime source of the alienation and underachievement of the students. The teachers were lacking in understanding and sympathy for black and minority ethnic students.[15] The structures and procedures of the school and the low expectations of the majority of the teachers in inner city areas were highlighted to offset and to countervail deficit theories of the student and his home background. While the emphasis of this work in urban education did begin to shift attention away from the cultural deficiencies of urban blacks and away from the need for compensatory education and towards the need for curriculum reform and new models of educational experience, the focus of the analysis was still limited. In particular such studies frequently lacked an historical or wider structural sense of the function and location of the urban school. The analysis for all its interpretive detail and sense of vivid reality was locked into a present time and small scale focus. Such studies tended towards a search for solutions at the level of changed institutional procedures and attitudes and changed interpersonal relations[16] without reference to the economic or the political as possibly constraining such changes.

The politics of urban education

The late 1960s and early 1970s saw an increased recognition given to the economic and the political in the field of urban education. Gittell and Hevesi in *The Politics of Urban Education* (1969) produced an important text which brought together 'political theory' readings in community politics and power, in association with educational readings concerned with school segregation and desegregation and issues of community control of urban schools. Their analysis suggested that the 1954 US Supreme Court decision ordering integration of public schools had 'propelled public education into the open political arena' and that political conflict had taken place between black and white activists both for and against the integration of public schools. The perceived failure of integration and of compensatory education programmes by the late 1960s had led to a new phase in the political struggle: 'community leaders and ghetto dwellers who reject administrative reform, demand a complete redistribution of power; to effect such a redistribution they stress the techniques of decentralisation of school systems and community control' (Gittell and Hevesi 1969: pp. 7–8). At the centre of the urban education question from this viewpoint was a major political struggle between the integrationists and the exponents of community control. In the struggle for power and control over urban schools 'an increasing number of groups oppose community control because they fear it is a euphemism for black racism' (Gittell and Hevesi 1969: p. 10). Gittell, in concluding that 'the political failure of the school system is fundamental' (Gittell and Hevesi 1969: p. 364), provided an important counterbalance to a body of urban education writing which had looked primarily at the cultural, the microinstitutional and the interpersonal. However, it is important to be clear about the notion of politics used in this study and in others of this genre concerned with greater community participation. What is being referred to is the politics of city schools as realised through the struggle for community control which 'implies a redistribution of power within the educational subsystem' (Gittell and Hevesi 1969: p. 365). The interest groups involved in the struggle are identified as educational administrators, increasingly militant teacher organisations, civil rights groups, community activists and ghetto leaders. In other words, although issues of power and of control over institutions and resources were discussed, urban education studies in America in the early 1970s which concerned themselves with politics were very delimited in the range and focus of their analysis. The suggestion for instance that urban schooling only entered the open political arena after 1954 and in relation to the desegregation issue revealed a blindness to the earlier political struggles which had characterised the development of urban schooling in America.[17] The concentration upon the struggles of interest groups in the educational 'sub-system' without reference to features of class structure and the wider distribution of power and control in society illustrated the limitation of the particular forms of political science which were being utilised in the analyses.

The dominant themes of urban educational study in America during the 1970s were political and economic although always refracted through the lens of the race question. Such themes had to do with the conflicts between local communities or between local communities and centralised bureaucracies for control over city schools or with the struggles and problems caused by various forms of financial crisis in the cities. Studies of this genre are epitomised in texts such as Levin's *Community Control of Schools* (1970); Katzman's *Political Economy of Urban Schools* (1971); Peterson's *School Politics: Chicago Style* (1976) and Yarmolinsky *et al.*'s *Race and Schooling in the City* (1981). Despite the limitations arising from the system-style concepts of politics and economics used in these studies, taken together they represent a shift of emphasis away from culture as a fundamental explanatory category in urban education inquiry towards power and resources as fundamental categories.[18] Thus, by 1979 Ravitch was representing the urban education problem in these terms.

> The dilemma facing urban schools today and for the foreseeable future is that their objective needs grow larger as their financial capacity diminishes. The middle class exodus from the city reduces the city's tax base and its ability to generate revenues for the schools and other public purposes. . . . When the big cities turn to the state government for aid, they tend to get an unsympathetic response from legislatures dominated by a suburban and rural majority with little interest in paying more taxes to subsidise city schools. The political power of the cities is impaired by their loss of population, by the rising proportion of the politically inactive people in the cities, as well as by the cities' inability to create coalitions with non-urban interests, thus leaving the cities as politically isolated claimants for more state aid. The fact that the city schools are perceived as non-white enclaves that are inefficient,

Urban education: policy science or critical scholarship? / 17

ineffective, poorly disciplined and infinitely capable of consuming tax money without producing tangible results merely confirms the predisposition of state legislatures not to provide additional subsidies. Even in the Congress, the political strength of the urban bloc has waned; the cities lost congressmen in the reapportionment that followed the 1970 census and they are likely to lose more after the 1980 census (Ravitch 1979: pp. 76–7).

Although in this passage Ravitch grasps the essential importance for urban schooling of changes in the balance of power and changes in the balance of resources, her conclusions and recommendations for action, despite this, are largely concerned with possible changes in educational procedures coupled with a general call for 'the economic regeneration of the cities'. Therefore, although the most recent examples of urban educational writing in America do focus upon issues of power and resources, they are at the same time characterised by theoretical limitations in the scale of the analysis and by recommendations for action which are of a muted or general type.

Critique of American studies

Throughout this analysis of urban education studies in America, critical comments have accompanied the presentation of 'typical perspectives and key concepts'. Following the example of Mills (1943) it is now appropriate to draw these comments together into some form of overall critique. From the previous discussion, the limitations of urban education as a field of study and research have become apparent. They may be summarised as (a) an inadequate theorisation of the urban; (b) an overemphasis upon the cultural as an explanatory category and an underemphasis upon the structural; (c) a mode of inquiry dominated by various forms of abstracted empiricism or by micro-institutional studies; (d) an inadequate sense of the historical in the understanding of urban phenomena; and (e) limited concepts of power and resources expressed in a limited sense of the political. While the material and range of texts already presented exemplifies these limitations some further elaboration of this critical summary will be attempted in the following pages.

(a) Theorisation of the urban

It has been shown that such theorisation of the urban as can be found in the field of urban education has drawn largely upon the legacy of the Chicago School of urban sociology. Thus this School's emphasis upon the city as an analytical frame in itself; upon 'urbanism' as a distinct way of life and set of social relations; upon evolutionary models of urban growth; and upon moral and social cohesion in the city and the search for community, has had a profound influence upon urban educational writing. To this theoretical base has been added Havighurst's concept of 'metropolitanism' referring to certain contemporary polarising tendencies visible in major urban areas. Such theorisation of the urban has been marked by fundamental limitations, the most obvious of which is the abstraction of the city (and of city schools) as objects of investigation from the wider social, economic and political framework within which they are located. This has led to a consequent emphasis upon discrete 'urban problems'. It will be argued later that the study of the urban can be conceived of in broadly functionalist terms as the study of urban problems; in broadly Weberian terms as the study of urban conflicts or in broadly Marxist terms as the study of urban contradictions. American studies in urban education have largely confined themselves to the first category of the urban only (with recently some tentative moves into the second category). What this has meant is that the understanding of the urban which informs the analyses has failed to exploit the full theoretical resources available. A critical scholarship of the urban cannot emerge from such a restricted approach. A critical scholarship of the urban must not only draw upon the full range of urban theory but must be aware of the epistemological and theoretical discussions concerning the status of the concept 'urban' itself. Recent critical writing such as that of Castells (1976) which asserts that the language of the urban is ideological rather than scientific, challenges the whole basis for a field of urban education and yet many of those writing within this field appear entirely unaware of such challenges.

(b) Culturalist perspectives

The dominance of culturalist explanations within urban education studies is in one sense to be expected. Given that a central concern of such studies is the investigation of urban schooling and of the

Urban education: policy science or critical scholarship? / 19

processes of cultural transmission and cultural reproduction in urban school systems then a preoccupation with questions of culture must logically follow. This preoccupation has, however, been narrowly conceived. The culturalist approach within urban education in America has been powerfully influenced by notions of urbanism, derived from the Chicago School; by notions of the cultural deficiency of urban blacks and by social psychological theories of cultural deprivation and compensatory education. Much of the literature has been characterised by a social pathological and deficit view of the cultural forms associated with specific areas of the city, particularly the inner city, or of cultural forms associated with racial or ethnic groups in the city. In a very real sense such an emphasis which represents 'the cultural problem of the cities' can be seen as a contemporary and social scientific expression of an older tradition of moral concern about the quality of life of the urban working class and of immigrants in the city. As the work of Lazerson (1971) and of Kaestle (1973) has shown, urban schools in America were founded as part of a moral mission to the city, a mission in which notions of cultural conformity to the norms of established American life were powerful. The sense of deficit and the sense of cultural conformity has continued in modern studies in urban education but it has been distanced from the overt moral judgments of the past and from explicit statements of cultural intention. This distancing has been a result of the use of an apparently neutral social scientific language of cultural deprivation and disadvantage. Culturalist writing within urban education in America has suffered therefore from a perspective which has been relatively blind to its own historical context and to the limitations associated with this context. These limitations have shown themselves not only in a narrow and ethnocentric view of what constitutes culture (with a consequent underestimation of the strengths and complexities of other cultures) but also in a persistent tendency to isolate the study of culture from wider structural forces. The separation of cultural forms from their structural, economic and political location has led to an individualistic and depoliticised view of cultural issues in urban education. There has been little recognition that what is called urbanism could be seen as the cultural expression of capitalism and that what is called cultural disadvantage could be the expression of an exploitive economic and political situation. Separated from mainstream cultural theory[19] and dominated by educationists and social psychologists, the culturalist perspective within urban education has failed to grasp the range and variety of issues which have to be faced in any attempt to explain 'the failure of urban schools'.

(c) Mode of inquiry

In characterising the texts used in the study of social problems and social disorganisation in America in the 1930s and 1940s, Mills (1943: p. 166) noted that 'the informational character of social pathology is linked with a failure to consider total social structures. Collecting and dealing in a fragmentary way with scattered problems and facts of milieux, these books are not focused on larger stratifications or upon structured wholes.' Later, in describing such a mode of inquiry as 'abstracted empiricism', he argued that 'it does seem foolish to undertake any detailed studies of smaller-scale areas before we have good reason to believe that, whatever the results, they will permit us to draw inferences useful in solving or clarifying problems of structural significance' (Mills 1973:p. 77). A scrutiny of texts used in the study of urban education in America in the 1960s and 1970s reveals precisely those weaknesses which Mills highlighted in the social pathology of an earlier period. Considerable empirical 'busyness' has resulted in studies of urban and inner city communities, ethnic cultures and characteristics, ghetto schools, urban and educational intervention programmes, aspects of school administration and organisation, curriculum innovation, school finance, inner city classrooms, urban teachers and principals, school board politics, desegregation and community control. While such studies are not lacking in rich description and perceptive insights into particular situations, they remain as pieces of a social jigsaw that are never assembled into any coherent theoretical framework.[20] Typically, the particular issue under examination has been abstracted from its wider relations with class structure, with market economic forces, and with major political and ideological struggles and from a sense of its own history. Thus the mode of inquiry adopted in the field of urban education in America has led in practice to a narrow and fragmented view of the problems of urban schooling. For all its empirical activity the field of urban education either leaves the student with no clear sense of what is to be done or with a conviction that changes within the context of the education system or the urban system provide the necessary answers. At the point where the analysis of urban educational problems intersects with the larger issues of class, power and the organisation of economic life, the student encounters

Urban education: policy science or critical scholarship? / 21

significant closure. At the point in other words where urban phenomena begin to lead towards fundamental levels of causation, the student does not find the necessary theoretical or empirical elaboration but only silence.

(d) Sense of the historical

It would be misleading to suggest that there has been an absence of critical and scholarly work in the history of urban schooling in the USA. On the contrary, such writing has been more in evidence in America than it has been in Britain. The writings of Cohen (1964), Katz (1968, 1971, 1975), Lazerson (1971), Schultz (1973), Kaestle (1973), Tyack (1974) and Ravitch (1974) and recent collections such as Ravitch and Goodenow (1981) show the vitality of this particular field of historical inquiry. Such work has been characterised by a lively debate between the so-called 'revisionist' historians such as Katz and the so-called 'apologists' such as Ravitch.[21] The great value of this debate is that it has made visible an important ideological conflict concerning the origins and nature of urban schooling in America. It has also made much more salient such crucial issues as class, bureaucracy, racism and issues of social control in the appreciation of urban schooling. How then is it possible to argue that urban education studies have lacked a sense of the historical?

A scrutiny of urban education texts and journals reveals that despite the work undertaken by historians of education in America on the origins of urban schooling, very little of the substantive findings and very little of the theoretical debate appears on the agenda of urban education studies *per se*. No serious sense of the historical[22] can be found in such journals as *Urban Education* or *Education and Urban Society*. Widely used texts, for example, Miller and Woock's *Social Foundations of Urban Education*, begin their discussions with statements such as 'only since the 1950s have professional educators paid much attention to urban schools as special phenomena' (Miller and Woock 1970: p. 3). The absence of an historical sense of the urban question and of the 'problem of urban schools' within mainstream urban education studies is difficult to explain. It is perhaps another manifestation of the intellectually limiting effects of the present academic division of labour. The historical studies of urban schooling and the textbooks of urban education appear to have co-existed but not to have connected in any important degree.[23] The net effect of the absence of a serious historical dimension within urban education studies has been to cast this area of inquiry into a 'present crisis' perspective with heavy emphasis upon the race question in the city. Indeed, a strong and persistent thread of writing within urban education studies represents the central issue as essentially a racial one.[24] What a proper historical location of the urban problem would reveal is that the race question in the city is a dramatic present manifestation of an historical complex of issues to do with class, with domination and with exploitation in metropolitan cities. What it would also reveal is that the problem of the urban school is a contemporary version of historical struggles about the nature of education; struggles in which political, class and ideological elements were much more salient than in contemporary educational analysis.

(e) Sense of the political and economic

As already indicated, the 1970s saw a shift away from a primary emphasis upon the cultural, the microinstitutional and the interpersonal in urban education writing towards a concern with the political and economic. The particular notions of the political and the economic which characterised this shift have already been discussed. In essence, the politics referred to are either the politics of interest groups within the city or the politics of the school board and of interest groups within education. The economics referred to are the economics of collective consumption in the field of the social services. The strengths of this most recent writing are to be found in the recognition that issues of differential power and of differential resources lie at the base of the problem of urban schools and of educational underachievement in the cities. Thus Ravitch (1979) points to the fundamental significance of changes in the balance of power between the cities and the suburban/ rural areas in America in affecting the schooling question. The weaknesses of this work are to be found in a tendency to separate issues of collective consumption from issues of the wider organisation of economic life and of the mode of production, and a tendency to separate questions to do with the distribution of power between cities and suburban/rural areas from questions to do with the wider social structuring of power. Urban education writing in America has shared these characteristics with other aspects of urban studies in general. The thrust of recent critical writing on the urban question (Harvey 1973; Castells 1977, 1978) has been precisely to throw light

Urban education: policy science or critical scholarship? / 23

upon these separations and closures. It will be the concern of the final section of this chapter to take up these questions but before this is attempted some examination of the development of urban education studies in Britain must be made.

The development of urban education studies in Britain

Urban education studies in Britain have developed significantly in the last decade with widely diffused materials published by the Open University (Raynor and Harden 1973 a and b; Raynor and Harris 1977 a and b); influential conference collections edited by Field (1977) and by Marland (1980); important review articles by Herbert (Herbert and Johnson 1976) and by Williamson and Byrne (1979) and the beginnings of studies in the history of urban schooling by Reeder, in Reeder (ed.) (1977). These developments have been related to the growth of urban education courses at various levels within a range of institutions.[25]

The most obvious way in which to examine the 'typical perspectives and key concepts' of this corpus of writing is to ask the question, to what extent has urban education study in Britain reproduced the limitations, already outlined, of urban education studies in America, and to what extent has it been able to develop new agendas and new perspectives? This question can perhaps be most clearly answered by tracing first the continuities of these two fields and then by examining their discontinuities.

The course materials of the Open University's Urban Education course (E351) of 1973—4 show the continuities at their clearest. A scrutiny of the readers (*Cities, Communities and the Young* (Volume 1) and *Equality and City Schools* (Volume 2)) and of the supporting units reveals a pattern reminiscent of the Passow readers of the 1960s.[26] No systematic attempt was made to theorise the urban or the notion of urban education as a field of study. In so far as the material presented had a theoretical framework, it was provided by legacies from the Chicago School (articles by H.J. Gans and by L. Wirth); brief selections from the writings of British urban sociologists (Ruth Glass, John Rex and Ray Pahl) and an undeveloped stipulative definition of urban education from John Raynor. This lack of a coherent theoretical structure was compounded by an absence of any sustained historical treatment of the urban question or of the origins of urban schooling in Britain. In the whole of Course E351 (1973—4) a sense of the critical history of the urban can be found only in a seminal essay by Stuart Hall.[27] Given that Britain represents the *fons et origo* of large-scale capitalist urbanisation and given that the schooling of the British urban working class in the nineteenth century was a matter of considerable political and ideological significance,[28] this absence of historical location is remarkable. Both of these significant omissions, the theoretical and the historical, had the effect of introducing urban education studies into Britain with the 'present crisis' perspective which had characterised American work. However, unlike such work, the 'present crisis' perspective was not mediated through a strong preoccupation with race relations in the city. In its place, an important amount of attention was given to the sociology of the inner city, issues of planning and resources for urban areas, community development and community education and to the debate on compensatory education.

The early 1970s were characterised by a heightened and radical interest in the sociology of knowledge and in questions of cultural and social reproduction. Yet despite the appearance of Michael Young's crucial book *Knowledge and Control* in 1971, with important contributions from Bernstein, Bourdieu and Keddie, the culturalist perspectives within Course E351 drew heavily upon existing American sources. Articles by Frank Riessman, Martin Deutsch, Mario Fantini and Gerald Weinstein and Merle Karnes on various aspects of cultural deprivation and compensatory education, while juxtaposed with important critiques such as Norman Friedman, D.C. Morton and D.R. Watson and Basil Bernstein's 'Education cannot compensate for society', did not engage with the wider perspectives in cultural theory which were then available.

In these ways, the genesis of urban education studies in Britain was strongly marked by transatlantic influence. There were however discontinuities with the American pattern. The most striking of these is the absence of a strong preoccupation with the question of race in the city. Although in Course E351 there was material focused around Rex and Moore's (1967) study *Race, Community and Conflict* and a single (American) article concerned with black studies, the race question was not salient. Whether this is to be explained by the greater salience of class as an analytical category in British studies or by a general unwillingness in the early 1970s to recognise the existence of a race problem in the urban centres of Britain must remain open to speculation. For whatever reason race was only a marginal issue in studies in urban education. Much more central was the question of the distribution of resources in urban and particularly in inner city areas. Whereas in American work culturalist perspectives had been dominant, in the early development of British work, culturalist perspectives were equally balanced by a socio-political concern with resource allocation. In this can be detected the much stronger influence in British work of sociologists such as Pahl, Halsey and Williamson and Byrne. Urban education studies in Britain in so far as they were mediated by Course E351 placed high upon the agenda the examination of socio-spatial systems and of key urban bureaucrats (Pahl); and the examination of the material basis of educational underachievement in city schools (Byrne and Williamson). In other words the work was characterised by a neo-Weberian approach in which the conflicts of interest groups and the crucial importance of distributive mechanisms and bureaucratic procedures was recognised. Added to this were Halsey's reflections upon the educational priority area policy of 1968—72 and his recognition that 'too much has been claimed for the power of educational systems as instruments for the wholesale reform of societies which are characteristically hierarchical . . .' (Halsey 1977: p. 71). While this work therefore had a much stronger sense of the 'distribution problematic' than was the case with American writing and while it had a much stronger sense of the social structural in the explanation of the urban, the sense of the political remained muted. A contextual rhetoric of the political can be found in Course E351 but nowhere does it constitute, in the 1973/74 edition, a substantive emphasis. In so far as the political is represented in the field of urban education it is represented by the politics of the local system, and the politics of community.

Course E351 as the first formal presentation of urban education materials in Britain has been in a unique position to shape subsequent course construction and teaching in other institutions and to provide the general parameters and perspectives to be utilised. It is important therefore to note the extent to which this initial patterning has persisted or has been radically changed in the revision of 1977—8 which produced Course E361, Education and the Urban Environment.

New directions in urban education?

The revised Open University course in Urban Education appeared in 1977—8 in a social context marked by growing tensions and conflicts which focused to an important extent upon questions of economic decline and unemployment and upon questions of race relations in Britain. It appeared also in an educational and intellectual context which had been characterised for some time by an increase in radical and critical scholarship from Marxist and other sources. Within the sociology of education, the relations between the cultural and the material, the educational and the economic, the educational and the political had been brought into much sharper theoretical and empirical focus. Within urban studies, a powerful theoretical critique had been mounted by Harvey (1973) and the writing of Castells had been mediated by Pickvance's (1976) *Urban Sociology: Critical Essays*. In the 1975 edition of *Whose City?*, Pahl had opened an important debate between the neo-Weberian and the Marxist approaches to the urban question, which was developed in Harloe's (1977) *Captive Cities*. It is of some interest to trace the effects which these wider developments had produced in the pattern of urban education study as represented by Course E361.

A scrutiny of the revised course in urban education shows an important response to the changed social context of urban problems in Britain in the late 1970s. In particular, employment, unemployment and race relations issues had become much more salient and, significantly, were considered in close conjunction. Thus Raynor observed in the general introduction, 'we are today much more conscious of the difficulties of searching for a multicultural education in a period of economic recession and unemployment when the racism which lies so close to the surface, manifests itself in hostility towards minorities' (Raynor and Harris 1977a: p. 2). These new priorities were signalled in the structure of the course itself with units assigned to education and work relations (with special reference to the young unemployed in the inner city); immigrants and the labour market; race and the urban child; and race and education. In addition to this a complete section of the reader *Schooling in the City* was assigned to race and education relationships.[29] But if the changes in the course in response to certain immediate concrete social issues with dramatic urban manifestations can be seen to have been considerable, the responses at the level of theoretical development were uncertain and tentative. The fundamental theoretical weaknesses of the earlier course remained substantially unaltered. These were in theorising the nature of the urban; in advancing a rationale for urban education as a field of study; in developing a notion of the political and in clarifying and locating the

Urban education: policy science or critical scholarship? / 27

idea of culture. Course E361 provides the student with no systematic introduction to the urban as a language of analysis, despite the existence of a lively theoretical literature concerned with that very subject. At the same time, and more incredibly, it provides the student with no developed rationale for the activity of urban education in itself. The irony is that, while the general introduction to the course *denies* that 'Urban Education is nothing more than a loose collective title for a number of disparate topics' (Raynor and Harris 1977a: p.2), substantively nothing is presented which falsifies that picture.

Theoretical limitations and theoretical distancing

As with the American work, this influential course in urban education has developed at too much of an academic distance from a necessarily informing debate in other branches of intellectual work. This can be demonstrated both in relation to its treatment of politics and power and in its treatment of cultural issues. At first sight, politics appears to have become a major focus of the 1977—8 course. One of the three course readers is assigned to *The Political Context* (Volume 3) (ed. P. Raggatt and M. Evans) and two units are assigned to notions of participation (Block IV). But closer examination shows that 'urban politics' are taken to represent 'the questions raised by the priorities, activities and judgments of urban decision-makers in terms of physical planning, city governance and educational policies' (Raynor and Harris 1977a: p. 2) and the discussion of participation is based largely upon the definitions and formulations of governmental and official publications. These central concepts are in other words simply assumed within a narrow and untheorised framework. The student is given no introduction to a spectrum of theorising about the nature of politics and power either from Parsons's (1967) view of power as 'a means of effectively mobilizing obligations in the interests of collective goals' to Poulantzas's (1973: p. 104) view of power as the 'capacity of a social class to realise its specific objective interests'. An urban education view of politics is constructed which is entirely distanced from crucial debates in political theory between pluralists such as Dahl (1961) and critics such as Bachrach and Baratz (1970) and no reference is made to Lukes's (1974) important book *Power: A Radical View* which summarised and developed this debate. Given that Dahl's study in New Haven focused upon city decision making process to do with urban redevelopment and with public education and that Bachrach and Baratz's influential notion of 'non-decision making' was developed in a study of poverty and race relations in Baltimore, such omissions from a course with an urban focus are even more startling.

Such distancing is again apparent in Course E361's treatment of cultural questions in urban education. What are referred to as 'curriculum issues'[30] are presented without reference to the historical struggles over cultural transmission in British urban schooling and without reference to major concepts in the study of cultural and social reproduction. Thus no reference is made to Bernstein's classification and framing principles in the study of curricula; to Bourdieu's concepts of 'symbolic violence' and 'cultural capital'; or to Gramsci's discussion of the nature of hegemonic dominance. An urban education view of the curriculum is constructed which, while attentive to the community education debate and to the existence of conflicting educational ideologies in urban schooling, is in many respects insulated from mainstream discussions of cultural theory. These discussions are in no sense marginal to the consideration of the cultural problem of urban schooling but, on the contrary, are central to it.

While theoretical distancing and insulation is then a marked characteristic of the revised Urban Education course of 1977—8 it would be unfair and incorrect to suggest that the intellectual ferment of the 1970s was unrepresented. A thread of critical material can be detected throughout the course with contributions from Raymond Williams on urbanism, David Harvey on social justice and Bowles and Gintis on 'the long shadow of work' (in Volume 1) and from Stuart Hall on 'the crisis of the urban school' (in Volume 2). Within the unit material such perspectives can be found in Hamnett's treatment of 'multiple deprivation and the inner city' and in Street-Porter's examination of race, education and the city.[31] Although such critical material can be located in the structure of the course it is nowhere presented to the student as indicative of a major theoretical alternative to the distribution problematic which continued to feature as a dominant preoccupation of the course.

In analysing the American readers in urban education, a distinction was made between *contextual rhetoric* and *substantive emphasis* in the presentation of materials. It would be accurate at this point to say that critical materials in Course E361 have an analytical status between these two categories and that this status could best be described as that of 'sub-text' rather than as a fully developed oppositional position to the distribution problematic. Critical perspectives are present but in a fragmented, minor and unco-ordinated manner. This can perhaps be demonstrated most clearly in the use made of Harvey's important text, *Social Justice and the City*.

The epistemological status of Harvey's text is, in urban studies, probably unique. The first half of the book consists of a systematic attempt (in what is called 'Liberal Formulations') to work through a logic of territorial distributive justice according to principles of social justice set out by Rawls (1969, 1971). The second half of the book (in what is called 'Socialist Formulations') argues that liberal redistributive theory and practice cannot work in the context of capitalist urbanisation and calls for the development of a 'revolutionary theory' of the urban. The considerable significance of Harvey's work lies partly in the fact that it represents an intellectual or paradigm shift in the process of working upon the urban question. As Harvey himself asserts,

> The emergence of Marx's analysis as a guide to enquiry . . . requires some further comments. I do not turn to it out of some a priori sense of its inherent superiority . . . but because I can find no other way of accomplishing what I set out to do or of understanding what has to be understood. (Harvey 1973: p. 17)

In these circumstances it might reasonably be expected that students of urban education would be presented with not only 'Social Justice and Spatial Systems' (the last chapter of 'Liberal Formulation') but also with 'Revolutionary and Counter-Revolutionary Theory' (the first chapter of 'Socialist Formulations'). In fact, in Volume I of Course E361 they are presented with the liberal formulations only. Although of course there is nothing to prevent the diligent student from following the full span of Harvey's analysis, it is significant that in the formal structuring of the course this sort of closure should be evident.

Enough has now been written to demonstrate that urban education studies in Britain, in so far as they were mediated by the Open University Courses E351 and E361, were characterised by weaknesses of a fundamental nature. Despite a greater sense of the impact of wider structural forces upon urban phenomena than was the case in American work, nevertheless a limited distribution problematic, an undeveloped sense of the political, a narrow conception of the cultural and an insulation from many crucial theoretical debates effectively muted the emergence of a critical scholarship of the urban.

Going beyond the information given

The question which must now be examined is, to what extent did other sources in urban education in Britain extend the theoretical and empirical range of the core materials of the Open University courses? Herbert's (Herbert and Johnson 1976) review of the field concentrated primarily on contextual variables and school performance, compensatory programmes in the USA and upon evaluations of the educational priority programmes in Britain. Its frame of reference was essentially congruent with that of the Open University courses and it stressed the importance of 'expertise in spatial analysis', while avoiding a consideration of the political structuring of space, or of the implications of Harvey's work in this area.

Also unaffected by new developments in critical theory in urban studies were two collections of conference papers: Frank Field's (1977) *Education and the Urban Crisis* and Michael Marland's (1980) *Education for the Inner City*. In an interesting parallel with the early readers in urban education in America, both were the product of sponsored conferences on urban or inner city problems, the former sponsored by the Gulbenkian Foundation[32] and the latter by IBM (United Kingdom). Both of these readers were characterised by a preoccupation with urban policy and planning issues in inner city areas and by a search for 'positive' educational strategies in dealing with the problems of urban schooling. Both of them essentially abstracted such issues from wider structural and political considerations. In Brinson's (1977) paper the larger framework was acknowledged:

> During the last decade the urban crisis has come to be recognised as one of the major social problems of the day. We have seen how the deep social inequalities of our society — affecting income, housing, education and job prospects especially — can be seen in their most aggravated form within our cities. So the urban crisis becomes in turn a crisis of confidence in the processes of government and the priorities of society. Ultimately it calls in question the present social order — not without reason (Brinson 1977: p. 130)

But the implications of this insight were undeveloped. In the Marland collection the emphasis was upon positive action in the schools — 'what the schools can do for the inner city'. Papers from Widlake, Rutter, Kogan and Marland celebrated the potential for change and

Urban education: policy science or critical scholarship? / 31

progress in the inner city, arising from certain forms of educational practice. What may be observed in this reader is a strong 'grounds for optimism' orientation which takes as its adversary negative perspectives seen to be associated with sociological analyses of the inner city. A critical evaluation of this position will be made in the last section of this paper but it may be noted here that the uses and appropriations of the terms 'positive' and 'negative' have powerful ideological associations. In so far as the Marland collection pointed towards fruitful innovations in urban education practice, it usefully extended the scope of urban education studies. In so far as it implied that wider structural and socio-political analysis constituted a 'negative' approach it reinforced the already existing tunnel vision of urban education studies in Britain.

So far, it has been argued that other sources (to those of the Open University) did little to extend the range of theory, understanding and research in urban education. However exceptions to this general picture must be made in relation to Reeder's (1977) collection of papers *Urban Education in the 19th Century* and in relation to Williamson and Byrne's (1979) paper, *Educational Disadvantage in an Urban Setting*. The former work was important in two senses. In the first place it did much to overcome the lack of an historical consciousness in urban education studies in Britain by providing crucial perspectives on education and urban politics (Fraser); the educational ecology of nineteenth century cities (Marsden) and studies of urban working class children and youth (Reeder). In the second place it presented a scholarly and critical overview by Sol Cohen of American historical work on urban schooling, which had the effect of alerting students of urban education in Britain to this important corpus of writing. In short, Reeder's contribution marked a significant advance in urban education studies in Britain.

A further advance was marked by the analysis of Williamson and Byrne (1979), which constitutes one of the first attempts to extend the theoretical range of urban education studies by drawing upon the work of critical writers such as Gray (1976) and Cockburn (1977). In an evaluation review of urban educational deprivation, Williamson and Byrne pointed out that the 'spatial structuring of educational opportunities in Britain is the outcome of social, economic and political processes with historical roots which are part of a changing structure of a capitalist society' (Williamson and Byrne 1979: p. 186). Failure to recognise this total framework had, in their view, been a consequence of a muted or even a hypocritical orientation to the 'political' in the study of the urban.[33]

With the exception of the work of Reeder and of Williamson and Byrne, urban education studies in Britain in the 1970s showed only a modest advance from the range of earlier American work. This modest advance was constituted primarily by the applications of sociological perspectives derived from the work of Pahl, Halsey and others, which stressed the necessity of appreciating urban education problems and conflicts in a wider social structural and economic frame. In all other respects, historical, political, cultural, pedagogic, institutional and ideological such work remained distanced and insulated from major theoretical and empirical developments. Why this should have been so in a decade marked by vigorous theoretical dispute in sociology, in education, in geography, in aspects of history, in urban studies and in political economy is something of an enigma. Part of the explanation must be found in the influence of expectations emanating from various institutions and agencies that urban education studies would be a version of policy science with an agenda designed to clarify policy issues and to indicate practical initiatives to deal with an immediate crisis situation. Such an emphasis already identified in American studies can be detected in the development of urban education in Britain. The effect of a policy science emphasis is to bracket out the consideration of theoretical disputes, historical location and wider socio-political reference, in a close and 'positive' concentration upon the technical and the immediately realisable.[34] In so far as policy science is dominant in any area of inquiry or of action, it inhibits both the development of a sense of critical scholarship and a sense of radical action. Urban education in Britain shows all the signs of having been marked by both of these inhibitions.

Urban education: a possible reformulation of the field

It has been suggested throughout that the weaknesses of urban education study have arisen because of theoretical distancing, empirical abstraction and a policy science emphasis in its orientation and writing. It has been further suggested that the time has come for urban education studies to transcend these limitations and move towards forms of critical inquiry and critical scholarship.[35] What would such a development imply? From the previous analysis it is clear that it would involve theorising the nature of the urban and establishing a coherent rationale for urban education study; recovering a sense of the historical in the study of urban schooling; confronting the political and the economic in a more radical way; engaging with a wider range of cultural and pedagogic theory and attempting to situate empirical inquiries in relation to these wider frameworks. All this would need to be attempted while resisting the ideological charge that such activity was negative and marginal (i.e. lacking in the essential qualities of 'being relevant' and 'being positive') to the immediate problems facing urban education systems, inner city schools and teachers, parents and pupils in such localities. The scope of this paper does not admit an elaboration of each of these areas but an outline agenda can be suggested.

Urban theory and urban education

It is perhaps a truism to say that all students in urban studies need to be introduced to the theoretical spectrum and the theoretical debate which centres upon the nature of the urban question. This spectrum is characterised by functionalist perspectives which suggest a relatively delimited view of urban systems and 'urban problems'; by neo-Weberian perspectives which point to a more structurally related sense of 'urban conflicts' and by Marxist perspectives which provide a critique of existing formulations and suggest that 'urban contradictions' are indicative of the wider structural contradictions of capitalist societies. In other words, students need to enter this intellectual field equipped with a full range of the language of the urban if they are to make their own sense of the concrete phenomena before them (some attempt to provide this range is offered here in Chapter 3, 'Theorising the urban'). This implies that students should have some broad background knowledge of the ways in which the work of Durkheim, of Weber and of Marx and Engels relates to the city in the context of the growth of capitalism. It implies also a closer engagement with the work of the Chicago School and its successors; work in contemporary urban systems theory; the work of neo-Weberians such as Pahl (1975, 1977, 1978, 1979) and the work of contemporary Marxists such as Harvey (1973) and Castells (1976, 1977, 1978).[36] Urban education courses at present provide only a contextual rhetoric of the urban rather than a substantive emphasis upon it. This practice has shown that nothing is to be gained by rushing into an engagement with the problems of urban schooling before the very categories to be used have been subject to some critical scrutiny.

But this still leaves unresolved the nature of urban education as a specific field of inquiry. What is the relevance of this wider theorising to the elucidation of such a field? A survey of social theory and the urban question soon makes it apparent that there are a number of competing formulations of this field. In the first place, from a functionalist or systems perspective, urban education becomes *the study of a range of pathological problems manifest in the structure, processes and achievements of urban (and particularly inner city) schooling.* Urban education is here a species of policy science charged with the investigation of a particular sector of the contemporary urban crisis and with the formulation of 'within-the-system' remedies. For a field defined in this way the key concepts are urban system, urban ecology, urbanism as a way of life, cultural norms, cultural deprivation, compensatory education, disadvantage, urban intervention programmes, racial and ethnic integration, educational management and administration, community, participation and communication, and positive action. As we have seen, this has been the dominant construct of the field. From a neo-Weberian or conflict perspective, urban education becomes *the study of the distribution of authoritative,*[37] *cultural and material resources in urban schooling arising out of the manifest conflicts of social, political and ethnic interest groups and bureaucratic agencies in the city, conflicts which have profound consequences for the structure, processes and achievements of urban schooling.* Within this formulation, the analytical focus is upon the city as providing the most dramatic contexts in which such conflicts become visible but it is at the same time appreciated that the study of the urban is not an end in itself but, 'an arena, an understanding of which helps in the understanding of the overall society which creates it' (Pahl 1975: p. 235). Conceptions of urban education in this perspective, while they may start with the manifest conflicts of urban schooling, are bound in the logic of their analysis to move beyond the framework of the city to consider the wider structures which are in a necessary relation to these conflicts. For a field of urban education defined in this way, the key concepts are urban structure — social structure relations, interest groups,[38] bureaucracies, resources, distributive mechanisms and decision making, socio-spatial systems, distributive and territorial justice, urban conflicts and race relations.[39]

From a Marxist position, the study of urban education may at first sight be characterised as no legitimate field of inquiry at all but rather as an ideological diversion and a mystification. Such a view will be taken in so far as urban education study implies that the urban may be considered analytically in independence from wider structures and in so far as it implies, through 'the ideology of a special area approach', (Castells 1977) that problems may be localised and dealt with in specific urban areas. However while Marxist sources provide an important ideology critique for all forms of urban study, it is apparent that writers such as Castells take the view that a critical scholarship of the urban is both possible and necessary. In this way it can be argued that a Marxist study of urban education would emphasise *the field of urban working class schooling as the site of an historical process of attempted ideological domination and cultural control; as the site of visible schooling contradictions arising out of socio-political contradictions and as the site of a continuing struggle between agencies for hegemonic domination and forms of resistance generated by various groups to such domination.* Thus the key concepts which emerge here are structural contradictions, historical process, ideology, hegemony,[40] class relations, alienation and resistance; for which urban schooling provides one critical lens.

It is clear that these three possible constructions of the field of urban education study have been presented in ideal-type form but that in practice such analytical distinctions are not so neat and that a good deal of interweaving of them actually takes place. Nevertheless, the point of such an exercise is to suggest that students should have available such a conceptual mapping before they engage with the close detail of the structures, processes and achievements of urban schooling. A reformulated field of urban education must make such clarification a first priority.

Recovering a sense of the historical

Urban school systems arose in particular historical conditions and as the outcome of a complex of forces. These had to do with changed class and political relations in cities; concern for social and cultural cohesion; the ministrations of philanthropy, religion and moral mission; the imperatives of bureaucratic rationalisation and with a range of middle class and working class expectations for the powers of formal schooling. The determining effects of particular forces can be seen to have varied over time and also in relation to the dynamics of various societies. A serious study of urban education, even where its prime concern is with the problems of contemporary urban schooling, cannot escape engagement with such questions. It is important for students of urban education to examine accounts of city school systems which suggest that 'today's educational structures are historical products; they represent patterns that have become deeply embedded in American society and are enormously resistant to change' (Katz 1975: p. xvii), and also to scrutinise the argument that 'historical scholarship during the last decade has exposed the myths obscuring the origins of public schooling. Public education neither emerged in a blaze of egalitarian and humanitarian zeal nor did it alter patterns of inequality. Rather the development of public education cannot be understood apart from social relations between classes, anxieties about disorder, attempts to shore up a social structure under stress and the invention of modern forms of bureaucracy' (Katz 1979: p. 256). At the same time, it is important that students should examine the antithesis to this view, which suggests that urban education constituted from the start a serious attempt to realise democratic-liberal aspirations in a pluralist society (Ravitch 1978).

Students of urban education need to locate their contemporary discussions in a framework which is sensitive to issues of continuity and change. This requires some consideration of the extent to which the introduction of urban working class schooling was related to questions of social control in the cities and to a suggested 'crisis of hegemony'[41] in the wider institutions of society. Was it the case that this enterprise constituted 'an enormously ambitious attempt to determine, though the capture of educational means, the patterns of thought, sentiment and behaviour of the working class' (Johnson 1970: p. 119)? To the extent that the origins of urban education were marked by preoccupations of control and class-cultural transformation, have such preoccupations significantly changed or do they still exist in modern and transmuted forms? On the other hand, has a concern with cultural imposition and social control in the history of urban schooling overlooked the ways in which sectors of the working class *used* provided education for their own ends[42] or developed their own oppositional forms (Simon 1974; Laqueur 1976; Johnson 1979)? Does the contemporary situation of urban schooling reveal any continuities with these themes?

Historical materials on urban schooling make explicit, in ways which contemporary materials rarely do, the confident expressions of intent by the providing classes and the robust statements of resistance from the receiving classes. Such materials make salient the crucial importance of class relations (which are also power relations) and instances of ideological conflict in the provision of schooling. Performing as they do this vital function, they provide an absolutely necessary counter to the superficial, the bland, the apolitical and the 'present crisis' focus of much urban education writing. In short, it becomes apparent that there cannot be a sense of critical scholarship in urban education if such history is not recovered.

Confronting the political and the economic

It is a characteristic of a wide range of educational studies that discussions of the 'political' and of the 'economic' and of the ways in which these relations impinge upon school systems, is either avoided entirely or strictly delimited in extent. That this should be so is itself a fascinating problem in the sociology of knowledge and one which has considerable implications for the study of ideology.[43] For as Stuart Hall observes,

> Education might be thought of as the pursuit of politics 'by other means'. . . . education is precisely the means in modern societies by which men and women are formed and shaped as social individuals, . . . it is not therefore by chance or in error that every major change in the education structure needs to be understood as being intimately connected to a shift in power. . . . (Hall 1974: p. 49)

An urban education view of 'political' questions exists which is in effect concerned with the actions of interest groups and decision makers within urban school systems. An urban education view of 'economic' questions exists which is in effect concerned with the distribution of resources to urban (particularly inner city) schools when compared with suburban schools or with other social services. Discussion of these issues is legitimated because the frame of reference remains either within education as a 'sub-system' or within the city as a 'social system'. Such delimited concepts of the political and the economic are inadequate for a fundamental understanding of urban school problems. The weaknesses of urban education in this respect precisely repeat those of an earlier phase of urban sociology. While such investigations are a necessary first step in analysis they inevitably lead (or logically should do) to a consideration of the wider distribution of power and of the organisation of economic life. Students of urban education therefore must confront these relations which cannot be divorced from the crisis of the urban school, and they must be prepared to address a much more radical set of questions. They need in other words to overcome the inhibition (ideological barrier?) which suggests that such questions are not the legitimate concern of educators. Questions such as, if Merson and Campbell's (1974) view is correct, that the defining feature of inner city residents is their powerlessness, what mechanisms have produced such powerlessness and what can urban educational institutions do about this? What are the political and economic principles and mechanisms which have produced in America a political and economic crisis of the cities[44] with determinate effects upon inner city schools? What sorts of transformations would be necessary to solve such crises? Is David Harvey correct when he asserts that in the examination of all urban problems (including schooling) 'we discuss everything except the basic characteristics of a capitalist market economy. We devise all manner of solutions except those which might challenge the continuance of that economy' (Harvey 1973: p. 144)? If he is *not* correct, then what are the political and economic redistributive agencies which will establish territorial and social justice and the conditions for equality of educational opportunity within urban schooling?

To begin to answer such questions, students of urban education will need access to debates about the nature of power and decision making (Saunders 1980); about the political economy of the urban question (Pahl 1977; Castells 1977) and about the relations between the local and the central state (Miliband 1969; Poulantzas 1969; Cockburn 1977; Jessop 1977). These debates may appear to be a long way from the realities of the urban classroom but these same realities are, in part, an attenuated consequence of such power relations.

It is also necessary, as Pahl so rightly emphasises, that the comparative dimension within urban study is not neglected. In what senses for instance is the capitalist city different from the socialist city?[45] In what senses do the problems of urban schooling take on a different complexion according to different political and economic arrangements? At present, such questions are easier to raise than they are to carry forward into empirical inquiry. Nevertheless they point the direction in which a serious comparative political economy of urban schooling ought to be moving.

Cultural and pedagogic theory

If the city in general can be viewed as an arena for the making visible of fundamental social conflicts and contradictions, then it is certainly the case that working class inner city schools make visible a wide range of cultural and pedagogic conflicts and contradictions. These conflicts and contradictions provide an important focus for urban education study. Much of the existing culturalist and pedagogic writing within urban education (especially in America) has been within a framework, sometimes implicit and sometimes explicit, of deficit theory. There have been two dominant categories of deficit theory. The first has located the relative cultural and pedagogic failure of urban working class schools in features of the pupils, the family or the local community. The second (apparently more liberal) version has located such failure in the deficiencies of urban teachers and the arrangements of urban education administrators. The limitations of such approaches have been pointed out by Bernstein:

> deficit theory fails to examine how the distribution of power and the principles of social control regulate the distribution of, the reception of, the participation in and the change of dominant cultural categories . . . the debate the research has triggered off in the USA has been, on the whole, conducted at a fairly trivial level, because it has not been placed in the wider problematic of cultural reproduction and change. (Bernstein 1977: pp. 27–8)

What would placing such a debate in the wider problematic of cultural reproduction and change involve within urban education? It would seem to involve in the first place a careful examination of the historical mission of urban working class schools as agencies of cultural transmission. What principles can be discerned in such schools underlying the structuring of the curriculum, of the pedagogy and of the social relations of schooling in the nineteenth century? What sorts of responses, both in terms of accommodation with or resistance to such principles become apparent in different fractions of the urban working class when such research is undertaken? It can be expected that such sociohistorical inquiry will reveal that judgments about the cultural and educational 'effectiveness' of such schools were a subject of fierce controversy from the start.

Against this necessary background of the contested nature of cultural and pedagogic principles in urban schooling, it would then be possible to trace the changes in such principles and in the forms of curriculum, pedagogy and social relations in city schools in the twentieth century, relating such changes to shifts in educational theory, economic developments and socio-political features.[46] By this procedure a continuing ideological conflict over the contents and structure of the curriculum, the mode of pedagogy and the nature of social relations within urban schooling would become visible. It would be no longer possible for students of urban education to imagine that issues of curriculum and pedagogy and issues of underachievement were simply part of a technical problem of the inner city school. It would become apparent that judgments about whether a particular curriculum or a particular pedagogic approach was 'working' would be linked to conflicting socio-political ends and not simply to some consensual version of an educational or individual norm. In these ways students would be brought to recognise the conflicts and contradictions associated with the cultural role of inner city schools. These contradictions arise from sets of expectations all of which claim legitimacy. Contradictions arise for instance between an historic function of conservative cultural reproduction and a contemporary potential for the celebration of cultural variety; between a curriculum and pedagogy concerned with critical consciousness and a curriculum and pedagogy concerned with domestication;[47] between a curriculum for achieving 'within-the-system' successes or with a curriculum for 'against-the-system' resistances.[48] In order to be able to evaluate these positions students of urban education will need some access and introduction to a spectrum of theorising including the work of Apple, Bantock, Bernstein, Bourdieu, Freire, Gramsci, Lawton, Sharp, and Young. Using such literature they will need to attempt to clarify the linkages between cultural and pedagogic arrangements and wider political and social arrangements. In doing so they will need to formulate what seems to them to be a curriculum structure and a mode of pedagogy particularly suited to the conditions of the inner city school.[49] But theorising alone will not be sufficient without the discipline provided by empirical engagement and empirical inquiry. Bernstein recognises this when he says, 'conceptual elegance is attractive but only when it has the living quality which comes from empirical exploration' (Bernstein 1977: p. 4). Therefore it is to empirical exploration in urban education study that we now turn.

Empirical exploration

What sort of empirical exploration is required in a reformulated field of urban education study? There is no shortage of work to be done in various categories of inquiry and at various levels, but there are dangers to be avoided. The student of urban education needs to avoid the abstracted empiricism of 'a scatter of requests for scattered information, statistical or otherwise, about a scatter of individuals and their scattered milieux' (Mills 1973: pp. 77–8). Also to be avoided is the type of empiricism which substitutes for critical theorising: 'mapping even more evidence of man's patent inhumanity to man is counter-revolutionary in the sense that it allows the bleeding-heart liberal in us to pretend that we are contributing to a solution when in fact we are not. This kind of empiricism is irrelevant' (Harvey 1973: p. 144).

In other words, we need forms of empirical inquiry in urban education which, at their best, will be historically and theoretically situated on the one hand and generative of critical action[50] on the other. Given these necessary conditions, what sorts of projects appear to be significant? This paper has already indicated the work which needs to be done in recovering a sense of the historical; confronting the political and the economic; and deepening the treatment of cultural and pedagogic theory applied to the study of urban education questions. At community, institutional and classroom levels another sector of inquiry opens up. For instance, can community education in inner city areas do anything to overcome the sense of alienation and powerlessness among inner city residents?[51] To what extent does an effective community education programme require the support of agencies beyond the school including universities, political parties, trade unions, ethnic organisations and tenants' organisations, and to what extent has this sort of co-ordination been accomplished?[52] Even where accomplished, is community education in practice a modern version of gentling the urban masses, or might it produce the dynamic for the emergence of urban social movements?[53] These are the sorts of questions which a serious study of urban education would pursue with some empirical vigour. At the level of the inner city school such questions would be: what are the ways in which racism and sexism are manifest in structures, processes and relations? What school policies exist to counter racism and sexism and in relation to the former, what is the effectiveness of policies of multicultural or multi-ethnic education?[54] Is multicultural education a modern form of gentling the black urban masses, as Stone (1981) and Mullard (1982) suggest, or does it have real potential for effecting change?

Given the continuing ideological conflict over what constitutes a 'good' urban school and a 'good' teacher and a 'good' pupil within such schools, there is much scope for refined and discriminating study in this area. While in Britain Michael Rutter *et al.*'s (1979) study of the relative successes of twelve inner London secondary schools has provoked a considerable critical debate,[55] it has not provoked those researchers who are critical of its assumptions, methodology and findings to engage in what might be called 'oppositional inquiry'. Such oppositional inquiry is much needed in urban education. If there *are* other models of the good school than those suggested by Rutter then they will need to be demonstrated empirically. The same applies to other models of 'good' teaching in the inner city school[56] and to other concepts of the 'good' pupil. It is not enough simply to assert the case without the discipline of empirical engagement.

Finally, at the level of the classroom, the sorts of questions raised by Sharp and Green's (1975) study need to be pursued in inner city schools. In what ways do the constraints of the classroom as a workplace undermine the teacher's pedagogical intentions? What unconscious forms of exclusion or partial attention to certain categories of pupil result from the constraints of time, space and numbers? Do conflicts arise for teachers between expectations for pastoral responsibility and individual welfare work on the one hand and expectations for the intellectual development of pupils on the other? In the case of conflict, how do teachers in practice find a strategy for coping? Such classroom research within inner city schools will need to capture also something of the perspectives of a range of pupils. Paul Willis's (1977) study provides an excellent model for this in its rich ethnographic treatment of the culture of resistance among 'the lads', which is then theorised for its wider structural significance. But the urban working class school does not consist only of 'the lads' even if they make a particularly dramatic impact within it. Ethnographic research is needed to chart a whole range of socio-cultural responses to different pedagogical regimes in different schools. The world-view of the 'conformists', black and white, male and female must be scrutinised as closely as that of the 'rebels'. In this way an ethnography of the urban school will emerge capable of illuminating a full range of pedagogical principles and cultural responses which are related to wider structural frameworks.

Critical scholarship and 'being positive'

The conventional justification for a policy science emphasis in any area of study is that it has the virtue of 'being positive' and of suggesting realisable programmes of action. Much of existing urban education study has been justified in these terms. The conventional attack on forms of critical inquiry is that it results in the 'negative' and engenders feelings of powerlessness and loss of morale. The ideological nature of these judgments should by now have become apparent. Freed from the inhibition that our thinking in education cannot be allowed to be structural or political then it becomes clear that the work of critical scholarship, rather than being sterile is, on the contrary, fruitful at an intellectual, professional and practical level. In a paper which owes so much to the inspiration of C. Wright Mills it is perhaps appropriate to close with his masterly statement on this subject:

> Certain types of critics, by the way, judge work in social science according to whether or not its conclusions are gloomy or sunshiny, negative or constructive. These sunshine moralists want a lyric upsurge, at least at the end: they are made happy by a sturdy little mood of earnest optimism, out of which we step forward fresh and shining. But the world we are trying to understand does not always make all of us politically hopeful and morally complacent, which is to say, that social scientists sometimes find it difficult to play the cheerful idiot. Personally I happen to be a very optimistic type, but I must confess that I have never been able to make up my mind about whether something is so or not in terms of whether or not it leads to good cheer. First, one tries to get it straight, to make an adequate statement — if it is gloomy, too bad; if it leads to hope, fine. In the meantime, to cry for 'the constructive programme' and 'the hopeful note' is often a sign of incapacity to face facts as they are even when they are decidedly unpleasant — and it is irrelevant to truth or falsity and to judgements of proper work in social science (Mills 1973: p. 89).

Notes

1 The editor of *Urban Education* argued in the first issue that urban education studies should be a focus for the application of existing disciplines rather than a particular specialism in itself. See *Urban*

Education, vol. 1, no. 1, Summer 1964, p. 2. In a letter to the writer he has suggested that 'topic of inquiry' is the most appropriate description.

2 It is perhaps significant in understanding the formation of urban education studies in America to note the very flexible academic identities of its founding scholars. Havighurst, for instance, is reported by Kopan as being a science educator in the 1930s, a psychologist in the 1940s and a sociologist in the 1950s. See A. Kopan, 'Robert J. Havighurst: the pursuit of excellence' in H. Walberg and A. Kopan (eds), *Re-Thinking Urban Education*, Jossey Bass, 1972.

3 Havighurst contributed also to the special edition of *International Review of Education*, vol. XIII, No. 4, 1967, 'The effects of urbanization on education'; and to the *World Yearbook of Education 1970*, 'Education in cities'.

4 For an example of a widely used text in urban education studies see H. Miller and R. Woock, *Social Foundations of Urban Education*, Dryden Press, 1970 (reprinted in 1973 and in 1978).

5 See H. Walberg and A. Kopan (1972), op. cit.

6 Pickvance (1976: pp. 1–2) writes,
   interest . . . in the field of urban sociology was given an extra impetus by the 'events' of May 1968 in France and their repercussions. Institutionally, this interest was helped by the French government's provision of finance for urban research in universities or independent research institutions following its interpretation of the 'events' as in part due to urban malfunctioning. That this finance has helped develop a new and critical approach not only within urban sociology but also in the form of political action regarding urban issues is a curious paradox.

7 Castells (1977: p. 77) comments on the significance of 'urbanism' in these terms:
   an attempt to define the characteristic features of an urban culture and to explain its process of production on the basis of the content of the particular ecological form constituted by the city. In all probability, it is the most serious theoretical attempt ever made, within sociology, to establish a theoretical object (and consequently, a domain of research) specific to urban sociology. Its echoes, thirty-three years later, still dominate discussion.

8 For discussions of the influence of the Chicago School, see Mellor (1977), Castells (1977), and Saunders (1981).

9 The notion of policy science is taken from B. Fay (1975), *Social*

Theory and Political Practice, London, Allen & Unwin. Fay defines policy science as
> that set of procedures which enables one to determine the technically best course of action to adopt in order to implement a decision or achieve a goal ... in this regard the policy scientist really is a type of social engineer who makes instrumental decisions on the basis of the various laws of science — in this instance social science — which are relevant to the problem in hand. The policy engineer ... is one who seeks the most technically correct answer to political problems. (p. 14)

10 As with the notion 'interdisciplinary', the notion of 'complexity' used in these studies is more rhetorical than real, i.e. the complexity of issues is not in fact substantively pursued in the analysis.

11 A close scrutiny of the Passow readers establishes this. Reader 1 (1963: p. 335) contained an influential article by Deutsch focusing upon the psychological products of social deprivation and providing a composite portrait of the disadvantaged child: 'his educational handicap, cultural limitations, inarticulateness, short attention span, undeveloped abstract thinking abilities and lack of motivation for academic success'.

In Reader 2, (1967: p. 9), Charles Silberman in an article called 'The city and the Negro' argued that even if racial discrimination was ended the 'Negro problem' would not be solved because 'the truth is that too many Negroes are unable or unwilling to compete in an integrated society.'

12 See A.H. Passow (1963) op. cit.

13 It is correct to note that the Passow readers did recognise a debate around questions of cultural disadvantage and compensatory education. A small thread of critical writing can be detected. See D. Dodson, 'Education and the powerless' and S. Wayland, 'Old problems, new faces and new standards' in Passow (1963).

Perhaps the most important contribution came from Basil Bernstein in 'A critique of the concept of compensatory education' which appeared in Passow (1972).

14 It is probably significant in appreciating the psychologistic emphasis of this work to note that Miriam Goldberg, Professor of Psychology and Education, had become Director of the Urban Education Project at Teachers College in 1968.

15 The American literature of urban education is marked by a continuing search for 'better teachers' and 'better administrators' for inner city schools, and for new ways of preparing teachers and administrators for work in such schools. See, for instance, V. Haubrich, 'Teachers for big city schools' and L. Kornberg, 'Meaningful teachers for alienated children', both in Passow (1963), op. cit.

16 While providing dramatic and vivid accounts of inner city schools such studies had the unfortunate effect of implying that the main problems in urban education lay in the sphere of interpersonal relations and that authoritarian and insensitive teachers were a prime cause of alienation in such schools. Thus although a 'blame the pupil' stance was avoided, a 'blame the teacher' stance often took its place.

17 See for instance David Tyack, (1974) *The One Best System: A History of American Urban Education*, Cambridge, Mass., Harvard University Press.

18 This new emphasis applied also to race as a fundamental cultural category in American studies in urban education. Whereas the studies of the 1960s viewed racial questions very much in culturalist and deficit terms (see 'The controversy over the black family' in Miller and Woock, 1970, op. cit., pp. 132–45), in the 1970s the emphasis began to change. In the 1970s, attention focused upon the effects of institutional racism and upon the consequences of desegregation measures in education. However a notable check to this development was caused by Jensen's (1969) reassertion of the genetic basis of black educational underachievement. That race continued to be a central preoccupation of urban education studies in America can be seen in such texts as C.V. Willie's (1978) *The Sociology of Urban Education*, which is *entirely* concerned with this question, despite its title.

19 It is important to note that while Bernstein's early work on language and class was incorporated in an oversimplified manner into urban education studies, his later work on cultural and social reproduction has been ignored in the texts. Also ignored has been the work of Young (1971), of Bourdieu (1971, 1977) and of Apple (1979).

20 Some writers have recognised the need for wider theoretical and historical frameworks in urban education study. See for instance Ray Rist (1973), *The Urban School: A Factory for Failure*, Cambridge, Mass., MIT Press.

21 See D. Ravitch (1978), *The Revisionists Revised: A Critique of the Radical Attack on the Schools*, New York, Basic Books. See also M. Katz (1979), 'An apology for American educational history', *Harvard Educational Review*, vol. 49, no. 2 pp. 256–66.

22 Individual historical articles can be found but comparatively rarely. They provide occasional historical insertions rather than an important framework against which contemporary urban issues can be appreciated.

23 See, for instance, H. Miller (1978), *Social Foundations of Education:*

An Urban Focus, New York, Holt, Rinehart & Winston. A third edition of a widely used text, it still opens with the words, 'only since the 1950s have professional educators paid much attention to urban schools.' No account is taken of the historical studies of urban schooling undertaken in the 1970s except for passing references to the work of Tyack and of Ravitch.

For an urban education text with an historical dimension, see W.W. Brickman and S. Lehrer (eds) (1972), *Education and the Many Faces of the Disadvantaged: Cultural and Historical Perspectives*, New York, Wiley.

24 See, for instance, R. Dentler *et al.* (1967), *The Urban R's: Race Relations as The Problem in Urban Education*, New York, Praeger; R.L. Green (1969), *Racial Crisis in American Education*, Chicago, Follet Corporation, and C.V. Willie (1978), op. cit.

25 Urban Education was offered as a third level course by the Open University in 1973—4. Many of the students were teachers studying for the BA in Educational Studies.

Urban Education options were subsequently developed within the structure of existing BEd courses, for instance at Bradford College, Leeds Polytechnic, Polytechnic of the South Bank, Trent Polytechnic and the Roehampton Institute.

Specialist Diplomas in Urban Education have been established at Edgehill College, Goldsmiths' College, Trent Polytechnic and the Urban Studies Centre (London) of the College of St Mark and St John.

An MA (Urban Education) course was started at King's College, University of London in 1976 and an MA (Education in Urban Areas) at the University of London, Institute of Education in 1977.

26 It should be noted that A.H. Passow appears as a course consultant for Urban Education: E351, and for the readers.

27 See Stuart Hall, 'Education and the crisis of the urban school' in J. Raynor (1974), *Issues in Urban Education*, Milton Keynes, Open University Press.

28 See, for instance, Gerald Grace (1978), *Teachers, Ideology and Control: A Study in Urban Education*, London, Routledge & Kegan Paul.

29 See J. Raynor and E. Harris (eds) (1977), *Schooling in the City*, vol. 2, London, Ward Lock, pp. 187—250.

30 'Curriculum issues' are examined in Raynor and Harris (eds), *Schooling in the City* (1977), op. cit., pp. 89—185 and in Block VI, Urban Schooling, Milton Keynes, Open University Press, 1978.

31 See Unit 4 of Block II, Inequality in the City (1978), and Units

48 / Gerald Grace

11–13, Block V, Race, Children and Cities (1978), Open University Press.

32 The introductory essay of *Education and the Urban Crisis* notes, The Calouste Gulbenkian Foundation sponsored two conferences around this theme for the following reasons. First, the Foundation thought it important to try and bring together information on the current trends in our inner city areas in order to judge whether British cities were slipping into a disorder similar to that occurring in the USA. Second, if our cities were beginning to follow the American pattern, the Foundation wanted to know what part our educational system could play in reversing the trend. (Field, 1977: p. 1).

The preface to *Education for the Inner City*, contains a statement from the Director of Personnel and Corporate Affairs, IBM (UK):
the problems of the inner city are receiving attention from central and local government and from voluntary organisations. It is appropriate too for business, with its interest in and concern for the stability and health of our society, to make a major contribution. (Marland, 1980: p. viii).

33 In a comment upon the use of the political in the study of the urban, Williamson and Byrne (1979: p. 187) make their position explicit:
these arguments are clearly contentious, complex and overlaid heavily with political debate. But to pretend that in some way this is avoidable, that the questions with which we have to deal are purely technical, seems to us to be an equally strong *political* stance.

34 Certain contemporary developments in initial teacher training in Britain show these characteristics.

35 Critical scholarship is characterised, among other things, by the practice of ideology-critique; by the investigation of those structural contradictions which underlie a whole range of visible socio-political conflict situations and by the investigation of historical process. For a useful discussion, see Fay (1975), op. cit., Chapter 5.

36 Given the crowded nature of urban education courses such a theoretical array may seem impracticable. However an excellent overview is provided in Peter Saunders (1981), *Society Theory and the Urban Question*, London, Hutchinson.

37 For a discussion of authoritative resources see A. Giddens (1979), *Central Problems in Social Theory*, London, Macmillan. For a discussion of the relationship between authoritative resources and the city, see Chapter 6, 'Time, labour and the city', in A.

Urban education: policy science or critical scholarship? / 49

Giddens (1981), *A Contemporary Critique of Historical Materialism*, London, Macmillan.

38 For a discussion of interest groups, see Chapters 1 and 2 of P. Saunders (1980), *Urban Politics: A Sociological Interpretation*, Harmondsworth, Penguin Books.

39 From a neo-Weberian standpoint, the work of John Rex is particularly important, combining as it does an historically situated view of race relations, located both theoretically and empirically in relation to the urban context.
See J. Rex and R. Moore (1967), *Race, Community and Conflict*, London, Oxford University Press; J. Rex (1970), *Race Relations in Sociological Theory*, London, Weidenfield & Nicolson; J. Rex (1973), *Race, Colonialism and the City*, London, Routledge & Kegan Paul; J. Rex and S. Tomlinson (1979), *Colonial Immigrants in a British City*, London, Routledge & Kegan Paul.

40 A helpful definition of hegemony is given by MacDonald (1977) in *The Curriculum and Cultural Reproduction* (Revision II), Open University Press, pp. 68–9:
> hegemony refers to a whole range of structures and activities as well as values, attitudes, beliefs and morality that in various ways support the established order and the class interests which dominate it. The concept of hegemony refers to the organizing principle or world view which is diffused through agencies of ideological control and socialization into every area of daily life. It provides the fundamental categories of thought and perception of the social world which binds individuals together within one society. To the extent that it is internalized by ordinary people it becomes part of their 'common sense'. . . . Through cultural hegemony 'spontaneous' consent is created. . . .'.

For other discussions of hegemony see Chantal Mouffe, 'Hegemony and ideology in Gramsci', in Chantal Mouffe (ed.) (1979), *Gramsci and Marxist Theory*, London, Routledge & Kegan Paul; and Raymond Williams (1977), *Marxism and Literature*, London, Oxford University Press.

41 See Richard Johnson (1976), 'Notes on the schooling of the English working class', in R. Dale *et al.* (eds), *Schooling and Capitalism*, London, Routledge & Kegan Paul.

42 Harold Silver (1977) has suggested that there has been too much concentration on social control 'intentions' and not enough examination of actual 'effects'. See 'Aspects of neglect: the strange case of Victorian popular education', *Oxford Review of Education*, vol. 3, no. 1, pp. 57–69.

43 For a good discussion of this, see Ted Benton (1974), 'Education

and politics' in D. Holly (ed.), *Education or Domination?*, London, Arrow Books.

44 See R.C. Hill, 'Fiscal collapse and political struggle in decaying central cities in the United States', and W.K. Tabb, 'The New York City fiscal crisis', in W.K. Tabb and L. Sawers (eds) (1978), *Marxism and the Metropolis*, New York, Oxford University Press.

45 For one discussion of this see 'Learning from others: cities and socialism', Part II in W.K. Tabb and L. Sawers (eds) (1978), op. cit.

46 For one provocative and interesting attempt to relate a major change in the principles governing the curriculum to features of the wider socio-political situation in Britain in the 1920s, see John White (1975), 'The end of the compulsory curriculum', in *The Curriculum*, the Doris Lee Lectures 1975, University of London, Institute of Education.

47 This position is particularly epitomised in the writings of Paulo Freire.

48 For the notion of a curriculum of resistance, see C. Searle (1975), *Classrooms of Resistance*, Writers and Readers Publishing Cooperative, London.

49 It can be argued that inner city schools do *not* require a 'particular' curriculum or a 'particular' mode of pedagogy but simply 'good' academic teaching. For arguments along these lines, but from different ideological positions, see Boyson (1975) and 'Right to Learn' (1974).

50 The notion of critical action used here follows the argument of Fay (1975), op. cit.:
    the translation of a critical social science into practice would necessarily require the participation and active involvement of social actors themselves in this process . . . the function of the social scientist is not to provide knowledge of quasi-causal laws to a policy scientist who will determine which social conditions are to be manipulated in order to effect a particular goal, but rather to enlighten the social actors so that coming to see themselves and their social situation in a new way, they themselves decide to alter the conditions which they find repressive. In other words, the social scientist tries to 'raise the consciousness' of the actors whose situation he is studying. (pp. 102—3).

51 The potential for this has been noted by Halsey (1972):
    educational programmes may make a considerable impact on the political consciousness of the poor, a process that has certainly accompanied the development of compensatory education in the United States. Such political awakening may

be the most effective means of ensuring that the gross
inequalities between social and ethnic groups are eradicated.
(p. 30)

52 For a discussion of some of the issues involved, see B. Ashcroft
and K. Jackson, 'Adult education and social action', in D. Jones
and M. Mayo (eds) (1974), *Community Work: One*, London,
Routledge & Kegan Paul.

53 The notion of urban social movement is taken from Castells
(1977), op. cit; see Part IV, 'Urban politics'.

54 For a range of critical perspectives on this question see J. Tierney
(ed.) (1982), *Race, Migration and Schooling*, New York, Holt,
Rinehart & Winston.

55 See B. Tizard *et al.* (1980), *Fifteen Thousand Hours: A Discussion*,
London, University of London, Institute of Education. See also
A. Heath and P. Clifford (1980), 'The seventy thousand hours
that Rutter left out', *Oxford Review of Education*, vol. 6, no. 1.

56 For one attempt to begin this process, by initial description at
least if not by detailed research, see Part 3, 'Developing alternatives',
in Geoff Whitty and Michael Young (1976), *Explorations in the
Politics of School Knowledge*, Driffield, Nafferton Books.

Bibliography

Apple, M. (1979), *Ideology and Curriculum*, London, Routledge &
Kegan Paul.
Apple M. (ed). (1982), *Cultural and Economic Reproduction in
Education*, London, Routledge & Kegan Paul.
Ashcroft, B. and Jackson, K. (1974), 'Adult education and social
action', in D. Jones and M. Mayo (eds), *Community Work: One*,
London, Routledge & Kegan Paul.
Bachrach, P. and Baratz, M. (1970), *Power and Poverty: Theory and
Practice*, New York, Oxford University Press.
Bantock, G.H. (1975), 'Towards a theory of popular education',
in M. Golby *et al.* (eds), *Curriculum Design*, London, Croom Helm.
Bantock, G.H. (1980), *Dilemmas of the Curriculum*, Oxford, Martin
Robertson.
Basini, A. (1981), 'Urban schools and disruptive pupils: a study of some
ILEA support units', *Educational Review*, vol. 33, no. 3.
Benton, T. (1974), 'Education and politics', in D. Holly (ed.), *Education
or Domination?*, London, Arrow Books.
Bernstein, B. (1972), 'A critique of the concept of compensatory
education', in A.H. Passow (ed.), *Opening Opportunities for
Disadvantaged Learners*, Teachers College Press, Columbia
University.

Bernstein, B. (1977), *Class, Codes and Control: Towards a Theory of Educational Transmissions*, London, Routledge & Kegan Paul (second edition).
Bourdieu, P. (1971), 'Systems of education and systems of thought', in M.F.D. Young (ed.), *Knowledge and Control: New Directions for the Sociology of Education*, London, Collier-Macmillan.
Bourdieu, P. and Passeron, J.-C. (1977), *Reproduction in Education, Society and Culture*, Beverley Hills, Sage.
Bowles, S. and Gintis, H. (1976), *Schooling in Capitalist America*, London, Routledge & Kegan Paul.
Boyson, R. (1975), *The Crisis in Education*, London, Woburn Press.
Brickman, W. and Lehrer, S. (1972), *Education and the Many Faces of the Disadvantaged: Cultural and Historical Perspectives*, New York, Wiley.
Brinson, P. (1977), 'Foundations and the urban crisis: a personal view', in F. Field (ed.), *Education and the Urban Crisis*, London, Routledge & Kegan Paul.
Brook, M. (1980), 'The "mother-tongue" issue in Britain: cultural diversity or control?', *British Journal of Sociology of Education*, vol. 1, no. 3.
Castells, M. (1976), 'Theory and ideology in urban sociology', in C. Pickvance (ed.), *Urban Sociology: Critical Essays*, London, Tavistock.
Castells, M. (1977), *The Urban Question: A Marxist Approach*, London, Arnold.
Castells, M. (1978), *City, Class and Power*, London, Macmillan.
Clark, K. (1965), *Dark Ghetto*, New York, Harper & Row.
Cockburn, C. (1977), *The Local State*, London, Pluto Press.
Cohen, S. (1964), *Progressives and Urban School Reform*, New York, Columbia University Press.
Cohen, S. (1977), 'The history of urban education in the United States', in D. Reeder (ed.), *Urban Education in the 19th Century*, London, Taylor & Francis.
Conant, J. (1961), *Slums and Suburbs: A Commentary on Schools in Metropolitan Areas*, New York, McGraw Hill.
Crecine, J. (ed.) (1970), *Financing the Metropolis*, Beverley Hills, Sage.
Cuban, L. (1969), *Teaching in the Inner City*, New York, Macmillan/Free Press.
Dahl, R. (1961), *Who Governs? Democracy and Power in an American City*, New Haven, Yale University Press.
Dentler, R. *et al.* (eds) (1967), *The Urban R's: Race Relations as the Problem in Urban Education*, New York, Praeger.
Department of Labor (1965), *The Negro Family: The Case for National Action* (Moynihan Report), Washington DC, US Government Printing Office.
Duncan, O. *et al.* (1960), *Metropolis and Region*, Baltimore, Johns Hopkins Press.

Engels, F. (1976 edition), *The Condition of the Working Class in England*, London, Panther Books.
Entwistle, H. (1979), *Antonio Gramsci: Conservative Schooling for Radical Politics*, London, Routledge & Kegan Paul.
Fantini, M. and Weinstein, G. (1968a), *Making Urban Schools Work*, New York, Holt, Rinehart & Winston.
Fantini, M. and Weinstein, G. (1968b), *The Disadvantaged: Challenge to Education*, New York, Harper & Row.
Fantini, M. et al. (1970), *Community Control and the Urban School*, New York, Praeger.
Fay, B. (1975), *Social Theory and Political Practice*, London, Allen & Unwin.
Field, F. (ed.) (1977), *Education and the Urban Crisis*, London, Routledge & Kegan Paul.
Freire, P. (1972), *Cultural Action for Freedom*, Harmondsworth, Penguin Books.
Freire, P. (1972), *Pedagogy of the Oppressed*, Harmondsworth, Penguin Books.
Fuchs, E. (1968), *Teachers Talk: A View From Within the Inner City Schools*, New York, Doubleday.
Gentry, A. et al. (1972), *Urban Education: The Hope Factor*, Philadelphia, Saunders.
Giddens, A. (1981), 'Time, Labour and the City', in *A Contemporary Critique of Historical Materialism*, London, Macmillan.
Gittell, M. and Hevesi, A. (1969), *The Politics of Urban Education*, New York, Praeger.
Golby, M. and Fleming, A. (1978), Urban Schooling (E361, Block VI), Milton Keynes, Open University Press.
Grace, G. (1978), *Teachers, Ideology and Control: A Study in Urban Education*, London, Routledge & Kegan Paul.
Gray, F. (1976), 'Radical geography and the study of education', *Antipode*, vol. 8, no. 1.
Green, R. (1969), *Racial Crisis in American Education*, Chicago, Follett Corporation.
Hall, S. (1974), 'Education and the crisis of the urban school', in J. Raynor, *Issues in Urban Education*, Milton Keynes, Open University Press.
Halsey, A.H. (1972), *Educational Priority: EPA Problems and Policies*, vol. I, London, HMSO.
Halsey, A.H. (1974), 'Government against poverty in school and community', in D. Wedderburn (ed.), *Poverty, Inequality and Class Structure*, Cambridge, Cambridge University Press.
Halsey, A.H. (1977), 'Political ends and educational means', in P. Raggatt and M. Evans (eds), *Urban Education 3: The Political Context*, London, Ward Lock.
Hamnett, C. (1978), Inequality in the City (E361, Block II), Milton Keynes, Open University Press.
Harloe, M. (ed.) (1977), *Captive Cities*, London, Wiley.

Harvey, D. (1973), *Social Justice and the City*, London, Arnold.
Harvey, D. (1977), 'Social justice and spatial systems', in J. Raynor and E. Harris, (eds), *Urban Education 2: The City Experience*, London, Ward Lock.
Havighurst, R. (1963), 'Urban development and the education system', in A.H. Passow (ed.), *Education in Depressed Areas*, New York, Teachers College Press.
Havighurst, R. (1964), *The Public Schools of Chicago*, Chicago, Board of Education.
Havighurst, R. (1966), *Education in Metropolitan Areas*, Boston, Allyn & Bacon.
Havighurst, R. (1967), 'Metropolitan development and the educational system', in A.H. Passow (ed.), *Education of the Disadvantaged*, New York, Holt, Rinehart & Winston.
Havighurst, R. (ed.) (1968), *Metropolitanism: Its Challenge to Education*, 67th Year Book, National Society for the Study of Education, Part I, Chicago, Chicago University Press.
Havighurst, R. (1970), 'Chicago: educational development in a metropolitan area', in J. Lauwerys and D. Scanlon (eds), *The World Year Book of Education*, London, Evans.
Hawley, A. (1950), *Human Ecology*, New York, Ronald Press.
Heath, A. and Clifford, P. (1980), 'The seventy thousand hours that Rutter left out', *Oxford Review of Education*, vol. 6, no. 1.
Herbert, D. and Johnson, R. (eds) (1976), *Social Areas in Cities*, vol. 2, London, Wiley.
Herbert, D. and Smith, D. (eds) (1979), *Social Problems and the City*, London, Oxford University Press.
Hill, R. (1978), 'Fiscal collapse and political struggle in decaying central cities in the United States', in W. Tabb and L. Sawers (eds), *Marxism and the Metropolis*, New York, Oxford University Press.
Howe, H. et al. (1970), *Racism and American Education*, New York, Vintage Press.
Janowitz, M. (1972), *Institution Building in Urban Education*, Chicago, Chicago University Press.
Jessop, R. (1977), 'Recent theories of the capitalist state', *Cambridge Journal of Economics*, vol. 1, No. 4.
Johnson, R. (1970), 'Educational policy and social control in early Victorian England', *Past and Present*, vol. 49.
Johnson, R. (1976), 'Notes of the schooling of the English working class', in R. Dale (ed.), *Schooling and Capitalism*, London, Routledge & Kegan Paul.
Johnson, R. (1979), 'Really useful knowledge: radical education and working class culture 1790–1848', in J. Clarke et al. (eds), *Working Class Culture*, London, Hutchinson.
Kaestle, C. (1973), *The Evolution of an Urban School System*, Cambridge, Mass., Harvard University Press.
Katz, M. (1968), *The Irony of Early School Reform*, Cambridge, Mass., Harvard University Press.

Katz, M. (1971), *Class, Bureaucracy and Schools: The Illusion of Educational Change in America*, New York, Praeger.
Katz, M. (1975), *Class, Bureaucracy and Schools*, (see above), 2nd edition.
Katz, M. (1979), 'An apology for American educational history', *Harvard Educational Review*, vol. 49, no. 2.
Katzman, M. (1971), *Political Economy of Urban Schools*, Cambridge, Mass., Harvard University Press.
Kohl, H. (1967), *36 Children*, New York, New American Library.
Kozol, J. (1967), *Death at an Early Age: The Destruction of the Hearts and Minds of Negro Children in the Boston Public Schools*, Boston, Houghton Mifflin.
Laqueur, T. (1976), *Religion and Respectability: Sunday Schools and Working Class Culture 1780–1850*, New Haven, Yale University Press.
Lauwerys, J. and Scanlon, D. (eds) (1970), *The World Year Book of Education: Education in Cities*, London, Evans.
Lawton, D. (1977), *Education and Social Justice*, London, Sage.
Lazerson, M. (1971), *Origins of the Urban School: Public Education in Massachusetts 1870–1915*, Cambridge, Mass., Harvard University Press.
Leacock, E. (1969), *Teaching and Learning in City Schools*, New York, Basic Books.
Levin, H. (ed.) (1970), *Community Control of Schools*, Washington DC, Brookings Institute.
Lukes, S. (1974), *Power: A Radical View*, London, Macmillan.
Lutz, R. (ed.) (1970), *Toward Improved Urban Education*, Belmont, Jones.
MacDonald, M. (1977), *The Curriculum and Cultural Reproduction* (Revision II), Milton Keynes, Open University Press.
Marland, M. (ed.) (1980), *Education for the Inner City*, London, Heinemann.
Mellor, R. (1977), *Urban Sociology in an Urbanized Society*, London, Routledge & Kegan Paul.
Merson, M. and Campbell, R. (1974), 'Community education: instruction for inequality', *Education for Teaching*, no. 93 (Spring).
Midwinter, E. (1975), *Education and Community*, London, Allen & Unwin.
Miliband, R. (1969), *The State in Capitalist Society*, London, Weidenfeld & Nicolson.
Miller, H. (1978), *Social Foundations of Education: An Urban Focus*, New York, Holt, Rinehart & Winston.
Miller, H. and Smiley, M. (eds) (1967), *Education in the Metropolis*, New York, Free Press.
Miller, H. and Smiley, M. (1968), *Policy Issues in Urban Education*, New York, Free Press.
Miller, H. and Woock, R. (1970), *Social Foundations of Urban Education*, Hinsdale, Dryden Press.

Mills, C. Wright (1943), 'The professional ideology of social pathologists', *American Journal of Sociology*, vol. 49.
Mills, C. Wright (1973), *The Sociological Imagination*, Harmondsworth, Penguin Books.
Moore, G. (1967), *Realities of the Urban Classroom*, New York, Doubleday.
Mouffe, C. (ed.) (1979), *Gramsci and Marxist Theory*, London, Routledge & Kegan Paul.
Mullard, C. (1982), Multi-racial education in Britain: from assimilation to cultural pluralism', in J. Tierney (ed.), *Race, Migration and Schooling*, London, Holt, Rinehart & Winston.
National Advisory Commission (1968), *National Advisory Commission on Civil Disorders* (Kerner Report), New York, Bantam Books.
Newitt, J. (ed.) (1979), *Future Trends in Education Policy*, Lexington, D.C. Heath.
Pahl, R. (1975), *Whose City?: And Further Essays on Urban Society*, Harmondsworth, Penguin Books.
Pahl, R. (1977), 'Collective consumption and the state in capitalist and state socialist societies', in R. Scase (ed.), *Industrial Society: Class, Cleavage and Control*, London, Tavistock.
Pahl, R. (1978), 'Castells and collective consumption', *Sociology*, vol. 12.
Pahl, R. (1979), 'Socio-political factors in resource allocation', in D. Herbert and D. Smith (eds), *Social Problems and the City*, London, Oxford University Press.
Park, R., Burgess, E. and McKenzie, R. (1925), *The City*, Chicago, Chicago University Press.
Parsons, T. (1967), *Sociological Theory and Modern Society*, New York, Free Press.
Passow, A.H. (ed.) (1963), *Education in Depressed Areas*, New York, Bureau of Publications, Teachers College, Columbia University.
Passow, A.H. (ed.) (1967), *Education of the Disadvantaged*, New York, Holt, Rinehart & Winston.
Passow, A.H. (ed.) (1968), *Developing Programs for the Educationally Disadvantaged*, New York, Teachers College Press, Columbia University.
Passow, A.H. (ed.) (1970), *Reaching the Disadvantaged Learner*, New York, Teachers College Press, Columbia University.
Passow, A.H. (ed.) (1971), *Urban Education in the 1970s*, New York, Teachers College Press, Columbia University.
Passow, A.H. (ed.) (1972), *Opening Opportunities for Disadvantaged Learners*, New York, Teachers College Press, Columbia University.
Perel, W. and Vario, P. (1969), *Urban Education: Problems and Prospects*, New York, McKay.
Peterson, P. (1976), *School Politics: Chicago Style*, Chicago, Chicago University Press.
Pickvance, C. (ed.) (1976), *Urban Sociology: Critical Essays*, London, Tavistock.

Poulantzas, N. (1969), 'The problem of the capitalist state', in J. Urry and J. Wakeford (eds), *Power in Britain*, London, Heinemann.
Poulantzas, N. (1973), *Political Power and Social Classes*, London, New Left Books.
Raggatt, P. and Evans, M. (eds) (1977), *Urban Education 3: The Political Context*, London, Ward Lock.
Ravitch, D. (1974), *The Great School Wars: New York City 1805–1973*, New York, Basic Books.
Ravitch, D. (1978), *The Revisionists Revised: A Critique of the Radical Attack on the Schools*, New York, Basic Books.
Ravitch, D. (1979), 'A bifurcated vision of urban education', in J. Newitt (ed.), *Future Trends in Education Policy*, Lexington, D.C. Heath.
Ravitch, D. and Goodenow, R. (eds) (1981), *Educating an Urban People*, New York, Teachers College Press, Columbia University.
Rawls, J. (1969), 'Distributive justice', in P. Laslett and W. Runciman (eds), *Philosophy, Politics and Society* (third series), London, Oxford University Press.
Rawls, J. (1971), *A Theory of Justice*, Cambridge, Mass., Harvard University Press.
Raynor, J. (1974), *Issues in Urban Education* (E351, Block I), Milton Keynes, Open University Press.
Raynor, J. and Barnes, J. (1978), *The Urban Setting* (E361, Block I), Milton Keynes, Open University Press.
Raynor, J. and Harden, J. (eds) (1973a), *Cities, Communities and the Young: Readings in Urban Education*, vol. I, London, Routledge & Kegan Paul/Open University.
Raynor, J. and Harden, J. (eds) (1973b), *Equality and City Schools: Readings in Urban Education*, vol. II, London, Routledge & Kegan Paul/Open University.
Raynor, J. and Harris, E. (eds) (1977a), *Urban Education 1: The City Experience*, London, Ward Lock.
Raynor, J. and Harris, E. (eds) (1977b), *Urban Education 2: Schooling in the City*, London, Ward Lock.
Reeder, D. (ed.) (1977), *Urban Education in the 19th Century*, London, Taylor & Francis.
Rex, J. (1970), *Race Relations in Sociological Theory*, London, Weidenfeld & Nicholson.
Rex, J. (1973), *Race, Colonialism and the City*, London, Routledge & Kegan Paul.
Rex, J. and Moore, R. (1967), *Race, Community and Conflict*, London, Oxford University Press.
Rex, J. and Tomlinson, S. (1979), *Colonial Immigrants in a British City*, London, Routledge & Kegan Paul.
Riessman, F. (1962), *The Culturally Deprived Child*, New York, Harper & Row.
Riessman, F. (1976), *The Inner City Child*, New York, Harper & Row.

'Right to Learn', (1974), *School Does Matter*, Organisation for Achievement in the Inner City, London.
Riles, W. (1970), *The Urban Education Task Force Report*, New York, Praeger.
Rist, R. (1973), *The Urban School: Factory for Failure*, Cambridge, Mass., MIT Press.
Rogers, D. (ed.) (1974), *Urban Management and Social Change*, Beverley Hills, Sage.
Rutter, M. (1980), 'Secondary school practice and pupil success', in M. Marland (ed.), *Education for the Inner City*, London, Heinemann.
Rutter, M. *et al.* (1979), *Fifteen Thousand Hours: Secondary Schools and Their Effects on Children*, London, Open Books.
Saunders, P. (1980), *Urban Politics: A Sociological Interpretation*, Harmondsworth, Penguin Books.
Saunders, P. (1981), *Social Theory and the Urban Question*, London, Hutchinson.
Schnore, L. (ed.) (1967), *Urban Research and Policy Planning*, Beverley Hills, Sage.
Schultz, K. (1973), *The Culture Factory: Boston Public Schools 1789-1860*, New York, Oxford University Press.
Sharp, R. (1980), *Knowledge, Ideology and the Politics of Schooling*, London, Routledge & Kegan Paul.
Sharp, R. and Green, A. (1975), *Education and Social Control*, London, Routledge & Kegan Paul.
Sheldon, M. and Rivlin, H. (eds) (1970), *Conflicts in Urban Education*, New York, Basic Books.
Silver, H. (1977), 'Aspects of neglect: the strange case of Victorian popular education', *Oxford Review of Education*, vol. 3, no. 1.
Simon, B. (1974), *The Two Nations and the Educational Structure 1780-1870*, London, Lawrence & Wishart.
Smith, L. and Geoffrey, W. (1968), *Complexities of an Urban Classroom*, New York, Holt, Rinehart & Winston.
Stone, M. (1981), *The Education of the Black Child in Britain*, London, Fontana.
Street-Porter, R. (1978), *Race, Children and Cities* (E361, Block V), Milton Keynes, Open University Press.
Strom, R. (ed.) (1966), *The Inner City Classroom: Teacher Behaviours*, New York, Merrill Books.
Tabb, W. and Sawers, L. (eds) (1978), *Marxism and the Metropolis: New Perspectives in Urban Political Economy*, New York, Oxford University Press.
Tizard, B. *et al.* (1980), *Fifteen Thousand Hours: A Discussion*, London, University of London Institute of Education.
Tyack, D. (1974), *The One Best System: A History of American Urban Education*, Cambridge, Mass., Harvard University Press.
Urry, J. and Wakeford, J. (eds) (1973), *Power in Britain*, London, Heinemann.

Walberg, H. and Kopan, A. (eds) (1972), *Re-Thinking Urban Education*, San Francisco, Jossey Bass.
White, J. (1975), 'The end of the compulsory curriculum', in *The Curriculum*, the Doris Lee Lectures, University of London, Institute of Education.
Whitty, G. and Young, M. (eds) (1976), *Explorations in the Politics of School Knowledge*, Driffield, Nafferton Books.
Williams, R. (1973), *The Country and the City*, London, Chatto & Windus.
Williams, R. (1977), *Marxism and Literature*, London, Oxford University Press.
Williamson, W. and Byrne, D. (1979), 'Educational disadvantage in an urban setting', in D. Herbert and D. Smith (eds), *Social Problems and the City*, New York, Oxford University Press.
Willie, C. (1978), *The Sociology of Urban Education*, Lexington, D.C. Heath.
Willis, P. (1977), *Learning to Labour*, Lexington, D.C. Heath.
Wirth, L. (1938), 'Urbanism as a way of life', *American Journal of Sociology*, vol. 44.
Wirth, L. (1964), *On Cities and Social Life*, Chicago, Chicago University Press.
Wisniewski, R. (1968), *New Teachers in Urban Schools*, New York, Random House.
Wright, N. (1967), *Black Power and Urban Unrest*, New York, Hawthorne.
Yarmolinsky, A. *et al.* (eds) (1981), *Race and Schooling in the City*, Cambridge, Mass., Harvard University Press.
Young, M.F.D. (ed.) (1971), *Knowledge and Control: New Directions for the Sociology of Education*, London, Collier-Macmillan.

2
Urban education and the current crisis
Rachel Sharp

A discussion of urban education in relationship to the current crisis in Britain, the United States and Australia may seem, at first sight, a daunting project in the space permitted here. From another point of view, however, it poses an exciting opportunity to use the comparative method as a means of elaborating an analysis, an impossibility with a single case study. Had the sociology of education learned some of the lessons of its founding fathers, Weber and Durkheim, some of its weaker theoretical formulations could have been avoided.

In this chapter the evolution of a discourse centring on an apparent crisis in urban education in the 1960s and 1970s will be traced, together with the reconstitution of that discourse and its consequences in the recent past. Central to the argument is the need to examine these phenomena in relationship to the phases of capital accumulation in the capitalist system and its particular manifestations in each national context.[1] Whilst acknowledging that capitalism in different national geographical areas has not had an identical history, our aim will be to single out common features of the capital accumulation process and attempt to relate these to their consequences in the sphere of schooling. Naturally, a full confirmation of the thesis requires a systematic consideration of the crucial differences in the development of education in each country, and the relating of the latter to the historically unique patterns of relations which have characterized capitalism's variable history across the globe.[2]

To focus on the accumulation process may invite the charge of economism by both Marxist and non-Marxist critics. It will be impossible here to debate such charges. Rather, one can only assert that capital is a social relation requiring ideological and political mechanisms to sustain it (Holloway and Picciotto, 1978). These, historically, may vary, albeit within certain key limits. The analysis may also evoke accusations of functionalism.[3] However, nowhere is it being suggested that capitalism must, or will, be preserved. The laws of capitalist development are not to be conceived as inexorable processes which mechanistically determine particular outcomes. They are tendencies only which can be counteracted and may not be realized in actual events (Bhaskar, 1979). Their realization often depends importantly, among other things, on the mobilization of classes and other historical agencies and the rich complexity of the play of their contests in the political and other arenas. That the developments which will be discussed below have occurred, does not mean that they had to occur, in that form, to that degree, or that history could not have been different. Fascism was not, in the early 1930s, inevitable, just as, through a different kind of politics, Thatcherism, Reaganism and Fraserism, could have been prevented . . . . We anticipate our conclusion . . . .

The unprecedented wave of capital accumulation which the Western world experienced in the 1950s and early 1960s, often known as the Long Boom of the twentieth century, was the result of the particular resolution of the last major crisis of the capitalist system in the 1930s. Fascism, and the developments to which it gave rise, played a crucial role in that process. The reorganization of class and political relations, on both a national and international plane, brought about during the war against fascism and the early post-war years, cemented a unique set of circumstances peculiarly favourable to the inauguration of a long period of growth and rising prosperity from which the economies of most Western advanced societies benefited.[4]

The end of the Korean War saw American hegemony firmly established over the capitalist system, despite the crucial losses of substantial sections of the globe, most notably in eastern Europe and China. Capital's drive for accumulation was given a free rein. American hegemony ensured, in the West, a stable economic and political outlook especially favourable to a rapid expansion of world trade. Key resources were in plentiful supply. Imperialist expansion in the nineteenth century had ensured that Western capital had access to minerals and energy reserves in the Third World which did not seem unduly threatened by decolonization movements in the 1940s and early 1950s. This economic and political stability was guaranteed through relatively reliable military alliances, ideologically legitimated through the rhetoric of the Cold War.

The war had provided a unique stimulus to the harnessing of science and technology which could subsequently service capitalist expansion. A major technological revolution was under way, which accelerated the transition from the formal to the real subsumption of labour power,[5] under capitalist control. This process was accompanied by a reorganization of production and the labour process such as to consolidate new and more effective forms of labour discipline which would have important consequences for class relations (Braverman, 1974; Sohn-Rethel, 1978). Meanwhile, the internationalization of capital was proceeding apace, undoubtedly assisted by the establishment of a number of supranational apparatuses to facilitate economic and political co-operation between the various capitalist states.

The post-war period also heralded a more active state intervention in economic affairs. Most capitalist states were moving towards Keynesianism: the use of demand management and other counter-cyclical strategies to control the business cycle, through the active use of monetary and fiscal policy. The timing of the adoption of Keynesianism varied in different countries, depending on their unique pattern of class and political relationships,[6] but by the late 1950s the commitment to full employment policies and sustained growth was fairly general. Similarly, the period saw a significant extension of the state's involvement in welfare provision, sometimes referred to as the social wage, both as an aspect of demand management and as a product of the state's mediation of the class struggle.[7] To a greater or lesser extent, the working class in the three countries under examination were co-opted and integrated into the forms and structures of bourgeois democracy: trade unionism, parliamentarism and formal schooling. Reformism was now the dominant motif of working class political mobilization. The Cold War, undoubtedly assisted by Stalinism, had largely discredited socialism. Gradualism and social engineering were the norms of the day. A new capital-labour accord was being forged, whereby, increasingly, working class interests could be identified with those of capital.[8] In so far as capital benefits, all can seem to share in the fruits of its prosperity.

Rising living standards, giving access to mass consumption for significant sections of the working class, gave credibility to such a stance. Welfare provisions cushioned the impact of economic insecurity deriving from having nothing to sell in the market place but one's labour. The shifts in the structure of the labour force, caused by the expansion of the secondary and tertiary sectors, led to the growth of the new middle class and meant that many shared in the benefits of social mobility, thus reinforcing the view that 'we have never had it so good.' This consciousness was reinforced by the progressive extension of the commodity form, saturating the experience of everyday life. The culture industry, especially with the generalization of television ownership, contributed to the weakening of the social supports for counter-hegemonic currents derived from the historical experience of earlier decades. An expanded phase of capital accumulation laid the economic and ideological foundation for a relatively high degree of political consensus.

The successes of Keynesianism – economic growth, rising living standards and full employment – led to a remarkable convergence in developments in state education systems in the 1950s and 1960s. The proportions of GNP devoted to educational expenditure increased rapidly. Demographic shifts, together with changes in the structure of the workforce, led to a demand for increased qualifications to which the state responded by initiating a major expansion of educational provision especially at the secondary and tertiary level. As a corollary of Keynesianism, the central state increased its role in planning, management, and financial provision, as well as orchestrating closer ties between the tertiary educational sector and corporate firms, through subsidizing research and development programmes and reorganizing and expanding higher education. At the national level, education expansion increasingly came to be seen as a component of investment, illustrated, for example, in the rise of human capital theory. At the individual level, education was seen to be the key mechanism for social mobility and personal economic betterment.

Had the Long Boom continued indefinitely, as the more optimistic of bourgeois commentators predicted, given the power of Keynesianism to abolish, if not minor fluctuations in the business cycle, at least the grossest swings of the pendulum[9] which had marked capitalism's development since the industrial revolution, the sub-discipline of urban education might never have emerged. By the 1960s, however, the pace of economic expansion was slowing down. A continuous growth in living standards no longer seemed quite so assured. Whilst it might have seemed reasonable to expect that all would eventually be pulled up by the inexorable logic of economic development and rising prosperity,[10] a halting of that logic increasingly forced the recognition that not all groups and social categories were sharing equally in the benefits enumerated above, nor, in the absence of outside intervention, could this be expected. This was particularly so for the urban semi- and unskilled working class, girls and members of ethnic minority groups. About this time was constituted, both at the level of public political discussion and in bourgeois social theory, the phenomenon of the 'urban crisis' together with various initiatives at the level of state planning. These were designed to resolve what were seen as significant social problems which tended to be geographically concentrated in cities, especially in inner city regions (Lee, 1979). Cities were seen as sites of poverty and low income, racial and ethnic tension, urban congestion and traffic pollution, suffering from deficiencies in the provision of social services, housing, health and education, vulnerable to economic changes which had led to a flight of capital and jobs to more salubrious pastures. In short, the urban inner city was perceived as a rude reminder of the manifest consequence of social and economic disparity. An unequal access to resources and life chances had led to the geographical concentration of social problems which were seen as a threat to social harmony and the principles of social justice to which the bourgeois state was now thought to be committed.[11] As a symptom of the public recognition of these phenomena, 'urban education' emerged in the political and theoretical arena, together with its academic advocates, specialists, university courses and departments, designed to offer theories and recipes for solving the educational manifestations of the urban crisis, and to redistribute educational opportunity in favour of those groups now identified as disadvantaged (Passow *et al.* 1967).

The social construction of these phenomena as exemplifying a 'crisis' rather than merely a set of problems to be resolved needs itself to be explained. It was no accident that the moral panic encapsulated by the term 'crisis' coincided with the emergence of a number of urban social movements whose political activities posed threats to the social harmony and political consensus orchestrated in the 1950s. This was particularly so in the United States, which experienced the development of the civil rights movement, racial riots, the anti-Vietnam demonstrations and the student movement, all of which threatened the stability of class relationships, especially in urban settings. After a long period of comparative political quiescence, urban regions were now the sites of numerous struggles over the extension of rights, over the terms of access to state provided services, over housing and ecological issues, over the forms of structures of citizen control over the factors which structure people's lives and life chances. Many of these mobilizing movements had the central or local state apparatus as their adversary, and the repressive arm of the state was not infrequently necessary to control the course of events. There was also a resurgence of working class militancy in the sphere of production, which, in some cases, was not merely directed to the terms of the wage contract but to the forms of control over the production process itself.

Through a variety of stages, mechanisms and processes in each of the three countries, the hegemonic consensus emerged that the essential crisis was an issue of distributive justice, the solution to which necessitated a shift of resources in favour of those groups who were seen to be disadvantaged. The state was accorded the special responsibility of intervening to effect a redistribution of goods and services to redress the balance, which the market on its own had failed to achieve. The sphere of urban schooling was seen as especially crucial, given its role in the determination of life chances. If one could intervene here and succeed in reversing what was now defined as a vicious circle, all would be well. Whilst the problems might be socially generated, the solutions were to be directed, in the main, towards the affected individuals, constituted as disadvantaged clients, with individual needs.

A common strategy, underpinned by similar theoretical paradigms, and differing only in the matter of timing and the rigour of the state's response, emerged. In the United States, for example, the federal administration initiated a direct funding of school districts, targeted at the economically disadvantaged. The system of school financing was reformed, to equalize the position of poorer school districts, as well as to improve the educational provision of poorer schools. Programmes for desegregation were accelerated and many schemes of affirmative action, affecting both blacks and women, were inaugurated by both public and private agencies with federal support. Countless compensatory programmes such as Head Start were implemented, frequently based on cultural deprivation theory. Enormous sums of money were made available for educational research, curriculum development, and the provision of ancillary services.[12] It was the heyday of the educational expert! Parallelling the more prominent role of the federal administration in education there developed, paradoxically, major experiments in local participatory democracy, which can, with hindsight, be seen as a significant way of co-opting and controlling the leadership of the new social movement.

Similar developments occurred in Britain, [13] legitimated by the long history of reformist research in the sociology of education and the deliberations of a series of official committees, of which Plowden was, perhaps, the most significant. The educational priority areas were established, marking a shift in funding towards schools in areas of disadvantage. The programme of comprehensive reorganization was accelerated, together with the raising of the school leaving age. Whilst benefiting all children, these latter were seen to be particularly important for pupils in inner city areas. Other central and local government schemes designed to improve the facilities and services in urban areas were initiated, among them, the Urban Programme of 1968 and the community development projects. New support services were established, with special central government financial support. A whole series of curriculum projects were devised, targeted to meet the needs of those of low socio-economic status. The beginnings of moves towards meeting the special needs of girls and blacks were made. All of these developments were accompanied by measures designed to ensure the increased coordination of national and local projects and initiatives.

Coinciding with the coming to power of the Labour Party in 1972, a similar reorganization of educational priorities took place in Australia. The period marks a major push of the Commonwealth government into the area of pre-tertiary schooling, both with respect to the orchestration of policy and as regards funding. The Karmel Report of 1973, a major survey of the existing structure of educational opportunity and an advocate of positive discrimination, encapsulates the thrust of Labour Party Policy which led to the establishment of the Schools Commission and the Disadvantaged Schools Programme (Musgrave, 1982). Overall expenditure grew dramatically until 1974, special programmes targeted for disadvantaged groups were developed, from which migrants, aborigines, women and inner city pupils would be thought to benefit. School- and community-based innovation was encouraged. The Curriculum Development Centre was established. Class sizes were reduced, state educational bureaucracies restructured, teachers' salaries raised and a host of paraprofessionals inducted into the schooling system. The slogan of the times were those of devolution of responsibility, equality of opportunity, diversity, community involvement, multiculturalism and recurrent education (Freeland, 1979; Pusey, 1979; White, 1973).

Whilst most of these trends in all three countries can be described as the educational policies of access (a preoccupation with institutionalizing equality of opportunity), what they represent is the outcome of a new social democratic settlement fashioned out of the political and social struggles which characterized the ending of the Long Boom. What had been brought about was a hegemony of reformist discourse on class, gender and ethnic struggles. This involved a reorganization of both the language of educational debate and the definitions of political reality (Gintis and Bowles, 1981). This reorganization was nowhere smooth or uncontested. It did not occur at exactly the same time in each country, because of the historically specific nature of class and political alignments between and within antagonistic classes and class fractions in each national context. However, the success of the policies devised depended, crucially, on a continued upward trajectory of economic growth and rising living standards: the *real* foundation, as opposed to the mere ideological articulation of, the Post-Industrial Society, the end of ideology, and all that. As will be explored below, however, the economic foundations for the new social democratic settlement were rapidly being eroded 'behind the backs' of the participants just as the spate of new plans, proposals and initiatives were rolling off the drawing boards.

The underlying motif of both the policies and the theories on which they were based continued that long tradition of 'gentling the masses' which has characterized the history of state schooling under capitalism (Hall, 1974). Amelioration of disadvantage, in the absence of any changes in the underlying structure of capitalist production relationships, could only mean management, containment and control. Far from calling the whole system into question, the theories developed in this period tended to naturalize and eternalize the key institutional forms of capitalist society, private property, the market, and commodity exchange, and look to a neutral state 'above society' to alleviate its worst excesses. The search for a chain of causal connections was arbitrarily arrested. The *effects* of the capital accumulation process were taken to be the *causes* of the low educational achievement of inner city pupils and a hierarchical structure of inequality seen to be unavoidable. What was aimed for was that those at the bottom should be 'raised up' along with all the rest of us and have 'a fairer go'. Justice was seen in distributional terms at the level of exchange rather than itself rooted in production relations (Williamson and Byrne, 1979).

It is not sufficient, however, to simply isolate the deficiencies of theory to which the urban education advocates were prone. We need an explanation of why the theory took that form, which itself relates to the social, political and ideological foundations and consequences of the Long Boom. Whilst an extended analysis is outside the scope of this chapter, we must refer to our earlier discussion of the elaboration and extension of the commodity form which occurred in the post-war period. Commodity fetishism fixates its victims at the level of the phenomenal forms, or surface appearances, of everyday life (Larrain, 1979). It is not that poverty, poor housing, low incomes, and job discrimination were not 'seen' but that they were seen as merely part and parcel of the structure of exchange relationships in which people are enmeshed. Improving the *terms* of the exchange is the issue, through ameliorative social engineering by activating, through pressure groups and otherwise, a potentially benevolent state.

'Urban education', as a discipline, had no theory of the context of urban schools. At best, it possessed a set of descriptions encapsulated in such phrases as 'an advanced industrial society', a 'post-industrial society', a society characterized by 'great complexity' and 'rapid social change'.[14] What needs to be stressed, however, is that some conceptualization of what constitutes 'the urban' is an essential prerequisite for the development of theories which explain specific social forms and practices such as those which comprise what we understand as urban schools (Castells, 1976; Saunders, 1981). Urban phenomena, in Western societies, are only comprehensible within the theory of the history of the production and reproduction processes of modern capitalism.[15] They are the manifestations of a particular form of class control over the industrialization process, the development of generalized commodity production and the primacy of exchange value over use value. Capitalist development produces a spatial concentration of production processes, the means of circulation and consumption in specific geographical regions which confront us in the form of modern Western cities. Moreover, the labour power on which the production process historically has depended is concentrated in cities.

Crucial to the history of capitalism was the development of the capitalist state. Not all the prerequisites for capitalist production can be provided by capital in their commodity form.[16] Some instrumentality was therefore functionally necessary for the provision of what Marx described as the 'general conditions of social production', including infrastructural and other services, an apparatus for maintaining political and ideological control over the workforce and a mechanism for politically organizing the relationships between antagonistic classes and class fraction to safeguard the essential requirements of capital accumulation (Folin, 1981). Given the geographical concentration of both production and labour power in urban areas, urban life has been profoundly structured by the history of state interventions.

The history of urban schooling is part of the history of capitalist development.[17] The patterns and forms of state schooling in urban

Urban education and the current crisis / 69

areas, the rules determining its selective provision, its content, and the social framework historically forged to guarantee its political control are intimately related to the changing conditions of production, the needs of accumulation and legitimation and the history of the mobilization of social groups and classes as they struggled for hegemony in both local and national contexts. Contemporary urban schools, for example, bear the imprint of capitalism in that everyday life in the communities for which they cater is profoundly affected by the key forms of capitalist social relations: commodification, atomization and individualization. Their catchment areas are deeply structured by the whole history of private locational and other decisions of firms, households and individuals making history — but not in conditions of their own choosing. Decisions are made by past and present urban actors within a structure of constraints fashioned by capital's tendencies, as this is historically mediated through class and other struggles in the arena of production, in the state, and in the local and national communities. We need only refer to the typical pattern of urban land use in contemporary cities: dense commercial cores, the geographical separation of production centres from residential centres, and socially segmented neighbourhoods differentiated according to lines of cleavage in the social division of labour (Harvey, 1977). These consequences of capitalist development deeply affect urban schools.

Whilst there are important variations between different countries in the conditions of production and reproduction which relate to the specificities of their own histories, the law of value produces across the capitalist mode of production a number of common tendencies and trends.[18] Of these, five will be singled out for special mention. Firstly, over time, capital undergoes a process of concentration and centralization, leading eventually to the internationalization of capital. Secondly, competition in the market place produces technological development which leads eventually to a rise in the organic composition of capital and periodic pressures on the prevailing rate of profit. Thirdly, more and more areas of social life become subject to the commodity form, thus leading to generalized commodity production. Fourthly, the division of labour will progressively be marked by horizontal and vertical divisions based on gender, ethnic origin, race and skill as a part of the process of capitalist control over the labour process and labour power reproduction. Finally, ideologies will emerge which will include as essential components themes which are necessary for, and compatible with, a market society, among them the ideas of freedom, private property, individualism, and equality of opportunity (Macpherson, 1964).

Capital accumulation, despite these common tendencies, is not evenly dispersed. Uneven development is the norm. This uneven development is produced, again by the law of value (Weeks, 1982) and the historical legacies of different phases of the accumulation process (Perry and Watkins, 1981). These phases of capital accumulation coincide with different phases of capitalist organization leaving their mark on the vitality or otherwise of cities (Harvey, 1977). The differences, for example, between cities in the sunbelt of the USA (Child, 1977; Gordon, 1977) compared with those of the northern frostbelt; between British northern industrial cities compared with those in the south east — (Massey and Catalano, 1978); between Australia's Newcastle and Wollongong on the one hand, compared with Brisbane or Albury — Wodonga on the other hand (Mullins, 1979), bear witness to important regional disparities which relate to whether their industries are in relative advance or decline. These national regional variations are overlain by international changes in the pattern of uneven development. All of these differences affect the character of urban schools and their variations across the capitalist mode of production.

Urban centres are also sites for the manifestations of capitalist contradictions. The capital accumulation process is necessarily contradictory, given that the social relations through which accumulation takes place are class relations, because of the private nature of appropriation of the surplus product, and the social nature of the conditions of its production; because of the inherent contradiction between use value and exchange value which produces a tension between the needs of accumulation and the requirements of reproduction and legitimation. The social relations in urban schools reflect the character of these contradictions. This is especially the case in countries where 'race' has played a vital role in differentiating the workforce. In many huge cities in America, for example, the results of suburbanization and white responses to desegregation initiatives have left the public schools predominantly catering for blacks and other ethnic minority pupils, with a white teaching force. The problems of teaching in such areas are illustrated in the phenomenon of teacher 'stress' or 'burnout' (Wilson, 1982).

But these are the effects of the *normal* process of capitalist development. The fact, for example, that inner cities were increasingly composed of the very poor and lowly paid, welfare recipients, the poorly housed, those without skills, blue collar service workers, oppressed minorities who have been the historic victims of institutionalized racism in its many forms, is no historical accident. It is itself the result of the continuing process of deskilling, the export of capital and jobs from old urban centres, the outmigration of skilled workers, the breakup of traditional communities through redevelopment schemes, traffic planning, and industrial relocation policies, all of which are characteristic of the recent history of cities under capitalism. The inadequacy of the facilities and services reflect the powerlessness of inner city populations to force local and central state apparatuses to change the pattern of distribution of goods and services in their favour.

The manifestations of the urban crisis which became visible in the 1960s were not symptoms of some isolated malfunctioning of the capitalist system but the outcome of its contradictions. Urban education policies and theories sought to attack the symptoms, whilst remaining basically committed or blind, to the very system which had produced them. The system was not even given a name.

As hinted earlier, the emergence of 'urban education' coincided with the actuality of, or the fear of, threats to the reproduction of labour power, caused by the beginnings of a new phase of mobilization of urban populations over some of the usual effects of capitalist industrialization: institutionalized racism and sexual discrimination, pollution, the destruction of the environment, bad housing, the exclusion from forms of democratic control, which coincided, not by chance, with an unprecedented resurgence of trade union militancy.

The fate of the new urban education policies, and the theories on which they depended, has now to be related to another normal feature of capitalism, its susceptibility to crisis. The accumulation process, since the foundation of capitalism, has been characterized by long phases of upward movement, followed by periods of slump or depression (Mandel, 1975; Wright, 1975). The very conditions which pave the way for a phase of expanded reproduction themselves produce barriers to the accumulation process in subsequent phases, giving rise to crises of accumulation. Crises are marked by overaccumulation in the sphere of production and realisation problems in the sphere of circulation. Crises, if they are to be resolved in favour of capital, are occasions for the restructuring of capitalist production, class and political relations, which thus prepares the way for a subsequent era of expanded reproduction. It is precisely the onset of such a crisis which marks the recent history of capitalist schooling.

The symptoms of major crisis in late capitalism are, by now, familiar: a serious decline in the rate of growth, leading to nil or negative growth in some capitalist nations; a massive increase in inflation, especially in the mid-1970s; rapidly rising rates of unemployment; instability in the world currency system; and the fiscal crisis of the bourgeois state. Whilst at the level of surface appearance all of them seem to stem from the steep rise in the price of oil in the early 1970s, their deeper causes lie in the normal operation of the law of value in the capitalist system itself and the contradictions of this mode of production.

The crisis of accumulation is marked by four important characteristics.[19] Firstly, the post-war trend towards a reliance on Keynesianism had led to a huge expansion in the level of both public and private debt, especially manifest in the inability of a number of Third World countries to service their loans from the international banking system (e.g. Mexico, Brazil, Argentina, the Philippines). Secondly, what Mandel has called the Third Technological Revolution, itself an important factor in the Long Boom, is producing a generalization of the application of new technology across the capitalist world leading to a rise in the organic composition of capital, an expulsion of labour from the production process, and pressures on the rate of profit. The consequence is a massive overproduction of exchange values, especially acute in steel, petrochemicals, automobiles, electrical goods and shipbuilding. The goods cannot be sold because of a lack of purchasing power. Thirdly, there has been some redistribution of surplus value to the property owning classes in OPEC and the Third World, itself the result of the economic and political changes during the Long Boom. Finally, capitalism has experienced aggravated social and political crises which in some cases have threatened bourgeois class relations (e.g. Vietnam, Iran, Southern Africa, Central and South America). This has produced a weakening of American hegemony over the capitalist system and been accompanied by an intensification of the arms race which has further fuelled the rate of inflation and caused a partial diversion of surplus value away from more productive sectors. Moreover the late 1960s and early 1970s, as we have noted, was a period which saw an intensification of working class struggles, not only over the individual and social wage, but over the control of production, the environment and other issues. The militancy of the working class has added to the pressure on the rate of profit and been an obstacle in the way of restructuring.

The crisis has affected all capitalist countries including the USA, Britain and Australia. It is especially visible in the manufacturing sector, and its effects are particularly acute in the declining regions and cities of the economy. However, there are some important differences between them, related, at least in part, to the way each of them is inserted into the world capitalist system. Both Britain and America, for example, have metropolitan status in that Department I (crudely, machinery and advanced technology) is of great importance. Australia, on the other hand, is a semiperipheral economy, supplying food and raw materials to the metropoles. Its own manufacturing sector, based primarily on import substitution and relatively inefficient, has developed historically behind high tariff barriers. It is particularly vulnerable to a world accumulation crisis (Brezniak and Collins, 1977; Cately and McFarlane, 1981). Britain's manufacturing sector, compared to that of America, has been suffering a long-term historic decline relative to those of the other EEC countries, Japan and the USA (Gamble, 1983; Glyn and Harrison, 1980; Overbeck, 1980), whilst on the other hand, American capital has gradually lost its overall hegemony in the face of the growth of the Japanese and West German capital. In addition, the structure of American capital has been far more affected by America's role as the main policeman and military protector of the capitalist world (Weisskopf, 1981; Castells, 1980; Bowles and Gintis, 1982).

It is beyond the scope of this paper to do more than mention some of the economic differences. These differences are complicated by significant political differences which have been produced by their unique histories. America and Australia have a federal political structure, for example, rather than a unitary state as in England. Moreover, in England, as Nairn (Nairn, 1977) argues, the bourgeois class failed to take full control of the state apparatus, whereas this has occured in the others. There are differences in the nature of the state apparatuses, variations in the patterns of political organizations, alliances and conflicts, specificities in the degree and manner of the incorporation of the working class into the framework of bourgeois institutions, variations in the strength of both the radical and conservative traditions as opposed to those of liberalism. In short, distinct histories have resulted in dissimilarities in the nature of the local hegemonic apparatuses, their institutionalized patterns and ideological themes for intervention in civil society. Whilst important, these must form the basis of another study. For what is at issue here is the structural imperatives produced by a crisis in capital accumulation which confront capital, whether it is British, American, Australian (or multinational, French, or Italian for that matter) as a structural constraint. Capital must find a means to effect a restructuring, if it is to remain in control, and bring itself eventually to a new phase of expanded reproduction. It is no part of the argument that such means *will* be found, or that they will take a specific form.

Capital's requirements (and these are essentially the same as those of the 1930s) are, firstly, a lowering of the wages of the working class and an intensification of the rate of exploitation, which will release more surplus value to capital. Secondly, capital must be restructured both to produce the above and to eradicate devalorized capital. This can be achieved through technological innovation, through a reorganization of the labour process, and through an acceleration of the concentration and centralization process via bankruptcies, mergers and takeover bids. In short, 'rationalization' and 'modernization'. This also may involve a geographical relocation of production processes into areas where the local social and political circumstances create conditions more favourable to accumulation. Thirdly, a cutting back of the social wage and a recomposition of state expenditure which will shift surplus value to capital, through regressive taxation, investment and export allowances, and the reduction of corporate taxes. In the present crisis this has also been associated with pressures to reprivatize areas of the economy potentially capable of, if not already marked by, an adaptation to the commodity form: health, education, postal and telephone services, for example.[20]

None of these changes can be orchestrated without a disciplining of the workforce. This can be achieved through an acceleration of the restructuring of the labour reserve army; an intensification of the horizontal and vertical divisions, in particular those related to income, skill, ethnic and sexual distinctions; and the weakening and disorganization of labour through an attack on the traditional concentrations of trade union power. Unprecedented levels of unemployment, a rise in the rate of bankruptcies, the assault on working class living standards, a progressive dismantling of aspects of the social wage structure, encroachments on the power of the union movement in all three countries all testify that this restructuring is taking place. How it is occurring must now be considered.

In order to satisfy the imperatives of capital restructuring, given the political and ideological currents in these three societies which developed out of the Long Boom, a recomposition of social and political forces has had to occur. This has involved a realignment of traditional patterns of class and other alliances and a disarticulation and rearticulation of popular political discourse. It is this latter which is particularly significant because it explains why the level of popular resistance to measures designed seriously to encroach on people's living standards has so far been so weak.

This shift in popular discourse has been brought about by the ascendancy of what is frequently described as the New Right. It is arguable how far the so-called New Right differs from the strands of authoritarian populism which gained such ascendancy in some of the key capitalist countries in the Depression and were of considerable saliency in others where the 'solutions' to that crisis of accumulation were not so extreme. The continuities and discontinuities between that era and the present deserve consideration in their own right and will not be discussed here.[21] It is only important to note that the structure of the capitalist mode of production both generate and allow only certain patterns of discourse to emerge and to engage in dialectical relationship with each other in a manner which parallels the distinct upturn and downturn phases of the accumulation process.

The key features of the New Right involve an articulation of neo-liberalism with aspects of a neoconservative ideological tradition.[22] At the centre of the former is economic 'man', the private individual, freely choosing among a range of alternatives to maximize 'his' utility in the market place. Individual self-reliance and initiative is stressed, on the one hand, whilst on the other, a reaffirmation of free enterprise, the sanctity of private property and the non-interventionist state. Neoconservatism forges a union of the cold rationality of capitalist economic 'man' with precapitalist traditions, in the affirmation of the family, religion and the nation, the non-market principles of social cohesion which can bind together the host of atomized, privatized economic actors which the sway of the market has produced. Neoconservatism involves a reconfirmation of 'old values' against all forms of permissiveness, sexual or otherwise, selfishness and indiscipline. Whilst the latter's main enemy might seem to be sex (not so with neoliberalism which tends towards a commodification of sex) they both share common enemies, on the one hand, the state, on the other, the unions, both of which are seen as synonymous with socialism. The state is opposed because of its interference with personal freedom and initiatives, as tending towards totalitarian control. The unions are opposed because they undermine the self-equilibrating processes of the market place. They are seen as vast agglomerations of economic power, pursuing narrow and sectional interests, which undermine the stability of the nation.

The power of this old/new discourse lies in its ability to resonate with people's experience; it provides a confirmation of that experience. The New Right appropriates deeply felt needs and aspirations, it offers ideals which transcend the war of all against all in the market place, and makes sense of generalized and very real frustrations.[23] It matters little whether the discourse is internally contradictory and composed of a series of incompatible separations. For everyday life *is* a life of contradictions and separations. People's experience under capitalism is split. The reality of frustration, dependence and powerlessness at work is compensated for by a feeling of power and autonomy in the field of consumption, a 'free choice over leisure and how to consume'. People know what they want. This illusion, deriving from the real world, of choice and autonomy, is reinforced by the geographical separation in urban areas of the place of work from the places of residence and leisure. Taxation *is* a constraint on personal freedom in the sphere of consumption and seems to provide the basis for the never-ending expansion of state expenditure.

At the level of visible reality, state expenditure appears to do little more than fuel the maintenance of a spawning, self-interested bureaucracy — the 'fat cats' of the Civil Service. The state is identified with inefficiency, bureaucratic regulation, corruption and oppression. Everyday experience confirms the remoteness of the state, its apparent inaccessibility to popular democratic control which has marked the shift of power to the executive. The automization and powerlessness which characterize the lives of bourgeois individuals and which everyday life confirms are disarticulated from their source in capitalist production relationships and reconstituted as an antagonism between the individual and the state, which requires a curbing of the latter as both economically necessary and morally desirable. The tax revolt thus has a very real foundation.

Moreover, economic decline is seen in some ways to be causally related to the retreat from traditional values embedded and sustained in the bourgeois family. The decline of the family can ideologically be related to state provision of welfare, to changes in traditional sex roles, to the increase of women in the workforce, and the trend towards sexual permissiveness resulting in abortion, promiscuity, homosexuality and divorce. Such a view, and the reassertion of traditional values, makes sense to those who experience the family as a defence against naked self-interest and personal insecurity. Whilst the symptoms of so-called family decline are the direct result of the extension of market relations which both tend to dissolve and to conserve precapitalist tendencies, the correlation of family decay with economic decline makes it fairly easy to see the one as the cause of the other.

Finally, the re-emergence of the secular myth of nationalism makes sense for those whose everyday life continually renders credible the thesis that everyone is out for him/herself. The appeal to nationalist discourse, that we should make sacrifices, pull together for the national good, buy British or Australian, 'smash the Argies' or whatever, captures and reconstitutes positive and genuine repugnance towards some aspects of bourgeois society. At the same time it provides the basis for striking at the power of the unions, who are 'always on strike' and undermining the national interest; for the intensification of anti-Communism which provides legitimacy for rearmament; and for the further consolidation of imperialist relations in the Third World. 'Common sense' dictates a reassertion of the strong state to arrest the historic decline of 'our' nation *vis-à-vis* others.[24]

Whatever the classes and class fractions whose real interests are furthered by the rise to ascendance of the New Right, its mass electoral appeal and the social basis for its support lie in the real foundations of everyday life under capitalism. It is not imposed 'from above', as a conspiracy theory might imply, but resonates with yearnings from below, from the contradictions in people's experience inherent in the social fabric of capitalism. Moreover it has successfully managed to detach significant sections of the working class and the new *petite bourgeoisie* from their traditional allegiance to social democratic reformism. Thus political life is reorganized under its banner.

The groundwork has now been laid for a consideration of the changes which have been taking place in the school systems in the countries under examination and the likely effects of these changes on those categories of disadvantaged pupils who formed the focus of the theories and practices of 'urban education'.

Given the centrality of schooling in the reproduction of labour power, for selection and allocation for the active workforce and the reserve army, and for the inculcation of the discipline appropriate to life in a market society, it is hardly surprising that schooling has figured prominently in ideological and political debate in recent times.[25] The restructuring of capital, if it is to proceed unproblematically in the interest of capital accumulation, creates pressure for a concomitant restructuring of the various political and ideological apparatuses and their practices. Thus, although there may be an element of smokescreen activity in the present ideological attacks on schooling and teachers, these attacks should not be seen as predominantly that (Frith, 1979). They are accompanied by significant financial cutbacks and pressures for a restructuring of the different levels of schooling. These cutbacks and attacks are not vindictive and illogical responses by capital and the state to social democratic gains won during the Long Boom. Rather, they are an attempt to reallocate the available surplus value to capital investment and thus assist the restructuring. By cutting state expenditure on the social wage (health, welfare, education, housing, urban and regional development, culture and recreation, etc.) the drain on surplus value is stemmed — the cost of labour power maintenance and reproduction is reduced — and the rate of exploitation is increased.

When applied to the specifics of schooling this response by the state exposes a major contradiction inherent in the state's provision of schooling. On the one hand, the absolute and relative expansion of technology produces a relative surplus population (unemployment) which must be absorbed to maintain social cohesion. This could be achieved through reducing the retirement age, hours of work and/or increasing the time spent in full-time schooling. However, the cost of an increased educational provision (or reduced hours of work without an equivalent pay reduction) produces an additional drain on surplus value, adds to the tendency for the rate of profit to fall, and hampers accumulation. The state must therefore seek to increase the quality and efficiency of that schooling provision. This is possible in that while schooling is not directly productive of surplus value, it has a variable indirect impact on the total amount of surplus value available for redistribution. Some aspects of educational expenditure can indirectly counter the drain on surplus value. Where emphases are placed on enhancing the basic skill and attitude training of productive workers, their increased productivity may offset the increased costs of their reproduction. Further, a redirection of educational expenditure into the applied sciences and engineering may result in more efficient technology which can offset its cost by increasing the productivity of labour.

To the extent that these moves to enhance the productivity of labour through schooling are successful, they help to revive the rate of profit. They also contribute to the creation of more 'technological' unemployment, a necessary expansion of schooling as a means of social control, a further drain on surplus value, and so on. In the arena of schooling, the capitalist state's orchestration of a cut in this aspect of the social wage can serve only to regenerate the problem of surplus population and a demand for more schooling. This basic contradiction of schooling cannot be avoided. It can only be reproduced within the capitalist system.

This contradiction is central to the present attacks on educational expenditure and schooling processes. The logic of capital accumulation demands a basic restructuring of the productive forces, and the state in each country is responding to this demand. As we shall illustrate below, a major restructuring of schooling is occurring which parallels that occurring in the productive sector. The state is attempting to curb educational expenditure and simultaneously make it more productive indirectly by placing a renewed emphasis on basic skills, values, technical and scientific training. There is a corresponding reduction of emphasis on the social democratic concerns of equality of opportunity, compensatory programmes and the liberal arts.

Within the inevitable political and ideological struggle around the nature and extent of the restructuring of schooling, the increasingly high levels of long-term, structural youth unemployment are crucial. This situation considerably weakens the processes of extended labour power reproduction. Schooling is essential to the overall reproduction process but a severe dislocation occurs if there is not a rapid transition from school to work. The longer the period of transition, the longer the period on the dole, the greater the dislocation. The hitherto existing socialization of the family and the school become increasingly irrelevant to the unemployed school leaver: the reproduction process is thrown into reverse and a counter-work culture of living on the dole develops. This counter-work culture poses a dual threat to the state and to the accumulation process; firstly, it presents a potentially volatile social stratum and secondly, it strikes at the very heart of the labour market. Capital, in this phase, demands that there exists an ever-ready reserve army of labour power. The state's political response to this demand and to youth unemployment is to place renewed emphasis on measures to bolster the work ethic and to make 'school products' more attuned to the demands of the labour market. Simultaneously the state must move to increase the school retention rate or develop an alternative institutional apparatus to maintain youth in a state of suspended readiness for the labour market. These responses of the state necessarily counter its equally essential moves to cut back schooling expenditure.

The state is faced with the necessity of schooling a greater number of people for longer periods of time and more productively (indirectly) with less money. However, the success of such a strategy depends on the capacity of the state to weld an alliance of class forces capable of suppressing, or dividing and demoralizing, the social forces opposed to the restructuring. Moreover, the state's capacity to effect these changes is limited by the state's inherently contradictory and fragmented nature.

All three countries, for example, are bourgeois democracies. This necessitates at least a partial responsiveness to demands from subordinate classes as well as to those emanating from capital (which itself does not always speak with a unitary voice). These subordinate groups have varying degrees of influence, pressurizing power and accessibility to the state's agents. However, the articulated demands of subordinate social categories may conflict with the need to functionalize the schooling system for capital. Secondly, the bourgeois state consists of a number of apparatuses which may work in different directions. State decisions reflect the outcome of a whole series of compromises between different interests and personalities at both the national and local level which frequently imply a less than unitary direction of state policy. Finally, the state's political decisions have to be translated into actions by agents in the educational bureaucracies, in schools and colleges and elsewhere. The intentions of policies may be frustrated in the manner of their implementation.[26] Be that as it may, however, some common trends and tendencies are now developing into a pattern in all three countries.

Central to this pattern is the reconstitution of the prevailing discourse about education which has parallelled a dramatic shift in the structure of everyday common sense among parents, employers, and indeed many teachers and educational 'experts'.[27] Again one should not be surprised at the ease with which this has occured. Whilst the state and the media have contributed to the representation of the crisis in accumulation as a crisis in schooling, this can only occur precisely because the explanations offered for the educational crisis seem credible and trustworthy, and the solutions proposed practicable, given the framework of people's experience. Bourgeois schooling does, for many, seem to give access to the good life, social mobility and economic betterment. If the successful transition between school and work does not occur, this must, in its obviousness, be something to do with inadequate schooling.

This new discourse about education, a sub-discourse of the New Right, has been organized around a number of ideological themes.[28] Progressivism, child centredness and a liberal preoccupation with general education have, it is alleged, led to a neglect of basic *skills* and a lack of vocational *training* in work related skills and attitudes. *Standards* are seen to be declining, both with respect to academic and behavioural matters. Schools, especially urban schools, are seen to have been neglecting *discipline*, as the level of truancy, drop-outs, and the decline in the respect for authority revealed in school vandalism and school violence confirm. The schools have not given sufficient emphasis to the issue of *accountability* to consumers (to the parents and employers, to the treasury or the nation of citizens). There needs to be more *efficiency, rationalization* and *planning*, more stress on *choice*, individual and family *responsibility*.[29]

Despite differing emphases and varying institutionalized means whereby the restructuring is being effected, the degree of convergence in actual developments in each country is quite extraordinary.[30] With respect to funding levels, for example, the policy of fiscal containment and balanced budgeting has led, at first, to a marked slowing down in the rate of growth in educational expenditure in the mid- and late 1970s, followed by significant cuts. In each country, this is legitimated through monetarism and demographic analysis, and has also led to actual or proposed changes in the method of government funding to achieve the same goal of cuts: see the proposal to return to the block grant system in Britain, to end it in the United States, and trends to defederalize in both the USA and Australia. The cuts in funding have been parallelled by a significant move towards privatization and the affirmation of the value of individual choice as a basis for public policy. Both in America and in Australia, there has been accelerating what has been described as a flight from the public schools which has led to the mushrooming of private schools, especially those of a Christian fundamentalist character. Britain has reintroduced the Assisted Places Scheme, Reagan's administration proposes tax credits for private schools, whilst in Australia federal funds for the private sector have dramatically increased (Marginson, 1982). All three countries have been flirting with educational voucher schemes.

These privatization tendencies link in with the enhanced role of the private sector in schooling, through the provision of 'work experience' and industrial training initiatives, in curriculum development, associated with the increased stress on new forms of educational technology, and even in some cases, in direct corporate funding of schools (see the recent Denver Adopt-a-School Plan).

This closer relationship between schooling and industry is only part of a greater stress on vocational education, with heightened emphasis on work experience programmes in the school curriculum, careers guidance, new training initiatives (Simon, 1982), and the fostering of employability. Closer control over pupils' performance is being orchestrated, involving the reintroduction or restructuring of examination systems (Whitty, 1982) and a proliferation of various testing schemes. In America, particularly, and to a lesser extent Australia, for example, there has been a big growth in the popularity of competency-based instruction and minimum competency testing. In Britain, the Assessment of Performance Unit was established to monitor changes in standards. Graded tests and pupil profiles are now very much on the agenda.

Teachers have not been immune from this attempt to reassert control. Proposals for core curricula or curriculum guidelines are either being implemented or seriously debated to curb the autonomy of teachers, sometimes affecting their political, religious or personal rights.

The banning of SEMP and MACOS in Queensland (Freeland, 1979), the Creation Science Controversy in the USA (Nelkin, 1982), the prohibition of political debate in the Youth Opportunities Programme in Britain, and the controversy over peace and disarmament studies (Rogers, 1982; Baylis, 1982; Broughton and Zahaykevich, 1982), are all illustrative of these trends. Perhaps even more sinister are the signs of a militarization of the schooling system, such as the call to reintroduce the cadet system in Australian public schools, the interest in and cooperation with the Department of Defence by the British Manpower Services Commission, the greater stress on patriotism in American schools, and the introduction of political education courses or 'citizenship education'.

The encroachment on what teachers define as their professional autonomy has been assisted by the cutbacks in educational funding levels, which in all three countries has led to sackings and retrenchments, a move towards more contract teaching and part-time employment, and various schemes designed to monitor teachers' 'performance'. An increasing reserve army of teachers' labour contributes to teacher insecurity, which facilitates greater control.

Many of these developments have led to a strengthening of the hierarchical stratification of the schooling systems to produce more rigid divisions between those destined for work and those who may well form the pool of the permanently unemployable. This stratification requires a reassertion of school discipline, with debates over the right to exclude unruly pupils in America, the requirement in New South Wales for all schools to develop a school discipline policy, and research into the incidence of school violence in Britain. Many of these changes, too, have involved the elaboration of various means of co-opting and controlling those who are seen to have an interest in education — among them parents, teachers and trade unions.

Of special importance, given our focus on urban education, has been the cuts in programmes targeted towards disadvantaged schools and pupils. In America, for example, the tax revolt has led to the cancellation of numerous special programmes and the retrenchment of educational personnel in urban areas. Moreover the proposed changes in the method of educational funding discussed above will have particularly adverse consequences for schools in poor districts (Vogel, 1982). In addition the defeat of the Equal Rights Amendment marks the retreat from programmes of affirmative action which is paralleled by moves to halt and reverse the desegregation trend. In Australia, the reduction of funds to the Disadvantaged Schools Programme and the changes in the composition and terms of reference of the Schools Commission, reveal similar tendencies (Freeland and Sharp, 1981). It is not necessary to enumerate the enormous impact that government cutbacks under both Callaghan and Thatcher have had on inner city schools in Britain.

Finally, there has been a big reduction of funding levels for educational research illustrated by the abolition in Australia of the Educational Research and Development Council, the reduced grants in Britain to the SSRC and the declining role of the federal government in funding educational research in the USA. Of the funding that remains, there has been a marked shift in its allocation to those research projects favoured by the New Right.

Few of these changes in schooling could have been brought about without a significant reorganization of the administration and control structures within the state itself,[31] sometimes involving the creation of entirely new structures such as the Manpower Services Commission in Britain and various educational commissions in several states of Australia. The creation of new structures has been particularly necessary where power centres represented in the old agencies have proved particularly resistant to change (Frith, 1979).

Finally, it is worth commenting on the changes in the bureaucratic language through which many of these developments are explained and legitimated. There is much talk of 'quality control', 'efficient delivery systems' and so forth — in short, the corporate language of the Harvard Business School!

What do all these developments mean? When considered alongside the non-educational aspects of the restructuring of capitalist class and political relationships discussed earlier, it is now apparent that they are part of the bourgeois state's attempt to engage in an increasingly repressive ideological and political offensive to control the workforce. To the extent that the restructuring succeeds, the illusion is sustained that the problems of the economy and the resulting unemployment levels are the result of the excesses of past social democratic experiments, individual pathology or industrial militancy.

We have now traced the evolution of a dramatic shift in the discourse through which the urban educational crisis is defined, and considered some of its consequences.[32] It remains only to focus again on the way in which these trends are affecting inner city schools. Despite the rhetoric of 'multiculturalism', equal opportunity, and women's rights, it is clear that these tendencies will merely accentuate the disadvantages of those of lower socio-economic status, the urban working class, blacks, ethnic minorities and girls. Urban schools, already the locale for containing a relative surplus population in the 1960s, are especially vulnerable. Their pupils are becoming increasingly irrelevant for the expanded reproduction of capital (Lee, 1979). Their structural location necessitates a heightening of the schools' role as agents of political control. The recent riots in Britain and America, and the spate of arson directed against school buildings in Australia, merely testify to the inherent contradictions of inner urban schooling which themselves have to be traced to the very processes of capitalist development itself.

Conclusion

The title of this chapter prompts the inevitable question: whose crisis? It is undoubtedly, as I have argued, a crisis of capital, a crisis of accumulation, as a result of which, certain fractions of capital will suffer, some fatally so. It is a crisis for its victims, particularly those expelled from the production process. Yet, in the three countries we have been considering, there is no evidence, as yet, that the bourgeois class, though its agents, is unable to effect its political rule. There are no deep fissures in the state's institutional system which might herald the end of bourgeois democracy and the rise of an 'exceptional state'.[33]

Although bourgeois freedoms are being gradually eroded in many sectors of civil society, a deep organic crisis has not yet materialized. On the contrary, the ruling class has been comparatively successful in capitalizing on the shifts in consciousness which are an inevitable function of a depression. Of course this recomposition of social life does not eradicate the fundamental contractions of the capital accumulation process. The latter are merely reproduced in altered form through the very solutions which the system itself throws up. Whilst it is difficult, at this stage, to identify when and how a renewed phase of expanded reproduction can be generated, it is clear that unless a new war of position can begin to be waged, the future for all but the strongest sections of capital, let alone the working class, looks grim. For those who claim to take the side of capital's victims, who struggle for reforms and amelioration, the time has now come to reconsider directions. The crisis is, first and foremost, a crisis for the left and for social democracy, as *Unpopular Education* (Baron *et al.*) has so penetratingly exposed. The left, along with others, is paying the penalty of the failure in the post-war era to develop an educative politics and a politics of education, as opposed to schooling, which could have resisted effectively and reversed the trends we have described. The costs of such political failures are severe indeed. But it is not too late for the regrouping of forces. It is not too late for the acute insight that what the old/new right has achieved at the level of popular discourse provides important lessons for a new old left.

All the slogans of the New Right's discourse could be dialectically rearticulated into a new educational discourse cementing a new and properly socialist form of pedagogy and of practice. (Not insignificant in this project might be the invention of a new name for that vision of the possibility of non-alienated social relationships towards which the left has historically striven.) The task lies before us. If we do not rise to the challenge, violent explosions in capitalist urban centres could materialize, bringing in their train profound fissures in the state's institutional structures and producing a deep organic crisis at the very centre of bourgeois society. Were this to happen, another bout of fascism and a repetition of the holocaust, this time with other victims, would be very much on the cards.[34]

Capital's recent adventures in the South Atlantic, and the Reagan administration's defence policies, demonstrate Brecht's prescience that 'the bitch that bore fascism "is" on heat again.' With the benefit of historical insight, we will not have the excuse that education has nothing to do with politics, that we did not know what was happening. *'Hic Rhodus, hic Salta'*!

Notes and references

1. Hargreaves's (1982), critique of such an approach would have been much stronger if he had demonstrated the empirical rigour that he calls for through the use of the comparative method and shown that across the capitalist world the political and social struggles which characterize the accumulation process do not crucially affect the forms and structures of schooling. For an interesting discussion of the state and education, see Shapiro (1982).
2. This work is under way. See Sharp (ed.) (forthcoming).
3. See Cohen's (1978) discussion of Marxism and functionalism.
4. The argument developed here is heavily dependent on the seminal work of Mandel, especially 1975. See also Weisskopf, (1981), and Bowles and Gintis (1982) for an analysis of the roots of American hegemony in this era.
5. Marx (1959) traces the essential elements of this transition as it began to emerge in the nineteenth century.
6. Exponents of monetarism were not silent in the post-war period. A full commitment to Keynesianism, for example, only emerged in the United States with the Kennedy administration, and in West Germany with the Grand Coalition of 1966.
7. Essential reading on the welfare state is Gough (1979), although the analysis is marred by his neo-Ricardianism.
8. The analysis in this chapter is heavily indebted to the work of the Birmingham Cultural Studies Centre Education group. See Baron *et al.* (1981). Acknowledgment of every insight would be impossible here. Despite adverse reviews of *Unpopular Education* it remains the single most penetrating appraisal of British post-war educational developments. It has also affected the recent work of Bowles and Gintis, and other American writers on education.
9. Bourgeois social theory frequently invokes the pendulum as part of the causal process at work. Needless to say, the pendulum itself explains nothing.
10. Not only the poor in the advanced countries would be pulled up, but also whole economies in the Third World, according to modernization theory.
11. This approach was still important for some in the late 1970s. See Field (ed.) (1977) and Marland (ed.) (1980).
12. It is impossible to list all the relevant literature published in this period. See Passow *et al.* (1967); Gittel and Hevesi (eds) (1969); Walberg (ed.) (1972); Cronin (1973); Miller and Woock (1973); Rist (1973); Hummel and Nagle (1973), as typical examples.

Urban education and the current crisis / 87

13 See Raynor and Harden (1973); Marland (ed.) (1980), Field (1977), Grace (1978), Robinson (1976) and Tyler (1977), for discussions of the changes.
14 These phrases have become little more than clichés.
15 This section owes much to the recent flowering of Marxist theoretical and empirical work on the urban phenomenon. See, especially, Pickvance (ed.) (1976); Harloe (ed.) (1977); Deer and Scott (eds) (1981); Harloe and Lebas (eds) (1981).
16 Wherever capitalism has invaded other modes of production, the state has played a vital role, often through the use of violence, in the provision of the 'free' labour force. See Aumeeruddy et al. (1978).
17 This issue has led to a particularly lively debate in America with the rise of the revisionist perspective in educational historiography. See Feinberg and Rosemont (eds) (1975) for a representative example, Cohen (1981) for a discussion of these developments and Ravitch (1978) for a liberal critique.
18 A proliferating literature on the law of value exists. The interested reader could start by looking at Marx (1959); Wright (1975) and Fine and Harris (1976).
19 Mandel (1975); Wright (1975); Weisskopf, 1981.
20 Privatization not only saves money but serves to depoliticize struggles over the provision of services and directs attention away from the state.
21 Particularly interesting studies around this problem have been done in Germany, centring around the journal *Das Argument's* studies of fascist ideology.
22 Hall (1979) and Wolfe (1981); Sawyer (1982). One of the best recent discussions of the New Right is Poole (1982), to whose analysis I am greatly indebted.
23 E. Bloch (1978) analysed this brilliantly with respect to fascism.
24 The rise of nationalism in the last few years can be illustrated by a few pertinent examples: American reaction to the Iran hostages affair, British activities in the South Atlantic, and the daily Australian medal count in the 1982 Commonwealth Games.
25 The analysis in this section is elaborated in much more detail in Freeland and Sharp (1981).
26 Freeland (1980) and other unpublished monographs by the same author has explored these issues in some depth with reference to the Australian government's youth training schemes.
27 See Johnston (1983) and Donald (1979).
28 As the Black Papers reveal, these preoccupations have had a long history. They did not become majority opinion, though, until the onset of the crisis.
29 In Australia, under the chairmanship of Bruce Williams, an official government committee deliberated on the problems of education and training, and published a major report in 1979 (Williams, 1979). These key ideological themes legitimated a major shift in

state policy since Karmel. See Freeland and Sharp (1981), for an analysis of the report.
30 For America, see Wexler *et al.* (1981); Litt and Parkinson (1979); Newitt (1979); Cirincione-Coles (1981); Gintis and Bowles (1981); Vogel (1982); Nelkin (1982). For Britain see S. Baron *et al.* (1981); Frith (1979); Salter and Tapper (1981); Donald (1979); Hall (1981); Stafford (1981); Williamson and Byrne (1979); Sarup (1982). For Australia see Bennett (1982); Freeland and Sharp (1981); Johnston (1983); Pusey (1979); Marginson (1982); Freeland (1979); Bannister *et al.* (1979), and the special issue of *Radical Education Dossier* on the future of public schooling, 18, 1982.
31 Well revealed in Salter and Tapper (1981), with respect to the role of the DES.
32 The old discourse continues but the forces for its support are severely weakened and its exponents seem to have lost most of their optimism. See Field (ed.) (1977) and Marland (ed.) (1980). As is common in a depression, social democracy proves its inability to hold its forces together.
33 See Jessop (1978) for a discussion of whether bourgeois democracy is the best possible political shell for capitalism.
34 Rosa Luxemburg's choice between socialism and barbarism is still pertinent today.

Bibliography

Aumeeruddy, A. *et al.* (1978), 'Labour power and the state', in *Capital and Class*, no. 6.

Bannister, H. *et al.* (1979), 'Literacy and the schools', in L. Johnson and U. Ozolins (eds), *Melbourne Working Papers 1979*, Melbourne, Melbourne University Press.

Baron, S. *et al.* (1981), *Unpopular Education: Schooling and Social Democracy in England since 1944*, (Education Group, Centre for Contemporary Cultural Studies, University of Birmingham), Hutchinson.

Baylis, J. (1982), 'Peace research and peace education', *Review of International Studies*, 8.

Bennett, D. (1982), 'Education: back to the drawing boards', in G. Evans and J. Reeves (eds), *Labour Essays 1982. Socialist Principles and Parliamentary Government*, Victoria, Drummond.

Bhaskar, R. (1979), *The Possibility of Naturalism: A Philosophical Critique of the Contemporary Human Sciences*, Brighton, Harvester Press.

Bloch, E. (1978), 'Non synchronism and its obligations to its dialectics', *New German Critique*, 9.

Bowles, S. and Gintis, H. (1976), *Schooling in Capitalist America*, London, Routledge & Kegan Paul.

Bowles, S. and Gintis, H. (1982), 'The crisis of liberal democratic capitalism: the case of the United States', *Politics and Society*, vol. 11, no. 1.

Braverman, H. (1974), *Labour and Monopoly Capital*, New York, Monthly Review Press.

Brezniak, M. and Collins, J. (1977), 'The Australian crisis from Boom to Bust', *Journal of Australian Political Economy*, no. 1.

Broughton, J. and Zahaykevich (1982), *The Peace Movement Threat*, Teachers College Record, vol. 84, no. 1.

Castells, M. (1976), 'Is there an urban sociology?', in C. Pickvance, *Urban Sociology: Critical Essays*, London, Tavistock.

Castells, M. (1980), *The Economic Crisis and American Society*, Oxford, Blackwell.

Cately, R. and McFarlane, B. (1981), *Australian Capitalism in Boom and Depression*, Chippendale, Alternative Publishing Co-operative.

Child, R. (1977), 'Capital accumulation and urbanization in the United States', *Comparative Urban Research IV*.

Cirincione-Coles, K. (ed.) (1981), *The Future of Education*, Beverley Hills, Sage.

Cohen, J. (1978), *Karl Marx's Theory of History: A Defence*, London, Oxford University Press.

Cohen, S. (1981), 'The history of urban education in the United States: historians of education and their discontents', in D. Reeder (ed.) (1977), *Urban Education in the Nineteenth Century*, London, Taylor & Francis.

Cronin, J. (1973), *The Control of Urban Schools. Perspectives on the Power of Educational Reforms*, New York, Free Press.

Deer, M. and Scott, A. (eds) (1981), *Urbanization and Urban Planning in Capitalist Society*, London, Methuen.

Donald, J. (1979), 'Green paper. Noise of crisis', *Screen Education*, no. 30.

Feinberg, W. and Rosemont, H. (1975), *Work, Technology and Education: Dissenting Essays in the Intellectual Foundations of American Education*, Chicago, University of Illinois Press.

Field, F. (ed.) (1977), *Education and the Urban Crisis*, London, Routledge & Kegan Paul.

Fine, B. and Harris, L. (1976), 'Controversial issues in Marxist economics', in *Socialist Register*.

Folin, M. (1981), 'The production of the general conditions of social production and the role of the state', in M. Harloe and E. Lebas, *City, Class and Capital*, London, Edward Arnold.

Freeland, J. (1979), 'Class struggle in schooling', *Intervention*, no. 12, April.

Freeland, J. (1980), 'Transition education: a case study in the state's response to youth unemployment', Sydney University, mimeo.

Freeland, J. and Sharp, R. (1981), 'The Williams report on education, training and employment: the decline and fall of Karmelot', *Intervention*, no. 14.

Frith, S. (1979), 'Education and industry', in *Radical Education Dossier*, no. 8.
Gamble, A. (1983), 'New Toryism. The rise of the resolute right', *New Socialist*, January/February.
Gintis, H. and Bowles, S. (1981), 'Contradiction and reproduction in educational theory', in L. Barton *et al.*, *Schooling, Ideology and the Curriculum*, Lewes, Falmer Press.
Gittell, M. and Hevesi, A. (eds) (1969), *The Politics of Urban Education*, New York, Praeger.
Glyn, A. and Harrison, J. (1980), *The British Economic Disaster*, London, Pluto Press.
Gordon, D. (1977), 'Capitalism and the roots of the urban crisis', in R. Alcaly and D. Mermelstein (eds), *The Fiscal Crisis of American Cities*, New York, Random House.
Gough, I. (1979), *The Political Economy of the Welfare State*, London, Macmillan.
Grace, G. (1978), *Teachers, Ideology and Control*, London, Routledge & Kegan Paul.
Hall, S. (1974), 'Education and the crisis of the urban schools', in Raynor, J. (ed.), *Issues in Urban Education*, Milton Keynes, Open University Press.
Hall, S. (1979), 'The great moving right show', *Marxism Today*, January.
Hall, S. (1981), 'Schooling, state and society', in R. Dale *et al.*, *Education and the State, Volume 1: Schooling and the National Interest*, London, Falmer Press and the Open University Press.
Hargreaves, A. (1982), 'Resistance and relative autonomy theories: problems of distortion and incoherence in recent Marxist analyses of education', *British Journal of the Sociology of Education*, vol. 3, no. 2.
Harloe, M. (ed.) (1977), *Captive Cities: Studies in the Political Economy of Cities and Regions*, London, Wiley.
Harloe, M. and Lebas, E. (eds) (1981), *City, Class and Capital*, London, Edward Arnold.
Harvey, D. (1977), 'The urban process under capitalism: a framework for analysis', *International Journal of Urban and Regional Research*, vol. 2, no. 1.
Herbert, D. (1976), 'Urban education: problems and policies', in D. Herbert and R. Johnson, *Social Areas in Cities, Volume 2: Spatial Perspectives on Problems and Policies*, London, Wiley.
Holloway, J. and Picciotto, S. (1978), *State and Capital: A Marxist Debate*, London, Edward Arnold.
Hummel, R. and Nagle, J. (1973), *Urban Education in America: Problems and Prospects*, London, Oxford University Press.
Jessop, B. (1978), 'Capitalism and democracy, the best possible political shell?' in G. Littlejohn *et al.*, *Power and the State*, London, Croom Helm.
Johnston, K. (1981), 'The production of conservative educational ideologies', *Discourse* 2 (1).

Johnston, K. (1983), 'A discourse for all seasons? An ideological analysis of the Australian Schools Commission Reports, 1973 to 1981', *Australian Journal of Education*, 27 (1).
Laclau, E. (1977), *Politics and Ideology in Marxist Theory*, London, New Left Books.
Larrain, J. (1979), *The Concept of Ideology*, London, Hutchinson.
Lee, R. (1979), 'The economic basis of social problems in the city', in D. Herbert and D. Smith (eds), *Social Problems and the City*, London, Oxford University Press.
Lipietz, A. (1982), 'Towards global Fordism', *New Left Review*, 132.
Litt, E. and Parkinson, M. (1979), *US and UK Educational Policy: A Decade of Reform*, New York, Praeger.
Macpherson, C.B. (1964), *The Political Theory of Possessive Individualism*, Oxford, Clarendon Press.
Mandel, E. (1975), *Late Capitalism*, London, New Left Books.
Marable, M. (1982), 'The crisis of the black working class: an economic and social analysis', *Science and Society*, vol. XLVI.2.
Marginson, S. (1982), *The Privatisation of Schooling in Australia*, Canberra, Australian Teachers Federation.
Marland, M. (ed.) (1980), *Education and the Inner City*, London, Heinemann Educational Books.
Marx, K. (1959), *Capital, Volume 1*, Moscow, Progress Publishers.
Massey, D. and Catalano, A. (1978), *Capital and Land*, London, Edward Arnold.
Miller, H. and Woock, R. (1973), *Social Foundations of Urban Education*, Dryden Press.
Mingione, E. (1977), 'Theoretical elements for a Marxist analysis of urban development', in M. Harloe (ed.), *Captive Cities*.
Mullins, P. (1979), 'Australia's Sunbelt migration: the recent growth of Brisbane and the Moreton region', *Journal of Australian Political Economy*, 5.
Musgrave, P. (1982), 'The sociology of education in Australia', *British Journal of the Sociology of Education*, vol. 3, no. 2.
Nairn, T. (1977), *The Breakup of Britain*, London, New Left Books.
Nelkin, D. (1982), *The Creation Controversy: Science or Scripture in the Schools*, New York, W.W. Norton.
Newitt, J. (ed.) (1979), *Future Trends in Educational Policy*, Lexicon, Lexicon Books.
O'Connor, J. (1973), *The Fiscal Crisis of the State*, New York, St. Martin's Press.
Overbeck, H. (1980), 'Finance capital and the crisis in Britain', *Capital and Class*, Summer.
Passow, A. et al. (1967), *Education of the Disadvantaged: A Book of Readings*, New York, Holt, Rinehart & Winston.
Perry, D. and Watkins, (1981), 'Contemporary dimensions of uneven urban development', in M. Harloe and E. Lebas (eds).
Pickvance, C. (ed.) (1976), *Urban Sociology*, London, Methuen.

Poole, R. (1982), 'Markets and motherhood: the advent of the New Right', *Intervention*, 16.
Pusey, M. (1979), 'The legitimation of State schooling systems', in Pusey, M. and Young, R. *Control and Knowledge*, Canberra, Education Research Unit, Australian National University.
Ravitch, D. (1978), *The Revisionists Revisited: A Crique of the Radical Attack on the Schools*, New York, Basic Books.
Raynor, J. and Harden, J. (1973), *Cities, Communities and the Young: Readings in Urban Education, Volume 1; Equality and City Schools: Readings in Urban Education, Volume 2*, London, Routledge & Kegan Paul, in association with the Open University.
Rist, R. (1973), *The Urban School: A Factory for Failure*, Cambridge, Mass., MIT Press.
Robinson, P. (1976), *Education and Poverty*, London, Methuen.
Rogers, R. (1982), 'Peace studies', *Where*.
Salter, B. and Tapper, T. (1981), *Education, Politics and the State: The Theory and Practice of Educational Change*, London, Grant McIntyre.
Sarup, M. (1982), *Education, State and Crisis*, London, Routledge & Kegan Paul.
Saunders, P. (1981), *Social Theory and the Urban Question*, London, Hutchinson.
Sawyer, M. (1982), *The New Right in Australia*, Macmillan.
Shapiro, H. Svi (1982), 'Education in capitalist society: Towards a reconsideration of the state in educational policy', *Teachers College Record*, vol. 83, no. 4.
Sharp, R. (ed.) (forthcoming), *Capitalist Crisis, the State and Education: Comparative Studies in the Politics of Schooling*.
Simon, J. (1982), 'Agenda for action: what price the new training initiative', in *Forum*, vol. 25, no. 1, Autumn.
Sohn-Rethel, A. (1978), *Intellectual and Manual Labour*, London, Macmillan.
Stafford, A. (1981), 'Learning not to labour', *Capital and Class*, no. 15.
Tyler, W. (1977), *The Sociology of Educational Inequality*, London, Methuen.
Vogel, M. (1982), 'Education grant consolidation: its potential fiscal and distributory effects', *Harvard Educational Review*, vol. 52, no. 2 2.
Walberg, H. (ed.) (1972), *Rethinking Urban Education*, Washington, Jossey-Bass.
Weeks, J. (1982), 'Equilibrium, uneven development and the tendency of the rate of profit to fall', *Capital and Class*, 16, Spring.
Weisskopf, T. (1981), 'The current crisis in historical perspective', *Socialist Review*, 57.
Wexler, P. *et al.* (1981), 'Deschooling by default: the changing social functions of public schooling', *Interchange*, vol. 12, nos. 2–3.
White, D. (1973), 'Create your own compliance: the Karmel Report', *Arena*, nos. 32–3.

Whitty, G. (1982), 'Examinations 1976–82: an exploration of some implications of the sixteen-plus controversy', in J. Ahier and M. Flude (eds), *Contemporary Educational Policy*, London, Croom Helm.

Williams Report (1979), *Education, Training and Employment*, vols. 1–3, report of the Committee of Inquiry into Education and Training, Canberra.

Williamson, W. and Byrne, D.S. (1979), 'Educational disadvantage in an urban setting', in D. Herbert and D. Smith, *Social Problems in the City*, London, Oxford University Press.

Wilson, H. (1982), 'The urban public school condition', in *Educational Forum* vol. XLVI, no. 4.

Wolfe, A. (1981), 'Sociology, liberalism and the radical Right', *New Left Review*, 128.

Wright, E.O. (1975), 'Alternative perspectives in the Marxist theory of accumulation and crisis', in *Insurgent Sociologist*, vol. 6, no. 1.

Wright, E.O. (1978), *Class Crisis and the State*, London, New Left Books.

3
Theorising the urban: some approaches for students of education

Gerald Grace

Urban social theory: problem, conflicts and contradictions

The term 'urban', like the term 'community', has become one of the potent legitimation symbols of our time. Urban (or its derivative 'inner city') prefaces the analysis of many of our contemporary ills and it provides a theoretical/ideological framework for policies and programmes devised by governments for the solution of these ills. As the urban context has been increasingly specified as the site of various crises in Western societies, an impetus has been given to all forms of urban study. There is, in other words, what Mellor (1977: p. 3) has called 'a lively sense of the urban problematic' which finds its expression in economics, political science, social administration, education, geography and history, and in the generic field of urban studies. It becomes apparent from the literature that there are very different ways of articulating or theorising the urban problematic. At the risk of oversimplifying a complex position it is perhaps possible, in ideal type form, to identify these differences around the organising constructs of problem, conflict and contradiction. The suggestion is made that much of the literature and discourse of the urban can be characterised from a sociological and urban education viewpoint in relation to these categories. Thus an emphasis may be discerned upon 'urban problems' which is underpinned by forms of functionalism and systems theory. In contrast to this, an emphasis upon 'urban conflicts' draws its inspiration ultimately from the work of Max Weber but more contemporaneously from the work of urban theorists such as Ray Pahl and John Rex. Challenging both of these constructs and the conventional wisdom of urban studies in general is the work of modern Marxists such as David Harvey and Manuel Castells where the emphasis is upon 'urban contradictions' as indicative of the wider contradictions of capitalism.

In practice these ideal type categories do not have such an analytically neat existence. There are theoretical intersections and writers on urban phenomena frequently use such categories in an eclectic fashion, but nevertheless it is maintained that they do encapsulate significantly different theoretical approaches which pattern all forms of urban study.

Urban study: the problem approach

In *The Division of Labour in Society* (1933), Durkheim recognised that urbanisation with its consequent effects on 'material density' and 'moral density' has potentially crucial implications both for social progress and for social disintegration. For Durkheim, the power of traditional hierarchies, of traditional restraints of custom and morality and of existing forms of social solidarity became attenuated as a result of urbanisation: 'Nowhere have the traditions less sway over minds. Indeed, great cities are the uncontested homes of progress . . . . When society changes, it is generally after them and in imitation . . . because the collective life cannot have continuity there' (1933: p. 296). While the weakening of the influence of the 'collective life' liberated the forces of social progress and of individual freedom in an industrialised and urbanised society, it liberated also the forces of moral and social anarchy arising from unrestrained egotism and individualism. It was Durkheim's concern to show that while the development of the division of labour contains within it the possibility of a new and stronger basis of social solidarity it might nevertheless come to be expressed through 'abnormal' forms. These abnormal forms and problems of transition within society as a whole would be most apparent within the great cities.

Although Durkheim did not himself develop a sociology of the urban and its associated pathology, his work provided an important source of inspiration for those who did attempt such an enterprise: the Chicago School of urban sociology. This School, taking the city of Chicago as its social laboratory, produced the first systematic formulations of urban theory and research methodology. As both Mellor (1977) and Saunders (1981) point out such formulations were to have a profound influence upon all subsequent types of urban study.

The theorising of the Chicago School followed the dual emphasis in Durkheim's work upon the urban as progress and the urban as pathological. The immediate concern of the School was however to identify the nature and range of urban problems in order to facilitate the generation of policies designed for their amelioration; 'Life in the cities was posed as a problem, a problem of social disorganisation caused by urbanisation and the immediate task of sociology as a science and as a practical enterprise was the elucidation of this social problem' (Mellor, 1977: p. 217).

As articulated by Robert Park, Chicago School urban theory was based upon the following premises and concerns:

(a) That the city is an organic system and organised unit in space whose structure and functioning is to be understood as 'produced by laws of its own'. In other words, the city constitutes a theoretical object for study in its own terms. The theoretical problem then becomes the elucidation of the 'laws' of urban development.
(b) The substantive problem posed by the city is that of social order and control. What are the necessary conditions under which new forms of social solidarity will emerge in the city?
(c) The city as a social form is characterised by a natural order of competition which is an elementary, universal and fundamental form of interaction. The struggle for existence identified by Darwin in the natural world has its counterpart in the city. Economic organisation and the grouping of populations is the outcome of this natural competition and produces a distinctive ecology of the urban.
(d) The natural order (urban structure) is to be understood as a consequence of processes of dominance, invasion and succession (derived from ecological study) whereby the entry of successive groups of immigrants to the city triggers off a predictable pattern of displacement and movement throughout the urban area. Such movements produce an ecological pattern which is related to differential land values. As Park (1952: pp. 151–2) puts it,

> The struggle of industries and commercial institutions for a strategic location determines in the long run the main outlines of the urban community ... the principle of dominance ... tends to determine the general ecological pattern of the city and the functional relation of each of the different areas of the city to all others.

(e) The separate communities of the city are the outcome of these processes. They are the 'natural areas' which make up the structural variety of the city, the quarters and neighbourhoods which segregate populations with broadly different racial, cultural and vocational interests. Although disrupted in successive phases of the city's growth it is expected that natural biotic balance and social equilibrium will reassert itself or can be assisted to do so.

(f) The moral order of the city is problematic and dependent upon the emergence of new forms of social solidarity. These are to be looked for as arising out of the division of labour and its necessary interdependencies ('competitive cooperation') and also in the form of an emerging locality-based sense of community in the 'natural areas' of the city.

This charter of urban theory was extended, modified and to some extent criticised by the work of Burgess (1967) which developed the concentric zone theory of urban growth, and by the work of Wirth (1938) in his classic essay, 'Urbanism as a way of life'. Wirth argued that new forms of socio-cultural relations ('urban culture') were emerging in metropolitan cities. Urbanism as a way of life was affected by number, density and heterogeneity of population. Influenced by the work of Simmel (1903), Wirth saw that,

> Whereas the individual gains, on the one hand, a certain degree of emancipation or freedom from the personal and emotional controls of intimate groups he loses, on the other hand, the spontaneous self-expression, the morale and the sense of participation that comes with living in an integrated society.' (Wirth, 1938: pp. 12–13)

Alienation was a potential problem arising out of the segmental, superficial and transitory relationships of the city.

While emphasising the city as a context for progress and recognising the richness of its structural and cultural variety, the Chicago School sociologists saw their professional mandate as contributing towards the understanding of what they regarded as temporary urban dysfunctions. They gave to the sociology of the city and to a range of similar studies a distinctive problems approach. Within a functionalist framework in which the city was regarded as tending towards biotic balance and social equilibrium the interest of urban researchers was focused upon what *impeded* such equilibrium. Substantively this led to a preoccupation with problems of social and cultural integration;

problems of special areas within the city; the emergence of a sense of community; problems of alienation and social relations and problems of social disorganisation and deviance. In so far as Chicago School sociology has shaped subsequent urban study, these concerns have been placed high upon the agenda of inquiry.

Criticism of the influence of the Chicago School is now widespread. Mellor, for instance, has argued that, 'the Chicago School tantalize in the pertinence of their observations and their insight into the social worlds of the metropolis and infuriate with the diversion of urban studies down an intellectual blind alley' (1977: p. 206). Forms of urban study based upon the Chicago School model have tended to take the city as a theoretical object in itself *without raising the question of its wider structural relations*. There has been a tendency to operate with a taken-for-granted notion of a capitalist market economy as constituting a natural order of competition, and in general, questions to do with community and the local world of consumption have been separated from their relations with the wider world of production. Much urban study has become preoccupied with ecological empiricism or with urban modelling of an increasingly statistical kind. Above all such studies have given low salience to questions concerned with the distribution of power or with the politics of urban conflicts. As Pahl (1975a: p. 238) observes, 'the Chicago of the second and third decades of this century displayed the capitalist order on the ground with startling clarity, but there is little discussion of inequality or class conflict by the Chicago School urban sociologists.' The theoretical and methodological limitations of the Chicago School have been reproduced in various categories of study from urban economics to urban education. While empiricism has been encouraged, the essential paradigm of the urban has escaped radical challenge until comparatively recently. Now the work of Pahl from a neo-Weberian perspective and the work of Harvey and Castells from a Marxist perspective provides such a challenge. Given that the field of urban education both in Britain and America has been powerfully shaped by Chicago School urban sociology it is obviously crucial that students of urban education appreciate the nature of these challenges.

The city: conflict, bureaucracy and distribution

New directions for urban study were originally suggested by Pahl (1975a) in a series of essays published as *Whose City?* In commenting upon the limitations of the Chicago School and the genre of urban study based upon it, Pahl has argued that a focus upon conflict over scarce resources and the crucial role of urban bureaucrats and managers in mediating this conflict should provide the basis for *a new paradigm in urban inquiry*. This paradigm should draw its inspiration from the writings of Weber; from Weber's conception of the sociology of the city as a means to the end of appreciating tendencies in the wider social framework; from Weber's sensitivity to the growing power of bureaucrats and managers in 'rational' society and from his insistence (against Marx) that the generation of interest groups and conflicts in the world of consumption was not necessarily directly related to the world of production. Within this paradigm a central process of the city is conflict and struggle. What has to be determined is 'the degree to which cities are simply arenas in which conflicts generated in the wider social structure are played out or whether new forms of conflict related to the nature of the city per se are generated independently of the encapsulating power structure' (Pahl, 1975a: p. 186). For Pahl, the city 'generates forms of conflict which are relatively distinct from the conflicts arising from the productive process', although he recognises at the same time that such conflicts of the city cannot be fully comprehended in abstraction from the wider political and economic framework. From this viewpoint, urban conflicts are not a direct manifestation of class struggle but the expression of a struggle among different groupings of the urban population for access to scarce social resources. These resources, housing, health service, education, transportation, social, cultural and recreational facilities constitute an important form of real income whose importance increases as wage differentials decrease. The city *concentrates* the process of collective consumption of these resources and in the process of concentration makes visible the patterns of inequality and generates the conditions for conflict. The crucial questions for urban study then become: who gets what share of these resources?; what are the distribution mechanisms and processes which operate in different resource markets?; what is the relation of the political and the ideological to the bureaucratic/managerial in determining different patterns of resource provision? Pahl has sought to express the dialectic of the socio-political and the spatial in examining these questions in his concept of the socio-spatial system.[1] This contribution to urban studies has been influential because in this formulation the relative blindness of the Chicago School to issues of conflict and inequalities of distribution has been transcended. The concept of an urban natural order has been replaced by the concept of an urban order (or disorder) constructed from a matrix of political, economic, social-spatial and bureaucratic elements. A problematic of urban distribution patterns and procedures has been articulated which it is claimed has its own existence, affected by, but distinguishable from the mode of production or the character of political or ideological governance. The epitome of this position is expressed in the following extract:

> The provision of public services and facilities has its own pattern of inequalities. It can be argued that the exploration of the systematic structuring of such inequalities provides a useful focus to students of stratification working in urban areas. The pattern of territorial injustice exemplified in the work of Davies for Britain can be found in every industrial society and the elimination of such inequalities could well be extremely difficult even in a post-revolutionary situation. The hidden mechanisms of redistribution operate in socialist as well as in capitalist societies: one of the tasks of a radical sociology might be to expose such mechanisms and to consider how an understanding of the urban redistribution system can be used to develop new theories of stratification in industrial society. (Pahl, 1975a: p. 168)

Much urban research and writing has been stimulated by such propositions, e.g. Webster and Stewart (1975) on distribution impact of local government policy; Byrne, Williamson and Fletcher (1975); Williamson and Byrne (1979) on educational resources and provision; Gray (1976) on allocative procedures of local authority housing managers; Pahl (1977) on the influence of managers and technical experts; Pinch (1979) on territorial justice and social services, and Tunley et al. (1979) on local government funding and educational provision.

The strengths of the new urban perspective formulated by Pahl lie in its explicit recognition of conflict as a central characteristic of cities (in opposition to the equilibrium or consensus models of the Chicago School); in its emphasis upon the importance of the sphere of collective consumption in cities and upon the making visible of inequalities in resource provision (in opposition to a descriptive ecological or culturalist emphasis in earlier work); in its emphasis upon the crucial role of mediating levels of bureaucracy and management in the understanding of urban distribution mechanism (in opposition to unduly micro or unduly macro explanations of this). Also fundamental is the recognition

Theorising the urban: some approaches for students of education / 101

that the study of the city is an important means to an understanding of wider political and social structures and the recognition that comparative studies of cities within different political and economic formations is crucial.

A similar theme has characterised the work of John Rex in urban sociology and the sociology of race relations. Here the focus has been upon the way in which cities and the relations of different groups of the urban population to a basic resource such as housing are involved in the generation of conflict including racial conflict. First expressed by Rex and Moore in *Race, Community and Conflict* (1967) the controversial concept of 'housing classes'[2] has been seen by some to be central to an understanding of city conflicts, related to but distinguishable from those of the workplace. Rex has criticised a tendency in urban studies to compound urban and racial conflicts: 'I want to insist that it is a gross oversimplification to say that the race relations problem is a problem of the cities purely and simply.' However Rex does argue that 'given pre-existing economically and historically caused tensions, the industrial city provides the social mechanism whereby racial confrontations are organised and racial conflicts ensue' (Rex, 1973: p. 151).

Urban sociologists of the Chicago School tradition were preoccupied, among other things, with the problem of city immigrants, a problem viewed essentially in functionalist and cultural terms. The Weberian mode of urban sociology and of race relations theory developed by Rex in publications such as *Race, Colonialism and the City* (1973) and (with Tomlinson) *Colonial Immigrants in a British City* (1979) has brought into the analysis the importance of metropolitan–colonial relations viewed historically; the nature of racism and the effect upon race relations of competitive struggle for resources and employment in different sectors of the city. For Rex, the city is not the generator of race conflict *per se* but it is the arena in which the sharpest expressions of race conflict become apparent.

The approach of Pahl and Rex to urban questions has generated a valuable corpus of empirical work but it has also attracted a growing set of criticisms. Harvey (1973) for instance, has criticised as 'typical of liberalism' the attempt to separate issues of distribution and social justice from issues of production when in his view 'production is distribution' and therefore the two cannot legitimately be separated. The focus upon the mediating levels of urban bureaucracy and management has been criticised for resulting in practice in too much concentration on the role of *individuals* in distribution processes to the neglect of structural and institutional relations and wider questions of power and its exercise.

Saunders (1979) also makes the point that concentration upon mediating levels of bureaucracy and concentration upon local government resource allocation tends to leave underdeveloped the effects of wider structures of political and economic constraint. Thus in his view 'the managerial approach in concentrating on studying the allocation and distribution of scarce resources fails to ask why resources are in scarce supply' (Saunders, 1980: p. 168). This is the fundamental question.

In responding to these criticisms, Pahl (1977) has recognised the need to locate the work of urban bureaucracy in a more explicit framework of political economy and in a theory of the working of the local state. However, it remains a basic premise of this position in urban theory that as the influence of the central state and the local state increases in both the world of consumption *and* the world of production then the mediating role of local state bureaucrats is crucial to analysis of the urban question *both in capitalism and in state socialism.*

Work in urban education has drawn extensively upon this type of urban theory and research. American studies have examined the operation of urban and school bureaucracies and the conflicts of different racial and ethnic groups within the city. The fiscal crises of various cities and of their public services have been scrutinised. British studies utilising Pahl's concept of socio-spatial system have examined the differential distribution of resources for urban schooling and the various policy initiatives which have attempted to redirect the flow of resources. Such studies have, in the main, tended to restrict their theoretical and empirical range to city conflicts and struggles distanced from wider questions of political economy and state power. The most recent work in urban theory has set out to make these connections explicit.

The political economy of the urban question

A major alternative to neo-Weberian forms of urban theory and inquiry has emerged in a critical Marxist literature which Pahl himself has acknowledged as 'a most powerful approach to the urban question'. This literature which is the creation of political economists, sociologists, geographers, political scientists and 'urbanists' has sought to provide a critique of contemporary urban study and to indicate a wider structural

Theorising the urban: some approaches for students of education / 103

and political framework within which urban phenomena are to be understood. In a comparatively short space of time an impressive range of theoretical and empirical studies has been produced to challenge the assumptions, procedures and preoccupations of established urban scholarship. Important examples of this work would include Harvey (1973), *Social Justice and the City*; Pickvance (1976), *Urban Sociology: Critical Essays*; Kapitalistate (1976), *The Urban Crisis and the Capitalist State*; Castells (1977a), *The Urban Question* and (1978), *City, Class and Power*; Harloe (1977), *Captive Cities*; Cockburn (1977), *The Local State*; and Tabb and Sawers (1978), *Marxism and the Metropolis*.[3]

While the range and variety of this literature has generated a host of contested issues, it would be true to say that it is united in its rejection of the problematic of resource allocation. From this stance, the emphasis upon conflict among different interest and status groups for control over resources is not enough. The urban does not simply reveal or even generate conflicts *per se*, it makes visible the fundamental structural contradictions of a capitalist society. The emphasis for a 'scientific and total' as opposed to an 'ideological and partial' study of the urban must therefore be upon the manifestation of such contradictions in a growing urban crisis which is itself part of a larger crisis of capitalist social formations everywhere.

It is necessary at this point to distinguish the use of 'conflict' in the literature from that of 'contradiction'. 'Conflicts' as the word is used in Weberian urban theory refer to *the struggles and oppositions of various social and interest groups within an urban population as they are expressed in different sectors of the market for resources*. 'Contradictions', on the other hand, refer to *structurally determined incompatibilities within a social and economic formation (generally identified with capitalism)*. Habermas makes the distinction in this way:

> according to Hegel and Marx, 'conflicts' are only the form of
> appearance, the empirical side of a fundamentally logical contra-
> diction . . . . We can speak of fundamental contradiction of a social
> formation when and only when its organisational principles
> necessitate that individuals and groups repeatedly confront one
> another with claims and intentions that are, in the long run, incom-
> patible. In class societies this is the case. (1976: pp. 26–7)

The work of David Harvey (1973) represents a sustained attempt to deal with the urban question in these terms. What makes his work particularly important to the student of urban studies is the way in which his analysis provides a theoretical bridge between a problematic of liberal redistribution and notions of social justice and a problematic of radical structural transformation. In *Social Justice and the City*, Harvey begins with a proposition derived from John Rawls (1971), that it is possible, given the appropriate thought and action, to establish for the city *'a just distribution [of real income], justly arrived at'*. His subsequent examination of the criteria, indices and mechanisms necessary to this attempt and his study of existing urban intervention programmes designed to accomplish this end, lead him to the conclusion that the 'liberal formulation' of the urban question is untenable. Harvey believes that both logic and history demonstrate that, 'programmes which seek to alter distribution without altering the capitalist market structure within which income and wealth are generated and distributed are doomed to failure' (1973: p. 110). Such a conclusion provides a major challenge to dominant strands of urban writing, discourse and policy which are based upon liberal assumptions about the possibility of rational solutions to urban conflicts *within* existing structures. The essence of Harvey's indictment of liberal conventional wisdom on the urban question may be represented as follows:

1 There is a fundamental contradiction between the imperatives of capital which require the priority of profit and the imperatives of social justice which require the priority of social needs.
2 In relation to cities, capital will flow in the direction of greatest profit, i.e. towards the suburbs and away from the inner city.
3 Government urban and inner city programmes which attempt to counteract that tendency operate against the imperatives of the market. As such they are always limited in funds and time-scale, intermittent in relation to specific crises and lacking in the power to accomplish any significant changes. At worst, such programmes and allocative devices are nothing more than face-saving or crises-dampening measures. At best, they are well-intentioned but ineffectual interventions against the grain of the socio-political and economic situation.
4 The history of urban intervention programmes both in Britain and America demonstrates the validity of this analysis.

From this paradigm, the conflicts and deprivations of the city are seen as the surface manifestations of the deep structure of capitalist contradictions and it follows from this view that surface solutions in the form of urban policy can never be successful in overcoming them. Harvey places the capitalist market economy at the centre of the urban question and in doing so argues that redistributive urban theory has uncritically taken for granted its central notion, 'scarce resources'. Scarce resources are themselves largely the product of that market:

> The concept of scarcity, like the concept of a resource, only takes on meaning in a particular social and cultural context. It is erroneous to think that markets simply arise to deal with scarcity. In sophisticated economies scarcity is socially organised in order to permit the market to function. We say that jobs are scarce when there is plenty of work to do, that space is restricted when land lies empty, that food is scarce when farmers are being paid not to produce. (1973: p. 114)

The relative blindness of urban studies to the world of political economy is exemplified, Harvey argues, by urban geographers and planners in their consideration of the 'problem' of ghetto formation: 'we discuss everything except the basic characteristics of a capitalist market economy. We devise all manner of solutions except those which might challenge the continuance of that economy' (1973: p. 144). For Harvey, such limitations in urban theory and discourse can only be overcome by a change of consciousness and the generation of a 'revolutionary theory'[4] which is not afraid to go to the heart of the urban question; which dialectically incorporates conflict and contradiction and which perceives the solutions and results of conventional urban theory as part of the 'problem'.

The beginning of such a *revolutionary theory of the urban* has come from the pen of Manuel Castells in a series of writings since 1968. The range and complexity of this work makes it necessary to produce a summary statement which is selective according to the focus of this paper. Castells argues that what urbanism is about is a relationship between society and space and this relationship is an expression of a specific organisation of the mode of production. Thus the capitalist mode of production realises a particular structuring of space and of social relations most clearly exemplified in the metropolitan city. This is what the Chicago School was describing without explicitly recognising it. In this way, 'everything described by Wirth as urbanism is in fact the cultural expression of capitalist industrialisation, the emergence of the market economy and the process of rationalisation of modern society' (Castells 1976a: p. 38). Urbanism as a discrete object of study is a myth.

The Chicago School, in Castells's view, did not in fact produce a sociology of the urban but a sociology of social integration in the city. Their preoccupation was with the question of social control in a time of rapid change, and with the sociology of community.

Urban sociology, Castells argues, has no claim to the status of scientific knowledge since it does not possess either a valid 'theoretical object' (a defensible conceptual schema) or a valid 'real object' (a determinate field of observation). The urban cannot be constituted as a legitimate focus of inquiry in independence of wider structures. Simply to demarcate the urban in terms of the city is to focus on something which cannot be defended either as a valid theoretical object or as a valid real object.

Existing urban sociology (and urban theory) has an ideological rather than a scientific character. Such work has a mystifying function in that it suggests that the problems located typically in inner city areas are problems which are city-generated and therefore amenable to various forms of urban policy and small-scale urban programmes. For Castells the 'urban crisis' is the expression of the structural contradictions of capitalism. Forms of discourse which preface with 'the urban' are likely to be diversionary from the proper location of the problem. They constitute 'the ideology of a special areas approach', i.e. the notion that there are only certain areas in the city that have to be dealt with and that urban policy has the capacity to deal with these problems.

In the light of these criticisms, Castells proposes 'a new theoretical field' which should take the place of existing urban theory: 'this field is not that of a new urban sociology but is simply a redefinition of the real problems tackled and the discoveries made within the ideological field described as urban sociology' (1976b: p. 71). As Castells sees it, this would be an end to an ideology of the urban and a beginning of a science of the urban.[5]

The new theoretical field of the urban which Castells has suggested, is expected to concentrate upon (a) the social structuring of space; (b) the organisation and mode of the institutions of collective consumption; (c) politics and the intervention of the state; and (d) forms of resistance. Each of these has considerable implications for the possible reformulation of inquiries in urban studies and in urban education.

(a) *The social structuring of space* Castells argues that space is not a physical given, it is not a neutral point of departure but a historically constituted social relation. The capitalist mode of production requires a spatial organisation which facilitates the circulation of capital, commodities and information. Therefore the social and spatial structuring of the city — the existence of the central business district, the smart metropolitan areas, the slum, the ghetto, the decayed inner city, the affluent suburbs — are produced essentially by the imperatives of various forms of capital. Contradictions do arise however when the imperatives of the various forms of capital (commercial, finance and property) conflict. An important focus for the reformulated field of the urban question is to examine the ways in which these various forms of capital shape the city; the relationship between these forms of capital and the formal planning agencies of the central and local state and the nature of the contradictions which emerge out of these processes.

(b) *The institutions of collective consumption* In Castells's view, conventional urban sociology 'has tackled a multitude of problems whose connection is that they belong to the sphere of collective consumption', e.g. to the provision of housing, education, health, transport, recreation. Thus urban sociology has played 'in the consumption sphere, the same role as industrial sociology in the production sphere' (1976a: p. 75). Such an emphasis is important but needs to be reformulated. The urban question conceived of as the organisation of the means of collective consumption makes visible an important site of contradiction in advanced capitalist societies. The contradiction arises because such 'social services' are required for the adequate reproduction of the labour force and are demanded through popular political action, while at the same time such services are generally unprofitable for capital ('expenses capital'). As pressures upon and expectations for such social services increase in metropolitan cities, the amount of expenses capital increases with the result that corporate interests attempt to resist such increases and in fact to reduce existing levels of provision. Such contradictions and crises have already revealed themselves dramatically in the fiscal crisis of several American cities[6] and they are emergent in major cities in Britain as a result of contemporary political and economic policies.

(c) *Politics and the intervention of the state* In an attempt to resolve these contradictions and their resulting conflicts, the state increasingly intervenes in the city both at the level of the social structuring of space (urban planning and development) and at the level of social services (through pressures upon the local state and its expenditure). This is what Castells describes as 'the intervention of the political'. Issues of power and politics become central concerns: 'it is politics which structures the totality of the field and determines how it is transformed . . . the heart of the sociological analysis of the urban question is the study of urban politics.'[7]

A reformulated field of inquiry in these terms must therefore examine the manifestations of the power relations between social classes in the city; the instances of state interventions in urban contradictions (where the state is conceived of as acting 'according to the relations of force between classes and social groups but generally in favour of . . . the dominant classes'[8]) and the attempts at resolution of contradictions in the spheres of planning, development and collective consumption.

(d) *Forms of resistance* Growing urban contradictions provoke not only increasing interventions from the state but also a growing resistance and opposition from different sectors of the urban population. This resistance is expressed in the emergence of 'urban social movements'. Reviewing Castells's use of this notion, Pickvance (1976) argues that organisations in the city can be placed on a scale of participation—protest—urban social movement. The crucial distinguishing feature of an urban social movement is that it has developed beyond the participation level, beyond organised (or spontaneous) protests on specific urban issues to the point of linking an immediately urban issue with a framework of wider struggle: 'it is only when an urban social movement unites economic or political contradictions with urban contradictions that the term in its strict sense can be said to apply' (Pickvance, 1976: p. 200).

A reformulated field of urban study, then, in the view of Castells, should investigate the political and protest movements which arise out of urban contradictions and increasing state interventions in these. These movements may be concerned with housing, the environment, redevelopment, health and education services etc. Initially such movements may have quite a limited focus but Castells predicts that 'there will be a significant development of urban social movements as a means of changing social relations and this will arise from urban contradictions' (1978: p. 127).

This, in very schematic form, is an outline of the new 'science of the urban question' which Castells has articulated. It attempts to replace the problematic of redistribution with the problematic of power. It moves the focus of urban study *beyond conflict* to structural contradiction. It is not simply a theoretical reformulation but also a call for empirical work[9] which takes a radically different focus from that of existing empirical work. It has provoked discussion, research and a wide range of critical response.[10]

Pahl (1975b), in making one such response, has pointed out that while the work of Castells has rightly placed the analysis of the urban question within the wider framework of political economy, it has restricted itself to the political economy of capitalism. Pahl argues that such a limitation is indefensible (and in itself not scientific but ideological) since there is an 'urban question' to be studied within state socialism as well as within capitalism. This urban question involves an examination of the mechanisms for the social structuring of space; the role of the urban bureaucracy; the role of the state in the sphere of collective consumption and the effects of technological developments, 'control of everyday life through the socialisation of the collective means of consumption takes place in all the advanced societies *notwithstanding ideological differences*. A common concern to increase the level of production and material wealth increasingly produces a territorial division of labour and a form of reproduction and social control of the work force which creates similar social problems and contradictions' (1975b: p. 17). Thus Pahl asserts again the need for comparative studies of the urban question, and argues that in this context 'the sociology of Max Weber appears the most radical.'

Theory and the 'real issues' of urban education

For those teachers, lecturers and administrators who are anxious to grapple with the challenges of the inner city schools, an examination of trends in urban theory may seem at best an interesting diversion or at worst a ritual academic preface which merely delays engagement with the real issues. Such a view is understandable in its impatience of 'theorising while the inner cities burn' but it ought nevertheless to be resisted. The rationale for the previous analysis is that no useful discussion of or even formulation of the 'real issues' in the inner city or in urban education can take place independently of theory. If such theory is not made explicit it will nevertheless continue to operate and shape the field covertly. There seems to be every advantage therefore in making it visible.

It will be apparent from the preceding pages that what is constituted as a 'real issue' in the study of the urban will vary according to particular theoretical standpoints and according to particular political and policy bases. Thus a view of urban education which is mediated through a problems perspective sets out a very different agenda to that which is mediated through an emphasis upon conflict theory or an emphasis upon the existence of structural contradictions. The weakness of the field of urban education has been its detachment from the theoretical debates and developments of urban social theory. Such detachment has restricted its ability to formulate a comprehensive agenda for study and a comprehensive range of theoretical tools to accomplish such study. Too often, the approach in urban education studies has been to start with a pre-given problem or set of problems of urban schooling and to work cautiously out towards what appears to be a sector of urban theory relevant to the pre-given problem. It is suggested here that an approach which *starts* with an appreciation of the range of urban theory is likely to produce a more profound formulation of the crucial issues in urban education.

Notes

1 See Pahl (1975a), p. 201.
2 See Rex and Moore (1967), pp. 6–7 and pp. 35–7.
3 Further examples of such work can be found in Harloe (1981) and Harloe and Lebas (1981) and in Dear and Scott (1981).
4 For a discussion of status quo, revolutionary and counter-revolutionary theory in urban geography and urban studies see Harvey (1973), Chapter 4.
5 Castells uses 'science' here in the sense of the science of historical materialism.
6 For one discussion of this see R.C. Hill, 'Fiscal collapse and political struggle in decaying central cities in the United States', in Tabb and Sawers (1978).
7 Recent works which have examined urban politics are Saunders (1979) and Dunleavy (1980).
8 For Castells's concept of the state, see Castells (1978), p. 3.
9 Castells argues that 'any new theoretical position that is not anchored in concrete analysis is redundant' (1977: p. 4).
10 For a critical appreciation, see Elliott and McCrone (1982), pp. 6–20.

Bibliography

Burgess, E. (1967), 'The growth of the city: an introduction to a research project', in R. Park and E. Burgess, *The City*, London, University of Chicago Press.
Byrne, D., Williamson, W. and Fletcher, B. (1975), *The Poverty of Education*, London, Martin Robertson.
Castells, M. (1976a), 'Is there an urban sociology?', in C. Pickvance (ed.), *Urban Sociology: Critical Essays*, London, Tavistock.
Castells, M. (1976b), 'Theory and ideology in urban sociology' in C. Pickvance (ed.), *Urban Sociology; Critical Essays*, London, Tavistock.
Castells, M. (1977a), *The Urban Question*, London, Edward Arnold.
Castells, M. (1977b), 'Towards a political urban sociology', in M. Harloe (ed.), *Captive Cities*, London, Wiley.
Castells, M. (1978), *City, Class and Power*, London, Macmillan.
Cockburn, C. (1977), *The Local State*, London, Pluto Press.
Dear, M. and Scott, A. (eds) (1981), *Urbanization and Urban Planning in Capitalist Society*, New York, Methuen.
Dunleavy, P. (1980), *Urban Political Analysis*, London, Macmillan.
Durkheim, E. (1933), *The Division of Labour in Society*, Toronto, Macmillan.
Elliott, B. and McCrone, D. (1982), *The City: Patterns of Domination and Conflict*, London, Macmillan.
Gray, F. (1976), 'Selection and allocation in council housing', *Transactions*, Institute of British Geographers, NS, I, pp. 34–46.
Habermas, J. (1976), *Legitimation Crisis*, London, Heinemann.
Harloe, M. (ed.) (1977), *Captive Cities*, London, Wiley.
Harloe, M. (ed.) (1981), *New Perspectives in Urban Change and Conflict*, London, Heinemann.
Harloe, M. and Lebas, E. (eds) (1981), *City, Class and Capital*, London, Edward Arnold.
Harvey, D. (1973), *Social Justice and the City*, London, Edward Arnold.
Herbert, D. and Smith, D. (eds) (1979), *Social Problems and the City*, London, Oxford University Press.
Kapitalistate Group (1976), *The Urban Crisis and the Capitalist State*, San Francisco.
Mellor, R. (1977), *Urban Sociology in an Urbanized Society*, London, Routledge & Kegan Paul.
Pahl, R. (1975a), *'Whose City?'*, Harmondsworth, Penguin Books.
Pahl, R. (1975b), 'From urban sociology to political economy', mimeo.
Pahl, R. (1977), 'Managers, technical experts and the state: forms of mediation, manipulation and dominance in urban and regional development', in M. Harloe (ed.), *Captive Cities*, London, Wiley.
Pahl, R. (1979), 'Socio-political factors in resource allocation', in D. Herbert and D. Smith (eds), *Social Problems and the City*, London, Oxford University Press.

Park, R. (1952), *Human Communities,* Chicago, Free Press.
Park, R. and Burgess, E. (1967), *The City*, London, Chicago University Press.
Pickvance, C. (1976), *Urban Sociology: Critical Essays,* London, Tavistock.
Pinch, S. (1979), 'Territorial justice in the city', in D. Herbert and D. Smith (eds), *Social Problems and The City,* London, Oxford University Press.
Rawls, J. (1971), *A Theory of Justice*, Cambridge, Mass., Harvard University Press.
Rex, J. and Moore, R. (1967), *Race, Community and Conflict,* London, Oxford University Press.
Rex, J. (1973), *Race, Colonialism and the City*, London, Routledge & Kegan Paul.
Rex, J. and Tomlinson, S. (1979), *Colonial Immigrants in a British City*, London, Routledge & Kegan Paul.
Saunders, P. (1980), *Urban Politics: A Sociological Interpretation*, Harmondsworth, Penguin.
Saunders, P. (1981), *Social Theory and The Urban Question*, London, Hutchinson.
Simmel, G. (1903), 'Metropolis and Mental Life', (first appearance in English) in K. Wolff (1950), *The Sociology of George Simmel,* Chicago, Free Press.
Tabb, W. and Sawers, L. (1978), *Marxism and the Metropolis,* New York, Oxford University Press.
Tunley, P. *et al.* (1979), *Depriving the Deprived,* London, Kogan Page.
Weber, M. (1958), *The City*, Chicago, Free Press.
Webster, B. and Stewart, J. (1975), 'The area analysis of resources', *Policy and Politics* (3), pp. 5–16.
Williamson, W. and Byrne, D. (1979), 'Educational disadvantage in an urban setting', in D. Herbert and D. Smith (eds), *Social Problems and the City*, London, Oxford University Press.
Wirth, L. (1938), 'Urbanism as a way of life', *American Journal of Sociology,* vol. 44, pp. 1–24.

Part II

Historical location

4 Reconstructing the history of urban education in America
Sol Cohen

> There is some danger in isolating a question for immediate and intensive research simply to meet urgent contemporary needs... there is no reason to believe that panic history will be more satisfying or enduring than panic policy-making. What is required now is the patient reconstruction of our entire urban past.
>
> R. C. Wade, 'An Agenda for urban history,' in H. J. Bass (ed.), *The State of American History*, Chicago, Quadrangle Books, 1970, p. 49.

I

In the late 1960s, after more than a half-century of neglect, the history of urban education in the United States finally emerged as the object of intensive historical inquiry and established itself as one of the liveliest and most significant sub-fields within the general field of history of education. What accounts for this development? There is always a close connection between the scholarship of a period and the fundamental concerns and characteristics of the society in which historians are living. But the nexus is professional as well as socio-political. The answer lies within the profession of history, the profession of history of education, as well as the 'urban crisis' which afflicted the United States in the late 1960s.

II

In 1890, the US Bureau of the Census announced that the Western Frontier was no more. Nevertheless, Frederick Jackson Turner's 'frontier thesis' cast such a long shadow over American historiography that for a long time afterwards the role of the city remained little explored or understood. In 1933 Schlesinger's pioneering *The Rise of the City, 1878–1898* appeared, putting forward bold claims for a history organized around 'the rise of the city.'[1] The volume however was little more than a 'collection of facts' as Charles Beard put it, rather than an urban synthesis. In 1940 Schlesinger submitted a plan for a 'reconsideration of American history from the urban point of view.'[2] Schlesinger's pioneering efforts found few followers for another two decades. Then, beginning in the early 1960s, there was a burgeoning interest in urban history, accompanied by an enormous and disparate literature in such genres as urban bibliography, urban historiography, general surveys of urban development, urban or city biographies, and period studies, along with what Lampard calls 'the orbis et urbis approach' to urban history, treating of 'virtually anything . . . and the City.'[3] Urban history quickly won for itself a place as a specialty in the broader field of history. Urban historians have greatly enriched our knowledge of urban history and of national history. Nevertheless, in the debates among the practitioners of urban history there surfaced considerable reservations about their new specialization.

One of the major issues is the 'problems' orientation of much urban history. To many urban historians the city was a 'problem,' a species of pathology. Perhaps the most forceful critic of his colleagues in urban history was Eric Lampard. 'Like beauty,' writes Lampard, 'problems exist in the eye of the beholder; they reveal more about the nature of the observer, perhaps, than about the object observed.' The 'problem' approach, observed Lampard in 1968, constitutes the conventional wisdom of American urban history. This sort of history focuses so much on contemporary problems, it becomes 'present politics.' This will not produce better urban history, nor a more decent urban politics. The 'crisis' that urban historians should turn their talents to, he advised, 'is not the urban crisis,' but 'the state of the literature and the art.'[4] Another issue which preoccupied practitioners of American urban history had to do with the vague and ill-defined boundaries of the specialty. Urban historians seemed to be groping for a distinctive subject matter, distinctive methods of research, and distinctive themes. What is the meaning of 'city'? The meaning of 'urban'? What is the difference between 'industrialization' and 'urbanization'? Should the historian study the city or the urban process? Is the city a singularly important phenomenon of itself or is it to be studied as a reflection of other movements or major currents in the mainstream of American history such as progressivism? Thernstrom complained that 'urban history apparently deals with cities, or with city-dwellers, or with events that transpired in cities, or with attitudes toward cities — which makes one wonder what is not urban history.'[5]

Hardly had urban history established itself as a reputable speciality when a group of American historians came forward to advance a 'new urban history.'[6] The new urban history was history from the 'bottom up,' the history of ordinary men and women. The new urban history borrowed extensively from the social sciences, especially sociology, and made imaginative use of historical sources such as city directories, tax lists, census returns, and artifacts such as photographs and the like. The new urban history explored the use of quantitative methodologies. The new urban history was concerned with new directories of inquiry: internal migration from country to city, patterns of social stratification and social mobility, the social consequences of technological change, and the evolution of the family, to name a few. Indeed, the 'new' urban historian was as much a social scientist as he or she was an historian. Here too, the misuse of the 'new urban history' was as much on the mind of some of its practitioners as its promise. Thernstrom, perhaps the most influential practitioner of the new urban history, warned especially against the uncritical use of social science concepts, the tendency of urban historians to do history with the 'urban crisis' uppermost in mind, as well as their penchant for making sweeping generalizations from limited evidence. For the present, Thernstrom cautioned in 1971, high priority must go to the careful description and analysis of particular communities and the processes which formed them, for little is known about the most elementary aspects of their history.[7]

III

The response of American historians of education to the rise of the city was until the late 1960s largely one of neglect or indifference. Why did it take so long for historians of education in such a heavily urbanized country as the United States to develop an interest in the history of education in its cities? The answer has largely to do with the dilemma of the historian of education in a professional education setting.

History of education as a special field of study in the United States dates back to about 1890 when it was one of the most widely offered courses in American teachers' colleges and schools or departments of education. From the beginning, however, American historians of education had to face the skepticism of academic colleagues towards the profession of education in general, the reservations of colleagues in schools or departments of education about the value of history of education in a professional program, while at the same time they had to cope with the general inadequacies of a field seemingly infinitely broad and indeterminate in scope, and prematurely specialized.[8] The mode of treating the field first took form in the late nineteenth century. The then-dominant content of courses in the history of education in American teacher training institutions was essentially European educational philosophy. Most of the textbooks in the field were histories of European educational thought, or studies of comparative European educational philosophy. A canon of major works had been isolated by tradition running from the pre-Socratics to Plato and Aristotle to St Augustine to Locke to Rousseau to Pestalozzi, Froebel and Herbart. History of education was study of this traditional canon with side trips to the 'Middle Ages,' the 'Renaissance and Reformation,' and the 'Age of Rationalism.' This is where Ellwood P. Cubberley made his contribution.

Cubberley's seminal *Public Education in the United States: A Study And Interpretation of American Educational History* broke with the idealist history of his predecessors.[9] Cubberley shifted the emphasis from intellectual history to social history, from European education to American education, from past problems to present problems. History of education, as hitherto written, Cubberley declared, 'had little relation to present-day problems in education,' and had 'failed to function in orienting the prospective teacher.' Cubberley presented his own history as an 'interpretation of American educational history' dealing with the 'larger problems of present-day education in the light of their historical development.' Cubberley deliberately aimed to inspire and guide. He wanted his readers 'to see the educational service . . . as a great national institution evolved by democracy to help it solve its many perplexing problems.'[10] Cubberley's great organizing themes were the great 'battles' to establish free, tax-supported and publicly controlled schools. Although *Public Education in the United States* placed educational developments in a social context, it was, in the Beardian tradition, the rise of industry that was central to Cubberley, not the rise of the city. In fact, the great 'battles' for public schools were waged not on the city but on the *state* level: our school systems are all state school systems' (italics mine).[11] This was the ultimate triumph of the public school wars.

Cubberley's notion of the function of history of education dominated the field for several decades, though never without challenge. Through the 1920s, 1930s and 1940s historians of education in the United States debated the question of whether and how history of education could be 'functional' in a professional school of education. In the meantime, some devoted their energies to writing highly specialized and antiquarian monographs or monographs with current educational problems uppermost in mind, ultimately hortatory in intent. Others wrote textbooks in a vain attempt to replace Cubberley's *Public Education in the United States*. Most historians of education never published at all, worn out by the multifarious demands of their professional teacher training responsibilities.[12] Some never budged from a commitment to history of education as the history of European educational ideas or the history of the philosophy of education but simply kept adding subject matter to satisfy critics. As late as 1950 one of the doyens of history of education, Thomas Woody, defined the historiographical frontiers of American education: primitive culture, the Christian era, Greek and Roman society, Renaissance, Reformation, Marxism, as well as education in India, Africa and the Soviet Union, also 'man (and woman) in society' (*sic*), and 'major problems' of American education.[13] Such boundless definitions of the field, and Woody is not unusual among historians of his generation, inevitably led to diffusion and fragmentation of energy. These circumstances severely retarded the development of any significant research interest in history of urban education.

American historians of education who in the late 1950s and early 1960s led the revolt against the Cubberley school of historiography introduced a variety of new subjects and approaches into history of education but interest in urban education was not part of their new outlook. The influential Committee on the Role of Education In American History ignored the history of education in cities while calling for study of the role of education in 'the building of communities on the frontier.' Bailyn urged historians to think of education 'not as formal pedagogy but as the entire process by which a culture transmits itself across the generations.'[14] Cremin's path-breaking *The Transformation of the School: Progressivism In American Education, 1876–1957* is not an urban interpretation of progressive education as might have been anticipated. Cremin is at pains to demonstrate that progressive education has its roots in rural as well as urban reform movements.

The vogue of urban educational history in the United States is scarcely fifteen years old. It arose at a particular moment of American political, social and intellectual history: the emergence of urban history as an exciting and accepted historiographical specialty, the turbulent social and political atmosphere of the 1960s, and the 'urban crisis'; the catalyst was the emergence of a radical revisionist school of educational history or, more accurately, of a critical school of history of education.[15] The critical revisionists comprise Joel Spring, Clarence Karier and Paul Violas among others, but its most notable practitioners are Michael B. Katz and David B. Tyack.[16]

The critical revisionists emerged on the American scene in the tail-end of the 1960s, that 'slum of a decade' in Richard Rovere's term. The sources of their radicalism were those which produced alienation and rebelliousness throughout American society in the late 1960s and early 1970s — the continuing war in Vietnam, racial discrimination, lawless politics, dehumanizing institutions, and the appearance of a whole range of dangerous and seemingly intractable urban problems.[17] They were greatly influenced by the New Left movement in politics and social thought, as well as by social and educational critics like Paul Goodman, John Holt, Jonathan Kozol, Ivan Illich and Theodore Roszak; the revisionist general historians John Higham, James Weinstein and Gabriel Kalko, and the Marxist economists Herbert Bowles and Samuel Gintis. James Wallace summed up the ideological thrust of the revisionist educational historians in the *Harvard Educational Review* in 1969. Wallace called for the publication of ' "anti-texts" in educational history' which would enable prospective schoolteachers to find 'a usable, but historically sound past.' Such an effort, Wallace conceded, 'will doubtless result in some over-written, over-simplified, and over-stated history.' But this is a risk which must be run, 'if history is to be relevant to a new generation of teachers.' As the American teacher becomes politically more radical, Wallace concluded, 'it would seem both desirable and inevitable that there be an accompanying radicalization of the discipline's bearing on education.'[18] Michael Katz had almost simultaneously precisely fulfilled Wallace's hope.

IV

In *The Irony of Early School Reform: Educational Innovation in Mid-Nineteenth Century Massachusetts*, Katz set the tone for much of the work in history of urban education in the United States for the late 1960s and early 1970s. *The Irony of Early School Reform* is essentially a topical study. Katz focuses on three aspects of educational reform in ante-bellum Massachusetts: the controversy over the abolition of the public high school in Beverly; the conflict between Cyrus Pierce and Horace Mann and the Boston schoolmasters over methods of teaching; and the arguments over the establishment of the state reform school at Westborough. Katz, however, is not really interested in these specific historical case studies as such. He is interested in them for what they reveal about the 'underlying dynamics' of American urban school reform generally, in the present as well as in the mid-nineteenth century.

Katz appealed to educational historians to cast off the 'myths' that have pervaded their accounts of the public school awakening. Katz rejects the view that popular education in the United States spread in response to the demands of an enlightened working class and the idealism of a handful of far-sighted academics, philanthropists, and social reformers. Katz questioned the motives as well as the aims of urban school creators. They were neither benevolent nor disinterested. School reforms were advocated by an elite of wealth and position largely for their value in the fight to help solve the problems of urban-industrial society. In alliance with this elite were the aspiring middle class who saw the school as an agency of social mobility for their children. Educators joined the fight for school reform to enhance their precarious professional status. The victory of school reformers was complete but it was a victory for the forces of reaction. A common school system was established but it was a system encrusted in a rigid bureaucracy, imposed upon the working class community which comprised its chief clientele, and conceived as an instrument of social control; a powerful agency for imposing the values of a dominant economic class upon the working class. The extension and reform of public education, Katz asserts, was not the outcome of 'a potpourri of democracy, rationalism, and humanitarianism.' It 'represented the imposition by social leaders of schooling upon a reluctant, uncomprehending, skeptical, and sometimes . . . hostile citizenry.'[19] Here is the 'irony' of the school reform. The very people in whose name educational reforms were sought, the working class, rejected them. Furthermore, urban school promoters of the mid-nineteenth century 'fostered an estrangement between the school and the working-class community that has persisted to become one of the greatest challenges to reformers of our own time.'[20]

Katz's use of social science concepts, especially quantitative techniques. is suggestive. However, it was Katz's moral passion, his polemical tone and apocalyptic rhetoric that was decisive. Katz conceived of *Irony of Early School Reform* as both a 'scholarly historical study' and 'a piece of social criticism.' The *Irony of Early School Reform*, however, 'emphasizes [the] connections between . . . past mistakes and the present disastrous state of formal education in American cities.' Katz offered no apologies for the partisan argument: 'the crisis in our cities must arouse a passionate response in all those who care about the quality of American life.'[21] To Katz, urban public schools possessed no redeeming features. They are irredeemably bureaucratic and structures of social control. Bureaucracy is anathema to Katz. He invariably uses the term as an epithet, heavy with odious connotations of rigidity, sterility and class domination. 'Social control,' the counterpart of 'imposition,' is the other *bête noire* of Katz. The schools are a potent social machine for the imposition of values and social control. That is why, states Katz, urban school creators were determined to foist their innovations upon the community, 'if necessary by force . . . the state [Massachusetts] passed compulsory school laws in the 1850s.'[22] School reforms, especially those reforms usually associated with educational progressivism, are another of Katz's targets.

School reform is an 'illusion.'[23] School reform is the opium of the working class. 'The diffusion of a utopian ideology that stressed education as the key to social salvation,' Katz asserts, 'created a smokescreen that actually obscured the depth of the social problems . . . and prevented the realistic formulation of strategies for social reform.'[24] Hence school reform movements are unacceptable; the fundamental reconstruction of American society is required. Here Katz's critique of the reform of urban schools becomes part of a broader polemic against 'liberalism' and 'progressivism,' and 'liberal' or 'progressive' historians of education, the 'consensus' school of American educational historiography.

To Katz, the function of history of education is to serve the cause of social and educational reconstruction. The major significance of the 'new' history of education, he asserts, lies in the way it 'links up with, and contributes to, the larger critical contemporary reappraisal of American life and institutions.'[25] In *Class, Bureaucracy and Schools*, the didactic intent is freely admitted. Katz ingenuously states, 'Our concerns shape the questions that we ask and, as a consequence determine what we select from the virtually unlimited supply of facts.'[26] Katz mines sources for a usable past. Where the evidence is not forthcoming, it is supplemented by Katz's explanation of 'real motives' and 'real functions' as opposed to stated ones. Like Cubberley's history, this is history in the service of ideological needs. Katz has merely substituted one kind of teleology for another, a Whig for a Protestant history. Instead of a recitation of battles waged and victories won for democracy and progress we are given a jeremiad lamenting decline, failure and victories won for reaction. *The Irony of Early School Reform* provides a blatant example of the activist historian deriving his history from his politics and thereby losing his respect for the pastness of the past.

The value of *The Irony of Early School Reform* lies not in its substantive content. *The Irony of Early School Reform* has been roundly criticized for its methodological and substantive shortcomings, specifically Katz's key study of the Beverly high school affair.[27] Furthermore, Katz's conclusions about urban school reform generally, as we shall see below, have been both implicitly and explicitly repudiated. The value of *The Irony of Early School Reform* lies in its contributions to the historiography of American education, which are two, one ephemeral, the other of lasting value.

Katz's integrating construct, 'social control,' became very influential among historians of education; for a time it was the prevailing interpretive framework for explaining school reform movements. The concept of 'social control,' at least as employed by Katz, has, however, very limited explanatory power. Of course the concept of social control helps historians to get at unstated motives and aims. But Katz's emphasis is exclusively on the evils of social control and such emphasis is naive and simplistic. As American sociologist Morris Janowitz points out, social control is a generic aspect of society. It is simply wrong to give it an exclusively pejorative connotation of conformity or coercion. In fact, social control is the obverse of coercive control.[28] Brian Davis observes that, by definition, the social is control. Social control, he observes, 'is not some dark opposite to liberation and freedom, it is the ubiquitous condition. . . .'[29] One does not choose to live in a society without social order and some forms of ensuring social order. Education is the social control system *par excellence*. The real question for historical investigation is what other functions does it perform.

Katz's permanent contribution to American educational historiography is that he provided an alternative, critical framework to the reigning 'progressive' one. *The Irony of Early School Reform* performed an invaluable service for American historians of education. It unfroze the tame, consensus mold into which history of education seemingly would be frozen, a mold from which even Cremin did not break. *The Transformation of The School* is in a key way very traditional. For example, Cremin viewed educational progressivism as 'part of a vast humanitarian effort to apply the promise of American life ... the ideal of government by, of, and for the people. . . . '[30] Cubberley would agree. It is not that in Cremin's view the 'transformation' occurs without conflict; but that the resolution of conflict is inevitably progress; the country and its educational system is unequivocally better off for educational reforms.

Before the publication of *The Irony of Early School Reform*, progressivism was the only historiographical tradition in the history of American education. Historians of education in the 1960s were settling into their ivory tower when Katz rebuked their complacency and disturbed their contemplation with the noise of current events. Katz shifted the focus from harmony and consensus to conflict and social strife. Katz brought involvement, indignation and a sense of injustice to the writing of educational history. If one of the tasks of the historian is to undo myths then the place of Katz in the history of American education is secure. Historians of education will not look at education in quite the same way again. Finally, *The Irony of Early School Reform* revitalized debate over the purposes of and results of schooling and aroused fresh interests in the history of American education, not only among historians, but among educational policymakers and the informed public.

V

In the late 1960s and early 1970s, stimulated by the work of Katz and the 'urban crisis,' a few books on urban educational history and perhaps a dozen articles of the 'orbis et urbis' genre made their appearance.[31] Still, they didn't add up to much. In 1973 Schultz started to write a comparative educational history of Boston, Chicago and St Louis. Struck with 'the paucity of respectable and useful historical writing on the establishment and growth of even *one* urban school system,' he abandoned the comparative project to concentrate on nineteenth century Boston (italics mine).[32] Due to the recency of interest, the paucity of the published work and its fragmentary nature, there was, remarkably, nothing on a city in the far west or the southern part of the country; such studies provided little cumulative knowledge of the history of urban education. Nevertheless, in 1974, David Tyack's *The One Best System: A History of American Urban Education* made its appearance. Here was an ambitious attempt at an interpretive history of American urban education by one of the country's most productive historians of education.

Tyack describes his study as an 'interpretive history of the organizational revolution' that took place in American schooling during the late nineteenth and early twentieth centuries.[33] In the latter part of the nineteenth century the local ward system—community control of schools with a vengeance — was prevalent in American cities, a legacy of earlier small town or rural patterns. Educational 'progressives' and their lay allies, an interlocking directorate of university presidents, professors of educational administration, leading businessmen and lawyers, and publishers of leading newspapers and journals of opinions, condemned the ward system as corrupt and inefficient. The ward system would be replaced by a system of management based on the model of the large-scale industrial or corporate bureaucracies rapidly emerging at the turn of the century. The reform watchwords were centralization, efficiency, economy and non-political control. School boards were to be small, nonpartisan, preferably composed of successful businessmen, and purged of all connection with political parties and elected officials.

The desire to bring order and efficiency to increasingly large and complex urban school systems prompted the move to centralization, standardization, systematization and bureaucratization. But the school professionals also sought greater power and status for themselves and their class. Their slogan was 'take the schools out of politics' and 'politics out of the schools.' But such slogans were largely window dressing. School reformers preferred a 'relatively closed system of politics' to 'pluralistic politics.' The drive to centralize the management of the public schools and to separate public school management from city government was a middle and upper class Protestant reform strategy to keep urban school systems from falling into the hands of the Catholic, working class, ethnic-dominated city political machines. In order to make 'the one best system' work, the schoolmen had also to classify children and to develop differentiated courses of study and standardized examinations. With classification and differentiated curricula came new job categories, new programs of professional preparation, more administrators, more bureaus: bureaucracy.

The tendency toward corporate-industrial models of management emerged first in school systems in cities in the American northeast, then spread south and west, and in time into rural and small-town school systems. Tyack concludes that educational leaders were able to develop a consensus in their search for the 'one best system,' and largely succeeded in securing its implementation. Their success, Tyack concludes, so framed the structure of urban education that the subsequent history of American urban schools 'has been in large part an unfolding of the organizational consequences of centralization.'[34]

Tyack discusses an extremely wide range of topics in *The One Best System*. There are interesting comparisons of school systems with police departments and other municipal organizations. Tyack's insights are frequently penetrating; for example, his description of the nineteenth century principal and his 'pedagogical harem' (his largely all-female faculty); his analogy between 'Black power' in American urban education in the 1960s and 'Catholic power' in urban education in the 1830s and 1840s; his observation that in the politics of urban education, what is frequently at stake are cultural issues as opposed to pedagogical ones; his depiction of the architecture of urban high schools—fancy Gothic structures to compete with the most ornate academies in attracting the attention (and the attendance) of the prosperous; his analysis of the close ties between city school superintendents and university presidents who frequently considered the city school superintendent a 'captain of education' like themselves.

The One Best System reveals many of the strengths, obviously, of the 'new' urban history. It also evidences many of the latter's deficiencies. Tyack's conception of urban education is so sweeping as to be virtually synonymous with everything that happened in city schools. Tyack's intention is to provide a new organizational synthesis for American urban educational history. Unfortunately, evidence is crunched to fit the construct. *The One Best System* is careless of historical detail. It is never clear who is doing what to whom and with what results and when. The historical agents are often vaguely 'they,' or 'the school managers,' or 'the centralizers,' or variations thereof. There is little sense of change or development over time. Further, Tyack's construct leaves too little room for struggle among conflicting tendencies within the same interest groups. Ravitch's case study of the politics of urban schooling in New York City reveals that there was conflict among school boards, between school boards and superintendents of schools, between the latter and their associate superintendents, between superintendents and principals, and between school leaders at different levels of the system.[35] Ronald Cohen's work on the Gary, Indiana, school system reveals that some generalizations about urban school systems break down when individual schools are examined![36]

For Tyack, the enlargement of our understanding of urban education will come only as we approach it with the new insights and methods of the social sciences. His work illustrates the dangers of indiscriminate borrowing. The distinctions between 'governance' and 'politics,' and 'centralization' and 'modernization' are crude and frequently blurred. Tyack's key integrative construct, 'bureaucracy,' is used with little sense of its complexity or denseness of meaning. Tyack conceives bureaucracy in largely invidious terms. Bureaucracy, concluded Tyack, resulted in 'displacement of goals.' Bureaucracy served to perpetuate jobs and outworn practices rather than serving the school's clients, the children.[37] Such conclusions need to be proven, not simply asserted. Many sociologists and political scientists hold positive or at least more neutral views of bureaucracy. Crozier argues that bureaucracy may not be antithetical to individual goals and may even provide more points of access for relatively powerless groups.[38] We learn from Hauser that bureaucracy is an ubiquitous form of organization in the city. Bureaucracy is an inevitable and indispensable concomitant of populations of large size and density and high levels of interaction, an indispensable tool in the functioning of a mass society. Bureaucracy is necessarily impersonal and requires the subordination of the individual to the organization. Bureaucracy may also produce greater freedom and may advance pluralism by providing points of access to government by minority and politically powerless groups.[39] Bureaucracy may be dysfunctional; it may also serve important functions in democratic society. Few generalizations can be made except on the basis of case studies limited to particular times, issues and locations for their focus.

The One Best System attempts to provide a usable past to serve as a guide to current educational policymaking. Tyack declares that he does not share the view that American urban schools have abysmally declined. But like Lord Byron's Julia, protesting that he never will, he does. Tyack's attempt to force history to contribute to the solution of the 'urban crisis' leads him to uncharacteristic hyperbole: 'schools have rarely taught the children of the poor effectively and this failure has been systematic, not idiosyncratic.'[40] Tyack portrays public schooling as 'racist,' and systematically so. Urban schools, he declares, 'did not create the injustices of American life, although they had a systematic part in perpetuating them.' In his desire to provide an immediately usable past to school policymakers, Tyack errs in the way he once warned against:

> Research arising from contemporary concerns may tempt scholars to read the present into the past, and to concentrate only on those features of our heritage which are pertinent to the problems of today. Disillusionment with institutionalized education and discouragement with the results of schooling in the present ... may prompt historians to tell a tale of woe as one-sided as the previous story of the public school triumphant.[41]

In the early 1970s, historians in the United States began to devote an increasing amount of attention to the 'organizational factor' in American history, to the development of those sprawling networks of large-scale organizations which dominate the United States and other industrial societies. Some historians envisioned 'organization' as the crucial ecological variable in urban history. Other historians have discerned an emerging organizational synthesis for the whole of modern American history, which seems destined to have enormous impact on urban history.[42] The 'organizational factor' draws our attention to very difficult questions of social change, to modes of decision-making, the balance between persistence and change in organizational forms over time, the relationship between cultural values, ideology and organization, and the interrelationship between social structure and organizational development. Historians of urban education will be indebted to Tyack for bringing the 'organizational factor' to their attention.

VI

Beginning in the early 1970s, a new generation of historians of urban education began to turn their attention to close monographic studies of urban schooling. In recent years the works of four of that new generation of scholars, Stanley K. Schultz, Carl F. Kaestle, Selwyn Troen and most recently Julia Wrigley, have made their appearance.[43] The subjects of Schultz, Kaestle, Troen and Wrigley, respectively, are the school systems of Boston, New York City, St Louis and Chicago. All abjure the premise that American public schools have been an unequivocal failure; all portray the schools as the focal point of idealism as well as self-interest. Together, they constitute a compelling refutation of the major assumptions and conclusions of the entire critical school of American urban educational historiography.

The point which emerges from these studies is that urban public school systems in the United States emerged as a response to the first shocks of modernization, which were felt earliest and most intensely in America's eastern coastal cities. Urban common school systems emerged as a response to the influx of immigrants and the social friction and social disorganization pursuant to rapid and disorderly urban growth. The public schools, tax-supported, publicly controlled, and free, were to be a major instrument in forging a new national cohesion. If the schools were to serve as general headquarters for a new moral and social discipline then all the children had to be got into the school and kept there as long as possible. The rapid expansion in the school population, the swelling economic investment in schools and the proliferation of schools and school teachers led to a demand for efficiency and economy, for systematization and bureaucracy. It was inevitable that the model for the nascent school systems would be the phenomenally successful New England factory system.

The advocates of public schooling set out to shore up their society. They were aided by schoolmen who found in the development of public schools a device by which they could enhance their own professional status and dominance. All believed, however, that education would improve the conditions of the poor. Bureaucracy, that is centralization, hierarchical organization, and efficiency and economy of operation, was essential if the system were to be universal. Finally, those who established school systems were not following some predetermined path. The process of urban public school system building went something like this: there was an urgent problem or 'crisis', followed by pressure on the schools, then hasty and makeshift solutions. The ramshackle creations of urban school system builders illustrate neither the working out of the inevitable spirit of progress nor the conspiracy of one class against another.

Kaestle's *The Evolution of an Urban School System* attempts to explain why and how the public schools of New York City became organized into a system: 'a single, articulated, hierarchical system that was amenable to uniform policy decision.'[44] In response to increasing immigration, vagrancy, intemperance, poverty, and crime, New York's leaders organized the Public School Society and turned to schooling as a deliberate instrument for the acculturation of the children of the poor.

The school system was expected to transmit not only literacy, but the cultural traditions and moral attitudes appropriate to the new urban America. The sheer numbers of children and schools dictated systematization. By the time the Public School Society turned over its school to the new, public, New York City Board of Education in 1853, 'schooling services in New York were consolidated, coordinated, and standardized in a process that one is tempted to call a bureaucratic revolution.'[45]

Regarding bureaucracy, Kaestle concludes that it was not so much class and cultural bias on the part of school leaders, but 'common sense' which mandated the bureaucratization of the schools. Of course schoolmen in New York were concerned with efficiency, economy and standardization, but there was more involved: 'the desire to be fair to all those who would accept the rules of the system, and desire to raise the quality of teaching.' Bureaucracy may cause alienation and stifle creativity, but bureaucracy also 'represents an effort to hold in check ... the personal prejudices and whimsical judgments of individuals.'[46] Kaestle concludes that New York's public school system is a reflection of the city's persistent institutional approach to urban problems, 'one which has aimed ideally to uplift, hopefully to reconcile, and minimally to control, its turbulent population.'[47]

Schultz's argument is in many ways similar to Kaestle's. The public school movement in Boston matured in response to what contemporaries viewed as an urban crisis; mounting concern over immigration, pauperism and rising crime rates. Voluntary and informal and discontinuous educational arrangements were unable to meet the challenge. Reformers turned to the school as a form of insurance to protect society. The purpose of public schooling 'was to secure order in a disorderly age.' City leaders championed education to secure social order. Still, Schultz concludes, to the extent that schools succeeded in reaching the children of the poor and foreign-born, they opened opportunities for social advancement.[48] In their attempt to create a 'system,' Boston schoolmen turned to the factories of New England. In their methods of organization schoolmen saw 'the perfect model for retooling the schools.'[49] Within this context, Schultz examines the continual struggle for funds, and the ethnic and religious tensions which complicated the problem of city school system building. Both Schultz and Kaestle make extensive use of quantitative evidence to demonstrate that children from a wide variety of socio-economic classes attended the public schools. Both show some awareness of European influences on the fledgling public school.[50]

Troen's study of the St Louis school system and Wrigley's of the Chicago schools provide invaluable mid-west counterparts to the more widely studied school systems of New York City and Boston. Troen rejects what he calls hostile analyses of urban school reform. Troen refers to the development of systems of public education as one of the great accomplishments of nineteenth century urban society.[51] Troen specifically dissents from any social control model of urban educational historiography. It simply does not apply to St Louis, he says. Troen also dissents from the view that bureaucratic reforms were an upper class attempt to seize the schools. Troen emphasizes rather the 'importance of the rationalizing processes that characterized modernizing institutions.'[52] It was imperative to structure school management if the system were to succeed in its program of expansion. Changes in city schools were not foreordained but rather 'flowed from the system's responses to changes in urban life, political pressures, educational theory, and the decisions of students and parents.'[53] Troen's summary of the shift in urban school governance in St Louis from laymen to experts is positive; administrative and curricular reforms were widely supported; they received widespread and enthusiastic endorsement as valid responses to difficult social and educational problems. That administrators were careful to educate the public to the system's work and to seek mass support made the transition relatively quick and free from conflict.

Wrigley's *Class Politics and Public Schools: Chicago, 1900–1950*, puts a period to an era in the historiography of American urban education. Wrigley refutes Katz's methodology and conclusions in the core case of the Beverly high school.[54] Wrigley directly challenges Katz's conclusion that public schools were fostered by an economic elite as a means of social control. She also challenges Katz's central notion that schools were imposed on the working class and its corollary, that labor was opposed to the public school movement.[55] Wrigley examines the conflicts over vocational education, financing, and control of the Chicago public school system. She concludes that business and professional groups, rather than conceiving of public education as a powerful agency of social control, which therefore should be expanded, often viewed the public school system as a drain on the finances of the city. Furthermore, they feared that over-education of the populace could create increased social frictions. Wrigley finds, on the other hand, that the Chicago labor movement provided consistent support for the public school system and fought for its expansion. Finally, the labor movement in Chicago was not 'imposed' upon. Far from being docile, the labor movement resisted reforms not in its interests and fought for its own educational ideals and reform programs: 'The history of educational development in Chicago is the history of struggle, compromise, and resistance, not of simple elite domination.'[56] And Chicago, as we now know, was not exceptional in this regard.

VII

Historians of education in the United States have always been under particularly acute tension. They carry commitments both to the discipline of history and to the professional education program. Their loyalties are claimed by the demands of both past and present. They are caught between their desire to count in the world and their desire to understand it, between their desire to do good and to do good historical scholarship, between their desire to create a 'usable' past and a 'historically sound' past. The problem is that such desires are at odds with each other, or that only within narrow limits are these desires compatible. The problem is, as Louis Morton has observed, that it is in dealing with the contemporary world that the historian is most vulnerable professionally, since it is in precisely this area that the qualities for which he is most valued and from which he draws his strength, 'perspective, objectivity, accuracy, and completeness,' are least evident.[57] The question is not that of creating a 'usable' past. All historians desire to write 'usable' history. Society may find history truly usable, if historians concentrate on scholarly work, increasing our store of knowledge and our understanding of the past. And since the past is never dead, it is not even past, increasing our understanding of the present as well. The critical historians of education were not able to control their moral passions and social purposes. Their work added little to our substantive knowledge of the history of urban education. To future investigators, much of their work will be relegated to the role of footnote to the 'urban crisis' of the 1960s.

In the late 1960s and early 1970s historians of urban education in the United States freed themselves from one myth, the 'pro-school' myth, then for a time, they became captive of a new myth, the 'anti-school myth'. They are freed now from both myths. In 1971, Thernstrom advised urban historians that priority must go to the careful description and analysis of particular communities. Wade was even more forceful:

> There is some danger in isolating a question for immediate and intensive research simply to meet urgent contemporary needs... there is no reason to believe that panic history will be more satisfying or enduring than panic policy-making. What is required now is reconstruction of our entire urban past.[58]

By the late 1970s, the time had arrived for American historians of urban education to follow their best advice. Many American historians of urban education are having second thoughts about making their specialty a form of social or political action; they are shifting their focus from the urban crisis to the crisis in urban educational historiography.

Though oversimplified, it may be helpful to view historiographical developments in the United States as a snake-like procession, with general historians as the head of the procession and historians of education as the middle part seeking to catch up with the head. Since 1975 there has been a renaissance in American local and community history. This development has fed upon and coincided with the dramatic upsurge in historical awareness within the United States encouraged by the American Revolution Bicentennial celebration. The origins of this trend must also be sought within the context of the rise of the 'new social history.' The new local or community history is an effort to write 'total history' within a manageable geographical framework, and in so doing illuminate the wider problem of change in history. Models of such in-depth studies are to be found in the work of the French School around Emmanuel Le Roy Ladurie, the English School of local studies centered at the University of Leicester, and the work of a group of American historians like John Demos, Philip Greven and Kenneth Lockridge, among others, focusing on New England towns in the colonial and revolutionary periods.[59] Within the last few years, and a few years after the head of the procession shifted its interest to localities and communities, the middle part, a small group of historians of education, turned their attention to in-depth local studies. The pioneer multidisciplinary and cooperative research projects in the new history of urban education are those currently directed by Michael Katz and Henry C. Johnson, Jr.[60] The results of their work lie in the future.

By way of conclusion, we may observe that in the United States the history of urban education is a relatively new venture, and we may claim for it the indulgence due to all new ventures. In the meantime, as Marc Bloch once remarked of history in general, the uncertainties of our discipline must not be hidden from the curiosity of the world.

Notes

1 A.M. Schlesinger, *The Rise of The City, 1878–1898*, New York, Macmillan, 1933.
2 'The City in American History,' *Mississippi Valley Historical Review*, vol. 27, 1940, p. 43.
3 E.E. Lampard, 'The dimensions of urban history: a footnote to the "urban crisis" ', *Pacific Historical Review*, vol. 39, 1970, p. 262. There is a huge literature here. A good overview is R.A. Mohl, 'The history of the American city,' in W.H. Cartwright and R.L. Watson, Jr (eds), *The Reinterpretation of American History and Culture*, Washington, D.C., National Council for the Social Studies, 1973, pp. 165–206.
4 Lampard, op. cit, p. 262.
5 S. Thernstrom, 'Reflections on the new urban history,' *Daedalus*, vol. 100, 1971, p. 359.
6 Ibid; S. Thernstrom and R. Sennett, (eds), *Nineteenth Century Cities: Essays In The New Urban History*, New Haven, Connecticut, Yale University Press, 1969.
7 Thernstrom, op. cit., p. 363.
8 For elaboration, see S. Cohen, 'The history of the history of American education, 1900–1976: the uses of the past,' *Harvard Educational Review*, vol. 46, 1976, pp. 303–8.
9 E.P. Cubberley, *Public Education In The United States: A Study And Interpretation of American Educational History*, Boston, Houghton Mifflin, 1919.
10 Ibid; pp. vii–x.
11 Ibid; pp. 487–95. For the concomitant but earlier interest in history of education at the state level see L.A. Cremin, *The Wonderful World of Ellwood Patterson Cubberley*, New York, Columbia University Press, 1965, pp. 19–23.

12 From a senior American historian of education:
It is difficult to do a really accurate and meaningful study in educational history, especially of the United States, if one has not been exposed to the joys and sorrows of daily classroom teaching; contact with children, adolescents and parents; cooperation or conflict with supervisors, administrators, boards of education and the community at large; and a multitude of other experiences which enable the historian to comprehend and appreciate the inner development of education. W.H. Brickman, *Guide to Research In Educational History*, New York, n.p., 1949, p. 215.

13 T. Woody, 'Fields that are white,' *History of Education Journal*, vol. 2, 1959, pp. 5—17.

14 The Committee on The Role of Education In American History, *The Role of Education In American History*, New York, Fund for the Advancement of Education, 1957, p. 18; B. Bailyn, *Education In The Forming Of American Society: Needs And Opportunities for Study*, Chapel Hill, North Carolina, University of North Carolina Press, 1960, p. 14.

15 The label 'radical revisionists' is an unsatisfactory one. All historians are revisionists, 'radical' revisionists even. Not all revisionists are critical of their society or its institutions. In spite of its shortcomings we will use the term 'radical revisionists' because of its familiarity.

16 See the following by M. B. Katz: *The Irony of Early School Reform: Educational Innovation in Mid-Nineteenth Century Massachusetts*, Cambridge, Mass., Harvard University Press, 1968; *Class, Bureaucracy, and Schools: The Illusion of Change in America*, New York, Praeger, 1971; *School Reform: Past and Present*, Boston, Little Brown, 1971; and *Education In American History: Readings In The Social Issues*, New York, Praeger, 1973. See also C.J. Karier (ed.), *Shaping The American Educational State, 1900 to the Present*, New York, Free Press, 1975; C.J. Karier, P. Violas and J.H. Spring, *Roots of Crisis: American Education In The Twentieth Century*, Chicago, Rand McNally, 1973; J.H. Spring, *Education and the Rise of The Corporate State*, Boston, Beacon, 1972; E.B. Gumpert and J.H. Spring, *The Superschool and the Superstate: American Education In The Twentieth Century, 1918—1970*, New York, Wiley, 1974; and D.B. Tyack, *The One Best System: A History of American Urban Education*, Cambridge, Mass., Harvard University Press, 1974.

17 J. O'Neill, *Coming Apart: An Informal History of America in the 1960s*, Chicago, Quadrangle Books, 1971, is helpful here. Also R. Berman, *America In the Sixties: An Intellectual History*, New York, Free Press, 1968; and T. Powers, *The War At Home: Vietnam and the American People, 1964—1968*, New York,

Grossman, 1973, Cf. D. Bell, *The End of Ideology: On The Exhaustion of Political Ideas In The Fifties,* Chicago, Free Press, 1960.

18 J.B. Wallace, review of *Progressive Education: From Arcady to Academe* by P. Graham, *Harvard Educational Review,* vol. 39, 1969, pp. 190–7.

19 Katz, 1968, p. 112.

20 Ibid; Preface.

21 Ibid., p. 214.

22 Ibid., p. 218.

23 The notion of school reform as an illusion is made more explicit in Katz's writings of the early 1970s.

24 Katz, 1968, p. 211.

25 'Comment,' *History of Education Quarterly,* vol. 9 (1969), p. 328.

26 Katz, 1971, op. cit., p. xxv.

27 See the reviews by Neil Harris in *Harvard Educational Review,* vol. 39, 1969, pp. 383–9; and Donald M. Scott in *History of Education Quarterly,* vol. 10 (1970), pp. 243–51. And see D. Ravitch, *The Revisionists Revised: A Critique of the Radical Attack on the Schools,* New York, Basic Books, 1978, especially pp. 116–26.

28 M. Janowitz, *The Last-Half Century: Social Change and Politics In America,* Chicago: University of Chicago Press, 1978. This volume is actually a history of the idea of social control.

29 B. Davis, *Social Control and Education,* London: Methuen, 1976, pp. 7–8.

30 L.A. Cremin, *The Transformation of The School: Progressivism In American Education, 1876–1957,* New York, Random House, 1960, p. viii.

31 For example, R.D. Cohen, 'Urban Schooling in twentieth-century America: a frame of reference,' *Urban Education,* vol. 8, 1974, pp. 423–37; W.W. Cutler, 'A preliminary look at the schoolhouse: the Philadelphia story, 1870–1920,' *Urban Education,* vol. 8, 1974, pp. 381–99; E.B. Gumpert, 'The city as educator,' *Education and Urban Society,* vol. 4, 1971, pp. 7–24; W.H. Issel, 'Modernization in Philadelphia school reform,' *Pennsylvania Magazine of History and Biography,* vol. 94, 1970, pp. 358–83; C. Kaestle, 'School reform and the urban school,' *History of Education Quarterly,* vol. 12, 1972, pp. 211–28; M. Lazerson, *Origins of the Urban School: Public Education In Massachusetts,* Cambridge, Mass., Harvard University Press, 1971.

32 S.K. Schultz, *The Culture Factory: Boston Public Schools, 1789–1860,* New York, Oxford University Press, 1973, pp. x–xi.

33 Tyack, op. cit., p. 3.

34 Ibid., p. 127.

35 D. Ravitch, *The Great School Wars: New York City, 1805–1973,* New York, Basic Books, 1974. See also J.M. Cronin, *The Control of Urban Schools,* New York, Free Press, 1973.

36 R.D. Cohen, op. cit., p. 437; R.D. Cohen and R.A. Mohl, *The Paradox of Progressive Education: The Gary Plan And Urban Schooling,* Port Washington, New York, Kennikat Press, 1979.

37 Tyack, op. cit., p. 11.

38 M. Crozier, *The Bureaucratic Phenomenon,* Chicago: University of Chicago Press, 1964; R.R. Alford, *Bureaucracy and Participation,* Chicago, Rand, McNally, 1969.

39 P.M. Hauser, 'Urbanization: an overview,' in P.M. Hauser and L.F. Schnor (eds), *The Study of Urbanization,* New York, Wiley, 1965, pp. 25, 28.

40 Tyack, op. cit., pp. 11–12.

41 D. Tyack, 'New perspectives in the history of American education,' in H.J. Bass (ed.), *The State of American History,* Chicago: Quadrangle Books, 1970, pp. 29–30.

42 L. Galambos, 'The Emerging Organizational Synthesis in Modern American History,' *Business History Review,* vol. 44, 1970, pp. 279–90; D. Cuff, 'American historians and the "organizational factor', *Canadian Review of American Studies,* vol. 4, 1973. pp. 18–31; R. Wiebe, "The progressive years," in Cartwright and Watson, op. cit., pp. 425–42.

43 Schultz, op. cit.; C.F. Kaestle. *The Evolution of an Urban School System: New York City, 1750–1850,* Cambridge, Mass., Harvard University Press, 1973; S.K. Troen, *The Public and the Schools: Shaping the St. Louis School System, 1838–1920,* Columbia, Missouri, University of Missouri Press, 1975; J. Wrigley, *Class Politics and Public Schools: Chicago, 1900–1950,* New Brunswick, New Jersey, Rutgers University Press, 1982.

44 Kaestle, op. cit., p. viii.

45 Ibid., pp. 159, 182.

46 Ibid., pp. 177–9, 190.

47 Ibid., p. 191.

48 Schultz, op. cit., p. x.

49 Ibid., pp. xi–xiii.

50 Cf. S.E. Fraser, 'British and continental education: American nineteenth century notes,' *Pedagogica Historica,* vol. 12, 1972, pp. 21–32.

51 Troen, op. cit., p. 224.

52 Ibid., p. 1.

53 Ibid., p. 4.

54 Wrigley, op. cit., pp. 4–13.

55 Ibid., p. 15.

56 Ibid., pp. 261–9.

57 L. Morton, 'The Historian and the policy process,' *History Teacher,* vol. 4, 1970, p. 23. In the early 1970s many historians voiced serious reservations about activist, presentist historiography. For example, I. Unger, 'The New Left, and American history: some recent trends in United States historiography,' *American Historical Review,* vol. 72, 1967, pp. 1237–63; R. Hofstadter, 'The importance of comity in American history,' *Columbia University Forum,* vol. 13, 1970 pp. 12–16; A.S. Kraditor, 'American radical historians on their heritage,' *Past and Present,* vol. 56, 1972, pp. 136–53; D. Deleon, 'The American as anarchist: social criticism in the 1960s,' *American Quarterly,* vol. 25, 1973, pp. 519–31; I. Susman 'History and the American intellectual: uses of a usable past,' *American Quarterly,* vol. 16, 1964, pp. 243–63. See also D.R. Warren, 'A past for the present,' in D.R. Warren (ed.), *History, Education, And Public Policy,* Berkeley, California, McCutcheon, 1978.

58 R.C. Wade, 'An agenda for urban history,' in J. Bass (ed.), *The State of American History,* Chicago, University of Chicago Press, 1970, p. 49.

59 K.N. Conzen, 'Community studies, urban history, and American local history,' in M. Kammen (ed.), *The Past Before Us: Contemporary Historical Writing In The United States,* Ithaca, New York, Cornell University Press, pp. 270–91; M. Kammen, 'The American Revolution Bicentennial and the writing of local history,' *History News,* vol. 30, 1975, pp. 179–90; L. Stone, 'English And United States local history,' *Daedalus,* vol. 100, 1971, pp. 128–32.

60 The 'orbis et urbis' tradition still persists. See, for example, D. Ravitch and R.K. Goodenow (eds), *Educating An Urban People: The New York City Experience,* New York, Teachers College, 1981, with its chapters on Jews, Roman Catholics, blacks, women's history, progressive education and teacher unionism, among other topics.

5
The university settlements, class relations and the city

Tony Evans

Any review of the history of urban education in Britain is likely to see the last decades of the nineteenth century as a crucial period of development. In those years we see the gradual transformation away from an education system based on voluntary enterprise to one in which the state comes to accept the overall responsibility for the education of the working class child. Harold Silver has argued that too much of our educational history has been limited to a few isolated areas such as policy formation, administrative organisation and legislation. What actually happened in urban education, the relationships and the processes involved, are by comparison undervalued (Silver, 1977). My intention in this article is to take one educational initiative of the period, the establishment of the university settlements in the poorer areas of the nineteenth century city, to explore the social context in which they operated and to see what is revealed about the nature of the relationships between the classes in the nineteenth century city. I hope too that this excursion into the history of a set of urban institutions can play some small part in demonstrating the value of an historical element in our approach to urban studies. The relationship between history and urban studies should be a mutually beneficial one. History provides a valuable testing ground for looking at our ideas and assumptions about urban society while the theoretical understandings being developed in contemporary urban studies should enhance our appreciation of what happened in the past.

The university settlements may be seen as just one aspect of a many-pronged response to the apparent threat to social stability posed by the existence of mass urban poverty. Other aspects of that response might be considered to include the development of the elementary school system as well as the gradual introduction of some control over housing conditions and the reform of local government. While the university settlements, of necessity, could play only a small part in tackling the problem of the Victorian city they attracted the interest and support of a sizeable part of the educated public and in so far as they represent the response of the products of the Victorian university to the problems of a class-divided society they provide a worthwhile focus of study through which our understanding of the relationship between class and education can be furthered.

Where attempts have been made in the socio-historical writing of recent years to analyse the class relationships at play in nineteenth century society much use has been made of the concept of social control. In his study of the development of elementary education in Spitalfields earlier in the century, for example, P. McCann entitles his article 'Popular education, socialization and social control: Spitalfields 1812–24' (McCann, 1977) and a wide-ranging survey of inter-class relations in a whole series of social areas – policing, government, the church and leisure activities, as well as education – was published in 1977 under the title *Social Control in Nineteenth Century Britain* (Donajgrodzki, 1977). In the most general terms these works draw a picture of a class-based society in which social order is maintained through the exercise of power by one class over another through a wide range of social institutions. Gareth Stedman Jones, however, has warned that scholars using the concept of social control should beware of being uncritically eclectic. In the reported discussion at the Society for the Study of Labour History's 1975 conference on 'The working class and leisure: class expression and/or social control' he expresses the view that the concept is derived from the sociological tradition of Durkheim and Parsons and implies acceptance of a model of static equilibrium, involving cycles of breakdown and of reimposition of dominance. In such a model the permanency of class conflict is denied and the role of the working class in actively shaping the social context is not acknowledged (Society for the Study of Labour History, 1976). In the introduction to the collection on social control Donajgrodzki admits the force of Jones's position but claims that the concept of social control is in fact trans-ideological and is quite compatible with approaches that are by no means consensualist or functionalist. He argues that used discriminatingly the concept of social control does not commit the historian to a simple reductionism in the analysis of relationships and that it can be used in ways that are quite compatible, for example, with Gramscian notions of hegemony (Donajgrodzki, 1977, Introduction).

In this context it is instructive to look at the way that the work of one of the historians most closely associated with the Birmingham Centre for Contemporary Cultural Studies has developed over the period of a decade. In 1970 Richard Johnson made an initial analysis of the development of educational policy in the nineteenth century in terms of social control. In an article entitled 'Educational policy and social control in early Victorian England' he argued that one of the major concerns of the nascent educational administration was to establish a closely guarded control over a working class population that was decadent in its behaviour and unable to bring up children in a socially reliable way. He concluded that

> The early Victorian obsession with the education of the poor is best understood as a concern about authority, about power, about the assertion (or the reassertion?) of control. This concern was expressed in an enormously ambitious attempt to determine, through the capture of educational means, the patterns of thought, sentiment, and behaviour of the working class. (Johnson, 1970, p. 119)

By 1976, when his 'Notes on the schooling of the English working class, 1780—1850' were published in the Open University course book *Schooling and Capitalism*, Johnson was still concerned to emphasise the way that the earliest educational administrators were effectively making a moral attack on the working classes but in the 1830s he now sees a 'crisis of hegemony' which is reflected in a class relationship which is typified by the cultural aggression of the bourgeoisie (Johnson, 1976, p. 50). Finally in 1977 Johnson's contribution to the Donajgrodzki collection contains a most valuable examination of the use of the concept of social control in an historical context. It is seen as 'a helpful point of departure' which, despite the vague, unspecific nature of its usage, allows for the consideration of authority relationships in social phenomena, such as education. However, he goes on to say that he sees it as an ambiguous concept 'in search of theory', and suggests that it can most usefully be employed in the debate about the state and its ideological functions in analysis of the many forms in which relations of domination can be disguised (Johnson, 1977, p. 78).

This debate about the conceptual tools used in historical analysis is far from being the arid theorising that traditional historiography would represent it as being. I believe that without such attempts to define the structural boundaries within which day-by-day events took place and without a workable basis of conceptualisation which allows valid comparisons to be made from one instance to another then our history is compartmentalised and of little more than antiquarian interest. In looking at the history of the university settlements and at the class relations embodied in them I have been particularly concerned to try to see in what ways domination, be it social or cultural, was being imposed by one class on another. On the other hand I have also tried to be aware of the potential liberatory force that might have been made available to members of the working class either through the settlements, or possibly in reaction to them. Inevitably an historical account is concerned with the individual event, a specific occasion, often with one person's actions, thoughts or motives. But it can also concern itself with wider issues which are illustrated by the particular instances in question and in this survey I have sought to raise the question of just to what extent the settlements can be characterised as being part of an apparatus of class-cultural control.

The first university settlements, Toynbee Hall and Oxford House, were established in the East End of London in 1884. In *Outcast London,* Jones warns against falling into the 'post hoc propter hoc' fallacy of simply seeing the settlement movement as a response to the social crisis of the early 1880s. He argues correctly that the ideas and practices institutionalised in the settlements were reflective of developments in thought and social action from the 1860s and 1870s (Jones, 1971, p. 259), and yet, having said that, the immediate social context is important in explaining the genesis of the movement. Even if the ideas behind the institutions were not new the realisation of crisis that occurred in those years was sufficiently different from what had gone before for the energy required to seek new solutions to be generated. Indeed Jones himself has allowed us to be able to see the crisis of the 1880s more clearly as the fusion of a number of long-term and short-term phenomena. On top of the long-term tendency towards industrial decline affecting the London economy the city experienced a period of trade depression, housing shortage and the apparent growth of socialist alternatives to traditional liberal ideology (Jones, 1971, Chapter 16). There is no doubt that respectable England was shocked by the successive revelations of George Sims, William Booth and Charles Booth in the last years of the century (C. Booth, 1892—97; W. Booth, 1890;

Sims, 1889). These had been preceded however, and probably outranked in terms of popular impact, by the pamphlet *The Bitter Cry of Outcast London*, published in 1883. Probably written by a Congregational minister, Andrew Mearns, it is a short and pungent piece of work. It complains about the inadequate presence of the churches in the poorest areas and about the evil effects of indiscriminate charity. It goes on to draw a picture of a 'seething . . . mass of moral corruption' in the city 'concealed by the thinnest crust of civilisation and decency'. It briefly surveys housing conditions, employment and the moral condition of the people and it calls for a 'lifeboat' to be provided in the shape of church missions. It was not on account of its offered solutions, however, that the pamphlet captured the public imagination. It received great publicity via Wickham Stead's *Pall Mall Gazette* and brought 'the condition of England' question to a new level of public concern (Wohl, 1970).

At Oxford the influence of the philosopher T.H. Green and more especially that of Arnold Toynbee, a junior colleague of his at Balliol, had created a receptiveness in the university to calls for tackling 'the social problem'. Thus when Samuel Barnett, Vicar of St Jude's in Whitechapel, put forward ideas for establishing in the poorer city area communities for university graduates from which they could work to devise programmes of educational and social benefit for the working class population his proposals were enthusiastically taken up. By 1913 forty-five settlements were operating in Britain (Barnett, 1918; Evans, 1982; Picht, 1914; Pimlott, 1935). Nor was the influence of the founding fathers limited to Great Britain. The example and inspiration of Barnett and other British pioneers is clearly acknowledged by social reformers both in Europe and in the United States. The work of Jane Addams, Stanton Coit and Robert Woods in the teeming cities of America has received rather more scholarly attention from historians than that of their British counterparts. Clearly there were very different circumstances at play in the American cities but many of the concerns of the settlement movement were shared internationally. A full analysis of the international links of the settlement movement has yet to be undertaken (Davis, 1967; International Conference of Settlements, 1922).

The primary objects of the movement in Britain can be adequately summarised by quoting those of Toynbee Hall. It was established 'to provide education and the means of recreation and enjoyment for the people in the poorer districts of London and other great cities; to inquire into the condition of the poor and to consider and advance plans calculated to promote their welfare' (Universities Settlement in East London, 1886). Some of the settlements, like Toynbee Hall, were secular institutions, whilst others, like Oxford House, were religious foundations of one denomination or the other. What all the settlements shared, however, was their chosen method of work, the voluntary effort of the settlement residents. These were young graduates who would come together in the poorer areas of the city, perhaps undertake some form of professional training in their chosen field, and work on the educational and social programme of the settlement in whatever time might be available to them. Most of the evidence used here is drawn from the experience of Toynbee Hall which, while not always typical of the movement as a whole, probably attracted the greatest public interest in the period under review.

At first sight there may appear to be problems in conducting an analysis of any set of nineteenth century institutions in terms of class relations between two polarised classes when there is no question that late Victorian society was riddled with minor social differences that would make apparent nonsense of such an approach. In a solidly working class area like East London minute gradations of status according to occupation, geographical origin and housing location played an important part in distinguishing between different groups of people and corresponding minor differences were just as apparent in the dominant classes. But a basic two-class picture was quite familiar to the educated Victorian and the whole point of 'settling' was that representatives of the cultured elite were deliberately choosing to go to live, as representative of their class, amongst the unenlightened. Indeed it is a curious fact that the consciousness of inter-class relations which is all-pervading in the writings of those involved in the settlement movement has often been lost in the writings of later historians. Canon Barnett himself, for all his consistent application of an individualist ideology, expressed his awareness of the importance of class in society. Writing in 1904 on how the division of labour had made the existence of classes inevitable he wrote, 'The classes in our great cities are many, but the terms "rich" and "poor", if not exact definitions, represent clearly enough the two great classes of society' (Barnett and Barnett, 1909, p. 26). This acknowledgment of fundamental social division was shared by his counterpart at Oxford House for much of this time, A.F. Winnington-Ingram, later Bishop of London. He felt it worthwhile to warn Cambridge students in a series of lectures published under the title *Work in Great Cities* in 1896, 'You will have to deal with a people whose traditions are totally different from our own' (Winnington-Ingram, 1896, p. 11).

If we accept that there was a fundamental division between the classes then a number of questions arise. The three main areas I want to explore in this article are as follows. What was it that motivated young university graduates to offer themselves 'in service' to the poor? How did the two classes react to one another when brought face to face with one another in such a setting? And underlying these, what does the experience of the settlement movement tell us about wider class relations articulated in an educational/cultural context, particularly in the light of the previous discussion on social control?

Before embarking upon these questions it is perhaps worth reflecting on the task facing the researcher tackling socio-historical problems of this nature. Any interpretation is dependent on the records left behind, by the institutions themselves and the individuals active in them. In looking at motives we can only examine consciously expressed thoughts. In looking at inter-class reactions we usually only have access to the words of individuals. Inevitably there are problems in using such evidence. Consciously expressed motives may tell only part of the tale. Individual reactions may or may not be representative of a wider group. In the end the historian has to make a judgment on the validity of using a particular piece of evidence based on his familiarity with the whole range of available evidence. However, unless such judgments are made we have no chance of building up an historiography that attempts to look at underlying social structures. It is important to me, therefore, that the arguments presented are based on publicly accessible materials which are open to reinterpretation by anyone who wanted to challenge the conclusions reached.

So what was it then that lay behind the attempts made by certain members of the educated classes to bridge the social divide? Certainly there was an indisputable strand of idealism in the motives of those involved. In the religious houses there was clearly an element of Christian zeal. But even in the non-religious foundations there was a sense of missionary purpose, to spread the benefits of culture to all. Writing just over ten years after the foundation of the first settlements Barnett explained,

> The establishment of settlements is the work of those who believe that the gifts to modern times are good; that culture is gain,

not loss; that cleanliness is better than dirt, beauty better than
ugliness, knowledge better than ignorance — Isaacs not to
be sacrificed. Settlements stand as an acknowledgement of the
claims of all the citizens to share in these good things . . . .
They express the desire on the part of those 'who have' to see,
to know, and to serve those 'who have not' (Barnett and
Barnett, 1909, pp. 259—60).

A clearer statement of an attempt to give practical application to Arnoldian notions of culture could not be asked for.

Observers less involved in the work of the settlement movement could be quite intemperate in their admiration. Sir Walter Besant in his book on East London saw them as 'lamps in dark places' which brought to the poor the chance of contact with the things they lacked:

the cleanly life, the power of acquiring knowledge, the possession
of, or access to, art of all kinds, more gentle manners, greater self-
restraint and in the cases before their eyes unselfishness and
the power of working without pay, without praise, without apparent
reward of any kind (Besant, 1901, p. 348).

This is not to say that those involved were not aware of elements of self-interest, or at least class self-interest, in what they did. T.H. Nunn was a resident at Toynbee Hall before making a wider mark on the life of the capital through the London Council of Social Welfare. Quoted in a survey of Mission work in the East End in 1906 he foresaw a forthcoming shift in political power in favour of the working class and argued that it was the task of the cultured minority to ensure that this shift in power should be achieved as painlessly as possible.

Whilst the balance of power still rests with those who care much
for the teaching and traditions of the past, they may learn
to understand and to prepare for their trust, those whose influence
must soon preponderate. There is yet time to bind the elements
of the society that is to be in the bonds of peace (Aitken,
1906, p. 137.

Philip Lyttelton Gell, the first chairman of Toynbee Hall, was a strong advocate of the centrality of the settlements' role as harbingers of social harmony. He believed that through individual contact and voluntary effort the dangers of social unrest inherent to a polarised class system could be overcome. His touchstone for measuring the success of a settlement's work lay in the answer to the question of whether visitors of any class left with their previous sense of class distinctions, class prejudices and class antagonisms effaced in a deeper conviction of human brotherhood and in the acknowledgment of a common responsibility for the common good (Gell, 1889, p. 61). Undoubtedly this call for inter-class cooperation which offered hope of social peace was central to the support the settlements received from the universities and other parts of the cultural elite.

Yet it is not difficult to see how this concern for social harmony and the wish to protect the cultural status quo can easily shift into expressions of fear of social upheaval. Sir John Gorst, MP, chose to give the Glasgow University Rectorial Address of 1894 on the subject of 'Settlements in England and America'. He expressed his concern that 'the destitute classes may swell to such proportions as to render the continuance of our existent social system impossible', and declared that society should be grateful to anyone who was willing to spend their life gaining the confidence of the masses 'and guiding their ideas into channels in which the common good of all is the prevailing influence' (Gorst, 1895, p. 6). The threat to public order and eventually to the stability of the state was clear enough to those who feared the rise of socialism and a rise of a working class population with its own political aspirations. While such sentiments were not on the lips of the founders of the settlement movement themselves it is possible to explain the widespread interest in their work in these terms.

On top of all this was a clear sense of guilt in many of the young middle class graduates. Beatrice Webb was a personal friend of the Barnetts and though never fully sympathetic to settlement work was a well-informed observer of developments in the early years. She sensed that behind the social ferment of the 1880s and in the genesis of the settlements in particular lay 'a new consciousness of sin among men of intellect and men of property' (Webb, 1926, p. 179).

Certainly Arnold Toynbee himself can be seen to epitomise this idea of class guilt. Toynbee died at the age of 30 after a hectic adult life of social service. His last public lecture was to a working class audience in Newman Street, London, where his criticisms of the single tax socialism of Henry George had been ill received. Toynbee's concluding remarks are worth quoting at some length.

Some of you have been impatient here this evening; you have shouted for revolution, but I do not think that that is the feeling of the great mass of the people. What I do feel is that they are justified, in a way, in looking with dislike and suspicion on those who are better to do. We — the middle classes, I mean, not merely the very rich — we have neglected you; instead of justice we have offered you charity, and instead of sympathy we have offered you hard and cruel advice, but I think that many of us would spend our lives in your service. You have — I say it clearly, and advisedly — you have to forgive us, for we have wronged you; we have sinned against you grievously — not knowingly always, but still we have sinned, and let us confess it; but if you will forgive us, nay, whether you will forgive us or not — we will serve you, we will devote our lives to your service, and we cannot do more (Picht, 1914, p. 22).

This intensity of feeling was echoed by Cosmo Gordon Lang, then Archbishop of York. He recalled on the occasion of Barnett's death in 1913 the impact of the early proposals for the creation of settlements on the undergraduate population of Oxford: 'Our conscience felt the rebuke of the contrast between the wealth of inheritance and opportunity stored up in Oxford and the poverty of the life lived amid the mean streets and monotonous labour of East London' (Barnett, 1918, Volume I, p. 310).

It would be nonsensical to attempt to find some overall measure of motivation distinguishing between elements of idealism, social and political fear and personal guilt and come to some easy conclusion about their relative order of influence. Clearly there was a whole range of reasons why different people supported the work of the settlements and no examination of conscious or unconscious motives can be settled incontrovertibly. Nevertheless, when we look at a society riven by class difference, where the threat to social stability was keenly felt, it does not seem to me to denigrate the spirit of service expressed by many of those involved to show that their concerns in that particular social context operated in ways that served the interest of the dominant class. Certainly one of the reasons that the settlements captured the imagination of the middle class was the importance of their implicit social function in defusing the threat represented by a massive working class population living in relative isolation from traditional social controls.

Having said that we then need to move on to explore the ways in which the two classes of late nineteenth century Britain reacted to one another when brought into contact with one another through the programmes of educational and cultural improvement put on by the settlements. Two of the movement's leading figures, Barnett and Winnington-Ingram, have been shown to be deeply conscious of the social divide across which they were working. Percy Alden, for some years a noted Radical in Parliament, was Warden of Mansfield House in Canning Town. He gave expression to the sense many urban reformers held about the impact of city life on the poor.

> The city, to some reformers, is no longer the objective embodiment of the higher life of man, but a terrible maelstrom of degradation, into which men and women are being rapidly sucked, and in which they are finally engulfed. Those of us who have lived in such districts have seen the process of demoralisation and destruction (Alden, 1904, p. 20)

From explanatory positions like this it is only a relatively short step to arguing for a deficit view of the local population. When describing the development of the educational programme at Toynbee Hall in her biography of her husband, Dame Henrietta Barnett remarks on the 'trying' arrogance of some of the working class students of the early years. She notes with satisfaction that these people 'saw themselves in the right perspective, when the Toynbee men unconsciously taught them nobler standards' (Barnett, 1918, Volume I, p. 326). Indeed Canon Barnett himself found little of merit in existing working class culture. He argued that settlements needed to be of a certain minimum size if they were to have influence for good in a neighbourhood. If they were too small 'they who come to represent [the] good' of the culture, knowledge and habits acquired at the university might be in danger of finding themselves giving way 'to the slovenliness and cheapness and want of manners which often distinguishes industrial neighbourhoods' (Universities Settlement in East London, *Annual Report*, 1890, p. 8). It was this wholesale dismissal of working class culture that lay behind the willingness to devise reforming schemes which intervened in all aspects of the lives of the urban poor – their education, their housing, their lack of thrift, their use of public libraries, the way they used their holiday treats, the way their children played.

Nevertheless, having said that, there is another strand in the thinking of the settlers which must not be ignored. There was some acknowledgment that the university graduate had something to learn from contact with the working man. In one of his most controversial articles, 'Labour and culture' published in 1906, Barnett recognised the rise to political maturity of the labour movement. 'The Labour Party is obviously the coming power. Its coming is welcomed because it brings with it the force gained in the discipline of work and the sympathy learned by contact with sorrow and suffering' (Barnett and Barnett, 1909, p. 215). The article went on to call for a radical redistribution of educational resources away from the ancient universities to be made available to meet working class educational needs so that the vision of a movement then mainly concerned with material advantage could be widened. In this and other later writings Barnett shows a much more sympathetic attitude to working class aspirations. If it is still an attitude permeated by patronising assumptions it does at least presuppose a dialogue with labour which was not shared by all middle class interests.

There had been a consciousness of the mutuality of the learning experience between the two classes from the earliest days of the settlements. The first prospectus advertising the foundation of Toynbee Hall sought to attract prospective residents in the following terms.

> There is indeed an abundance of work for the most varied abilities, and an experience of life invaluable for those who have to take part in forming the public opinion of their generation. Those who pass on to positions of responsibility in other localities to which their occupations may call them will be better and more useful citizens for the season spent in practical work and friendly intercourse with the working classes of East London. (Universities Settlement in East London, undated, p. 3)

When we try to uncover exactly how the young middle class residents reacted to the experience of being immersed, or at least partially immersed, in living in a working class neighbourhood it becomes possible to discuss two main types of reaction. I would suggest that one group moved on from the experience of living in areas like the East End to questioning the assumptions of the society they were living in and becoming involved in a variety of ways in trying to make some impact on social conditions generally. The second group probably more typical and about whom it is difficult to write with confidence seem to have moved on from their period of residence in the settlements back into the professional and managerial positions which they might otherwise

The university settlements, class relations and the city / 151

have been expected to pass on to after university E.K. Abel has analysed the destinations of 178 of the first residents of Toynbee Hall from 1884–1914 and found that 45 of these found employment in the civil service, 21 in the church, 18 in the universities, 15 in law, 14 in social services, and 13 in medicine. Journalism, politics and school teaching comprise the other significant areas (Abel, 1969, Chapter 2). For some of these the social distance between the classes was simply too great to be easily breached. This is difficult to illustrate but two recorded instances might offer some substantiation for this claim. In the very earliest years of activity one anonymous Toynbee resident reports on the political economy class he had been running at a Hackney Radical Club. He acknowledges the fact that his students had supplemented his teaching with their own practical experience as workers 'on matters of which a student fresh from Oxford must necessarily be ignorant'. But this generous sense of appreciation diminishes when he goes on to complain that when he invited the class to dinner at Toynbee Hall they came inappropriately dressed. He concludes 'Toynbee Hall will have done something for East London if it has taught a few people the virtue of "changing" ' (Universities Settlement in East London, *Annual Report*, 1886, p. 36). A similar sense of wounded pride is evident in the following complaint. A whole network of men's clubs developed from Oxford House through the Federation of Working Men's Social Clubs. However, following the 1894 final of the inter-club cricket competition G. Fiennes was forced to report,

> The committee of the Marylebone Cricket Club have up to the present year, kindly permitted the final to be played at Lord's. Unfortunately the privilege was abused last year, and a disgraceful scene took place owing to some supposed laches on the umpires' part. The Club this year felt compelled to refuse the privilege in consequence (Fiennes, 1895, p. 223).

But the reactions of the young middle class men who went as residents to the settlements were by no means uniform and it is worth looking at the group of residents who were radicalised by their experience as settlement residents. For some the radicalisation can be seen in cultural terms. C.R. Ashbee moved on from Toynbee Hall to establish the Guild and School of Handicraft in Mile End. This was a conscious attempt to put into practice some of the artistic ideas of Ruskin and William Morris in a cooperative production workshop

(Ashbee, 1976). For others the individualistic ideology of the settlement proved unsatisfactory and they sought involvement in collective political action. R.H. Tawney is probably the foremost intellectual example of this process though Attlee expresses this reaction at its most simple and direct.

> Some thirty years ago, when I was a young barrister just down from Oxford, I engaged in various forms of social work in East London. The condition of the people in that area as I saw them at close quarters led me to study their causes and to reconsider the assumptions of the social class to which I belonged. I became an enthusiastic convert to socialism (Attlee, 1949, p. 25).

A third group did not turn their backs on individualism or the current political status quo but carried the experience of their time in the East End into influential positions in the civil service where they played an important part in creating the machinery of the welfare state. Hubert Llewellyn Smith, Vaughan Nash, Cyril Jackson, Robert Morant and W.H. Beveridge might all be seen as examples of this tradition. Not necessarily radical in philosophy, the work they carried out in their respective government departments did much to change the relationship of the state to the poor. As Beveridge himself said in his autobiography, it was not that residence in a settlement inevitably led to the adoption of particular views but 'one would at least be in a position, having seen all sorts and conditions of men, to have reasonable views on all social proposals' (Beveridge, 1953, p. 31).

Equally when we turn to see how the working class population treated the arrival of a new school of philanthropists we find another wide range of reactions from those who wished passionately to take advantage of the educational opportunities on offer to those who were hostile to the intervention of young and inexperienced do-gooders. For some individuals the arrival of educated, cultured young men prepared to share and give of their knowledge was an exciting prospect. Thomas Okey, for example, was a Spitalfields basketmaker who had used the University Extension Society lectures, the free library at the Guildhall and the British Museum to widen his education and understanding. Toynbee Hall became the centre of his intellectual life and, particularly with the encouragement of Bolton King, he turned his gift for languages to teaching and translation purposes and ended his life as the first professor of Italian Studies at the University of Cambridge

(Okey, 1930). Frederick Rogers, the social and cultural campaigner who was central to the agitation for the introduction of old age pensions and who was the first chairman of the Labour Representation Committee, was another local man who became deeply involved in the life of Toynbee Hall. But Okey and Rogers were part of a long tradition of working class autodidacticism and arguably Toynbee Hall just happened to be the most convenient institution from which they could operate. Rogers in particular was in any case ambivalent about the settlement ideal. He had been involved in the foundation of Toynbee Hall but later recalled,

> What the young 'varsity man had to learn first of all in those days was that human nature was pretty much the same all round. They were amiable, friendly, charming and entirely well-meaning young fellows, but they surveyed life from a pinnacle, and needed to come down to earth (Rogers, 1913, p. 145).

Perhaps a more typical reaction of aspirant working class feeling can be discerned in George Acorn's *One of the Multitude*. Acorn never achieved the public distinction of Okey or Rogers. He was a master cabinetmaker, and through his settlement connections was asked to write his autobiography precisely because he was a supposedly ordinary man. His first contact with settlements had come at school where a Toynbee resident had been helping out. He recalls being invited to tea at Toynbee Hall and 'pouring out quaint fancies and opinions in return' (Acorn, 1911, p. 25). He acknowledges that this encounter had been important to him but also gives an insight to the lack of comprehension that must have been quite common amongst people with only casual contact with the settlements when he reports that this relationship simply came to an end, presumably because his Toynbee acquaintance had moved on elsewhere. It was to the library at the Webbe Club, one of the many clubs emanating from Oxford House, that Acorn pays tribute as his particular seat of learning. His comment on the settlement philosophy can perhaps be seen as a reaction of one of Matthew Arnold's aliens. 'Penetration of the lower classes by settlements is a splendid thing — the best way, I think, of raising the tone of East End life of all the methods I have seen applied' (ibid., pp. 25—6).

But not all local opinion was so well disposed, particularly amongst those in whom socialist ideas had found root. George Lansbury, another self-taught working class thinker, was far from sympathetic. He saw the settlements as palliatives, attempts to bridge the gulf between the classes with nothing more than smooth words and ambiguous phrases. He believed that the only accomplishment of Toynbee Hall was that 'men who went in training under the Barnetts, just as men and women who later came under the spell of the Webbs, could always be sure of government and municipal appointment' for within a few months they 'discovered themselves as experts on social affairs' (Lansbury, 1928, p. 130).

An anonymous labour activist writing under the pseudonym 'Persona' in the *Woolwich District Trades and Labour Council* magazine was equally convinced that the settlement movement was nothing more than a form of class conspiracy intended 'to teach the working man astronomy, electricity, botany and manners'. He goes on to build up a sophisticated notion of the sociological location of knowledge, arguing that the universities were 'not national, but upper-class and aristocratic centres of learning' and that 'political economy and historical science must alike justify and defend the present status of wealth and the conditions that ensure it.' One of the very first residents of Toynbee Hall, C.H. Grinling, was active in the labour movement in Woolwich at this time and the reply from 'An Oxford Man' in the next issue is likely to have been written by him. He points out that the settlements involved a mutual learning process and defends the work done. 'Persona', however, will have none of this.

> For 'An Oxford Man', whilst undoubtedly sympathetic with tne worker, is not one of them, one feels that his sympathy flows downwards, that his cautious emotion is somewhat in hand, that he half fears the class for whose well-being he would willingly serve (*Borough of Woolwich Labour Journal*, 1902, nos. 12–14).

But if local socialists were cynical about the settlements we must be careful not to lose sight of the fact that other leaders of the working class movement in East London worked with the settlement residents and were deeply appreciative of their work. Both in relation to the development of trade unions and other working men's associations such as the Order of the Phoenix and the club movement the settlements often acted as a resource and support. Both Tom Mann and Ben Tillett pay tribute to the assistance given by Toynbee Hall and some of its residents in the 1889 dock strike (Mann, 1923, p. 105; Tillett, 1931, pp. 136—7), and Toynbee for many years played host to a number of dockside and garment workers' unions.

Perhaps any attempt to describe the reactions of the working class population as a whole must be tentative. Certainly it seems that the appeal of what the settlements were offering to the local population was limited. Even in the 'boom years' of the 1880s and 1890s Toynbee Hall was not attracting a wide cross-section of the community. The young American visitor, Robert Woods, was enthusiastically reporting in 1892 that the 1,000 or so registered students 'are both male and female, young and old, and instead of being all well-to-do are really all poor' (Woods, 1892, p. 93). But the *Toynbee Record* was more tempered in its analysis. Schoolteachers and clerks were found to predominate amongst the student body, though 'a considerable and increasing proportion of artisans, especially in the science courses' was claimed (*Toynbee Record*, 1888, p. 10). Of the 1889—90 registration only 52 per cent of the student body had East London addresses, suggesting that the Toynbee classes were meeting a city-wide need for adult education classes and were not making much impact on the local population (Picht, 1914, p. 52).

Other small pieces of evidence help substantiate this picture of local indifference. Cyril Jackson indicated that suspicion of the visitors was widespread when he recommended the work of the Children's Country Holiday Fund for its effectiveness in communicating to parents that 'our aim in living among them is really that we may serve them, they begin to believe in our disinterestedness — an idea alas! which they are very slow to grasp' (Jackson, 1895, p. 104). The popular magazine *The Leisure Hour* in a review of the work of the settlements thought fit to comment,

> Many of the poor class, and those not of the lowest, resent the
> intrusion of successive batches of students, who come in
> the name of sanitary science, and bring only an intangible help.
> They too have the Englishman's notion as to his 'castle';
> and it is one that visitors of every order do well to remember.
> (Collings, 1895, p. 793)

So how finally are we to assess the inter-class relationship revealed in the experiences of Toynbee Hall and other settlements? Should they be seen as part of an apparatus of social control or is such a characterisation so far removed from actuality that it hides the truth of inter-class relationships? It is clear that on both sides of the class divide there were a whole range of experiences. The pioneers of the movement had come to East London with certain ambitions and the fact that the mass of the population were left untouched by these schemes means that they cannot be deemed to have been entirely successful. By some their intrusion was met with active hostility; probably to the vast majority their presence was largely a matter of indifference. By a small minority their offerings were eagerly welcomed and received.

To describe such a situation in terms of the concept of 'social control' seems to me to deny that range of reactions. In more general terms too it seems to offer inadequate scope to incorporate notions of resistance on the part of the working class population. In a two-class society in which power is distributed unequally any action by the dominant group affecting the dominated group is going to involve some form of imposition. However, we need to be able to distinguish between different types of imposition. In some spheres of action, and the political and economic spheres come to mind as examples, then control is probably the appropriate concept. In other spheres of action, and the cultural/educational sphere with which we are concerned when dealing with the settlements is surely such, social control is a less appropriate concept. It seems to me that we would do better to talk of 'attempted cultural imposition'. By using this term we do not make the assumption that intentions were successfully carried out and that some form of control was established. It then becomes possible to explore the full range of responses that actually took place. Certainly I believe it is helpful to look at the settlements as an example of 'attempted cultural imposition'.

In the end the most lasting influence of the settlements may not have been on the urban working class but on the middle class generators of the welfare state. For many of these the settlements were the generative context for their ideas on social and political affairs. The configurations of class relations in this country eventually came to be articulated through the bureaucracies of the state, providing education, welfare services, the 'planned economy'. Single institutions which offered the opportunity of direct cross-class experiences could only play a limited role in this new world, but for the turn of the century period I believe they do offer a fascinating focus for the exploration of class relations.

Bibliography

Abel, E.K. (1969), 'Canon Barnett and The First Thirty Years of Toynbee Hall', unpublished thesis, University of London.
Acorn, G. (1911), *One of the Multitude*, London, Heinemann.
Aitken, W.F. (1906), *Thirty Years in the East End*, London, S.W. Partridge.
Alden, P. (1904), 'The Problem of East London', in R. Mudie-Smith (ed.), *The Religious Life of London*, London, Hodder & Stoughton.
Ashbee, C.R. (1976), *A Few Chapters in Workshop Reconstruction and Citizenship* and *An Endeavour Towards The Teaching of John Ruskin and William Morris*, London, Garland Press.
Attlee, C.R. (1949), *The Labour Party in Perspective and Twelve Years Later*, London, Victor Gollancz.
Barnett, H.O. (1918), *Canon Barnett, His Life, Work and Friends*, (2 volumes), London, John Murray.
Barnett, H.O. and Barnett, S.A. (1894), *Practicable Socialism* (2nd edition), London, Longman, Green & Co.
Barnett, H.O. and Barnett, S.A. (1909), *Towards Social Reform*, London, T. Fisher Unwin.
Besant, W. (1901), *East London*, London, Chatto & Windus.
Beveridge, W.H. (1953), *Power and Influence*, London, Hodder & Stoughton.
Booth, C. (1892–1897), *Life and Labour of the People in London*, London, Macmillan & Co.
Booth, W. (1890), *In Darkest England and The Way Out*, London, International Headquarters.
Borough of Woolwich Labour Journal (1902).
Collings, T.C. (1895), The Settlements of London, *The Leisure Hour*, n.p.
Davis, A.F. (1967), *Spearheads for Reform: The Social Settlements and The Progressive Movement, 1890–1914*, New York, Oxford University Press.
Donajgrodzki, A.P. (ed.) (1977), *Social Control in Nineteenth Century Britain*, London, Croom Helm.
Evans, R.A. (1982), 'The university and the city: the educational work of Toynbee Hall, 1884–1914, *History of Education*, vol. II, no. 2.
Fiennes, G. (1895), 'Federation of working men's social clubs', in J.M. Knapp (ed.), *The Universities and The Social Problem*, London, Rivington, Percival & Co.
Gell, P.L. (1889), 'The work of Toynbee Hall', *Johns Hopkins Study in Historical and Political Science*, 7th series, no. 1.
Gorst, Sir J. (1895), 'Settlements in England and America', in J.M. Knapp (ed.), *The Universities and the Social Problem,* London, Rivington, Percival & Co.
International Conference of Settlements (1922), *Settlements and Their Outlook*, London, P.S. King.
Jackson, C. (1895), 'The Children's Country Holiday Fund and the

settlements', in J.M. Knapp (ed.), *The Universities and The Social Problem*, London, Rivington, Percival & Co.

Johnson, R. (1970), 'Educational policy and social control in early Victorian England', *Past and Present*, no. 49.

Johnson, R. (1976), 'Notes on the schooling of the English working class', in R. Dale, G. Esland and M. McDonald (eds), *Schooling and Capitalism*, London, Routledge & Kegan Paul and Open University.

Johnson, R. (1977), 'Educating the educators, experts and the state', in Donajgrodzki, A.P. (ed.), *Social Control in Nineteenth Century Britain*, London, Croom Helm.

Jones, G.S. (1971), *Outcast London*, Oxford, Clarendon Press.

Lansbury, G. (1928), *My Life*, London, Constable.

Mann, T. (1923), *Memoirs*, London, Labour Publishing Company.

McCann, P. (ed.) (1977), *Popular Education and Socialization in The Nineteenth Century*, London, Methuen.

Okey, T. (1930), *A Basketful of Memories*, London, J.M. Dent.

Oxford House in Bethnal Green (1948), *Oxford House*, London.

Picht, W. (1914), *Toynbee Hall and the English Settlement Movement*, London, G. Bell & Sons.

Pimlott, J.A.R. (1935), *Toynbee Hall – Fifty Years of Social Progress, 1884–1934*, London, J.M. Dent.

Rogers, F. (1913), *Labour, Life and Literature*, London, Smith, Elder & Co.

Silver, H. (1977), 'Aspects of neglect: the strange case of Victorian popular education', *Oxford Review of Education*, vol. III, no. 1.

Sims, G. (1889), *How The Poor Live*, London, Chatto & Windus.

Society for the Study of Labour History (1976), Conference Report, *Bulletin of the Society for the Study of Labour History*, no. 32.

Tillett, B. (1931), *Memories and Reflections*, London, John Long.

Toynbee Record (1888–1919), vols I–XXX.

Universities Settlement in East London (1886), *Memorandum and Articles of Association*.

Universities Settlement in East London (1885–1895), *Annual Reports*.

Universities Settlement in East London (undated), *Prospectus*.

Webb, B. (1926), *My Apprenticeship*, London, Congress & Co.

Winnington-Ingram, A.F. (1896), *Work in Great Cities*, London, Wells, Gardner, Darton & Co.

Wohl, A.S. (ed.) (1970), *The Bitter Cry of Outcast London*, Leicester, Leicester University Press.

Woods, R.A. (1892), *English Social Movements*, London, Swan, Sonnenschein & Co.

6
The urban, the domestic and education for girls
Mica Nava

The process of urbanisation in Britain during the nineteenth century which accompanied the development of capitalism can be related to a particular crystallisation of social divisions, not only between classes but also between men and women and between adults and children. In this article I want to look at some of the changes which took place during this period, and at their impact on the development of education for girls. My approach will be to isolate the broad outlines of certain phenomena and contradictions which can help illuminate specific educational outcomes and their connection to the city, rather than to trace the fine detail of the history. In doing so I shall draw on historical narratives which have hitherto remained relatively discrete. My object will be to try and knit these together in order to create a more comprehensive picture of the city and what it represented for women of different classes.

A number of writers have pointed out that in the earlier part of the nineteenth century working class boys and girls had a broadly similar experience of schooling, with a curriculum which was only slightly differentiated. (Silver and Silver, 1974; Delamont, 1978b; Marks, 1976.) Both boys and girls received on the whole only a rudimentary education appropriate to their station in life, in schools in which the emphasis was overwhelmingly upon inurement into habits of obedience. Girls in addition often received some instruction in needlework. This relative parity between the sexes was in marked contrast to the educational experience of children from the wealthier classes. The predominant pattern among the upper middle class was for girls to be instructed by governesses in their own homes in a limited range of feminine accomplishments designed to enhance their marriageability, while their brothers received a far more rigorous education in schools staffed by university-educated masters. However by the end of the nineteenth century, middle class women had in many instances won for themselves a secondary and university education in which the curriculum was identical to that provided for the men of their class, (Delamont, 1978b) whereas for children of the working class, the curriculum had become increasingly differentiated. By the turn of the century the schoolday of working class girls was heavily weighted with lessons in housewifery, cooking, laundrywork, needlework and child care while their brothers' was occupied with the study of maths, science, drawing and 'manual' work (David, 1980).

This transformation in the curriculum for girls was not internal to education and can only be understood through an examination of the wider social context in which the process of urbanisation plays a crucial part. A number of factors were to combine in the latter part of the nineteenth century which resulted in the consolidation and institutionalisation of this emphasis on the domestic in the curriculum of working class girls; some of the *same* factors simultaneously contributed to an expansion of opportunities and a slight erosion, or a redrawing, of the hitherto sharp divisions between the public and private spheres for the daughters of bourgeois and professional families. This contradiction not only indicates that there was no simple pattern of progress in the education of girls, it also reveals a degree of interrelationship between the advances made by middle class women and the domestication of the poor. These advances were not however to be wholly maintained: the early twentieth century saw certain setbacks in the education of middle class women which can again be linked with phenomena associated with the city.

The urban and the domestic as symbols

During the nineteenth century enormous changes were wrought upon the geographical and social map of Britain as a consequence of rural dislocation, and the expansion of industrial capitalism and urban trade. Not least among the changes of the nineteenth century was the massive increase in population which, in England and Wales, rose from nine million in 1801 to thirty-two million by 1901. The population of the County of London grew from less than one million at the beginning of the century to about five by the end (Sennet, 1977). The proportion of rural to urban dwellers also changed quite dramatically, thus the increase in London's population was indicative not only of the overall expansion but also of migration from the country to the city. By the end of the century 75 per cent of England's population lived in cities, and the proportion aged under 14 was between 30 and 40 per cent (Walvin, 1982).[1] Although northern industrial cities also grew very rapidly, by the middle of the century it was London in particular that had come to epitomise the urban 'problem'. London, more than any other city, was characterised by a geographical separation of classes, an erosion of traditional rural relations of deference and paternalism, great poverty, insanitary and overcrowded housing, and an enormous under-class or 'residuum' of casual workers, depicted as the morally dissolute and criminal, who threatened to disrupt the social order (Jones, 1976).

The early nineteenth century also saw considerable change in the organisation of domestic life. The increasing (though uneven) separation of the workplace from the home affected both the working and the middle classes. The widescale involvement of working class women and children in paid labour outside the home called into question the forms of paternal authority which had characterised eighteenth century family life in an economy based largely on domestic production. The absence of large numbers of working class women from the home was also to bring to the foreground in an unparalleled fashion issues of housekeeping. For the expanding bourgeoisie, the separation of the home from the place of work was to contribute to the gradual ascendance of a new ideal of family life in which the public and private spheres were clearly demarcated and men and women had their proper and naturally ordained place. The notions of separate spheres for men and women and of the moral influence of the home were promoted principally at the turn of the eighteenth century by Evangelicals who feared the influence of popular radicalism and the early stirrings of feminism (Hall, 1979). Yet by the second half of the nineteenth century these particular bourgeois Christian moralist ideas about what constituted appropriate behaviour for men and women had become so firmly established that the employment of women outside the domestic sphere, even those of the working class, was frequently considered unnatural, immoral and deleterious not only to their families but to the whole of society. A woman's place was increasingly perceived as a crucial aspect of the nineteenth century social crisis.

It is clear that in this context both the 'urban' and the 'domestic' took on an unprecedented symbolic resonance, particularly among the middle classes. As concepts they grew to possess meanings which transcended the complexity of regional, historical and class variation, and took no account of the pervasiveness of poverty and unrest in rural areas and of exploitation and conflict within the family. In this process the urban and the domestic became symbolic classifications of opposition and exclusion which attempted to impose a moral and cognitive order on a rapidly changing, volatile and incomprehensible world. As Mary Douglas has pointed out, 'It is only by exaggerating the difference between within and without, above and below, male and female, with and against, that a semblance of order is created' (1966, p. 4). The city in this schema represented chaos and pollution; the familial, harmony and purity.

Many authors have pointed to these symbolic associations, to the fact that 'the image of the human condition within urban and industrial capitalism ... was [of] social dissolution in the very process of aggregation' (Williams, 1975, p. 260). Raymond Williams points out also that during this period it was commonplace to identify the city 'as a source of social danger: from the loss of customary human feelings to the building up of a massive, irrational explosive force' (ibid., p. 261). For the poor, cities were grossly overcrowded and insanitary. Yet within the dominant nineteenth century conceptual framework, these structural aspects of the urban condition were transformed into issues of individual will: the problem of the city was perceived as *moral*. 'The evil to be combatted was not poverty, but pauperism ... with its attendant vices.' (Jones, 1976, p. 11). London in particular came to exemplify the problem of the pauper without bonds to the social order. 'The category of pauper functioned as a metaphoric condensation of a series of forms of conduct whose common feature ... was a refusal of socialisation: mobility, promiscuity, improvidence, ignorance, insubordination, immorality, in short a rejection of all those relations which are so essential in the formation of the social' (Rose, 1979, p. 23). Within the category of pauper it was prostitutes, 'literally and figuratively ... the conduit of infection to respectable society' (Walkowitz, 1980, p. 4) and destitute street children who particularly offended Victorian sensibility and confirmed the city as a pollutant and a symbol of social dislocation.

In opposition to this vision of the city were set both the rural and the domestic. As Davidoff, L'Esperance and Newby have pointed out, these were not only analogous concepts, they were interrelated —

the ideal home was situated in the rural village community (1976). Both symbolically exercised the power to resist the encroachment of disorder and evil. They represented traditional relations of patronage and hierarchy, integration, regulation, peace and innocence (ibid.). They were havens in a menacing and mercenary world. In contrast to the public sphere, the domestic was increasingly defined as private, moral and personal.

> During the 19th century the family came to appear . . . an idealised refuge, a world of its own, with a higher moral value than the public realm. The bourgeois family was idealised as life wherein order and authority were unchallenged. . . . As the family became a refuge from the terrors of society, it gradually became also a moral yardstick with which to measure the public realm of the capital city. (Sennet, 1977, p. 20)

Furthermore, in order to resist the chaos, pollution and immorality of the public sphere most effectively, the true home needed to be totally separated from the world outside. In 1865 Ruskin expressed it thus:

> This is the true nature of the home — it is a place of peace; not only from all injury, but from all terror, doubt and division. In so far as it is not this, it is not home; so far as the anxieties of the outer life penetrate into it, and the inconsistently-minded, unknown, unloved or hostile society of the outer world is allowed by either husband or wife to cross the threshold it ceases to be home. (1902 edition, p. 144)

Family life within this framework was above all defined as natural — part of the natural order of things. Women's role within this schema was not only decreed by nature, it was also quite pivotal. The wife represented the heart of the organic family,[2] it was in her persona that the superior morality of family life was invested. By her sweet and patient nature she was considered ideally suited to the task of upholding harmony and defending virtue. For women to venture outside the home for purposes other than social and charitable visiting was felt to be unnatural and improper. As symbols the urban and the domestic demanded a moral evaluation of physical space: thus women in the home were cast as angels, women of the city streets had 'fallen'.

It must be pointed out that this celebration of the rural and the domestic and this corresponding condemnation of the urban was, with some exceptions and variations, a theme which pervaded intellectual, social and literary commentaries of nineteenth century authors of both the right and left (and has continued well into the twentieth century (Davidoff *et al.*, 1976)). In much of this writing the urban and the domestic were inextricably linked not merely because they were cast as symbolic counterpoints. Domestic virtue was not only contrasted with urban vice and chaos, it was in addition frequently (and naively) conceptualised as a *solution* to the social menace of the nineteenth century city. That the bourgeois domestic ideal was both made possible by wealth generated in the public sphere and dependent for its continuing existence on the labour of the despised urban populace, that its 'purity' was maintained at the expense of the urban prostitute (Banks and Banks, 1965), were for the most part conveniently overlooked. The dualistic notions so often expressed in the discourse of the period tended to obscure these kinds of complex interrelations. Combined with other factors they also ultimately influenced — though in a contradictory and class-specific manner — the development of education for girls in the latter part of the century.

The domestic as a site of labour

The domestic sphere in the nineteenth century was of course a great deal more than its common representation as a symbol of harmony, tradition and womanly influence. During this period the middle class household was also a context in which an unprecedented number of men, women and children were employed.

> Large domestic staffs had, of course, characterised the great houses of the nobility for centuries past; what was new in the nineteenth century was the burgeoning of those 'of moderate incomes' —
> the manufacturers and merchants, the bankers, brokers, lawyers, doctors and other professionals whose incomes depended, directly or indirectly, on industrialisation and the rapid growth of towns that accompanied it. The large family, the large and over-furnished house, the entertainment of guests at lavish dinner parties, and the economic ability to keep one's wife in genteel idleness, all of which were essential attributes of the institution of the Victorian middle-class family, required the employment of domestic servants on a vast scale. (Burnett, 1977, p. 136)

Servant keeping was not confined to the wealthier sections of the middle class. Lower middle class families were also employers of domestic labour, though on a smaller scale, and contributed to the mid-century expansion of demand for servants which coincided with the decline of traditional rural occupations for both men and women. By 1851 a greater proportion of the population was employed in domestic service than in any other area except agriculture. One in four females in paid work were full-time domestic servants. Although many of these came from the countryside, the jobs were concentrated in urban areas, so that in London at the time of the 1851 census, one-third of the female population (of all classes) aged between 15 and 20 was employed in domestic service. Over the following twenty years there was an even greater upsurge of middle class prosperity and the numbers of female servants expanded by over 50 per cent (ibid.). At a time when the work of working class women outside the home (most particularly in factories) was increasingly subjected to criticism, domestic service remained exempt. Servants, it was felt,

> do not follow an obligatorily independent, and therefore, for their sex an unnatural career; — on the contrary, they are attached to others and are connected with other existences which they embellish, facilitate and serve. In a word, they fulfill both essentials of woman's being: *they are supported by and administer to men.* (author's emphasis) (Greg, 1862, quoted in Davidoff *et al.*, 1976, p. 168)

The employment of servants as a feature of Victorian middle class domestic establishments was in a number of different ways to bear upon the education and activities of both middle and working class women in the second part of the century. It was first of all to lead to pressure for a greater emphasis upon domestic subjects in the education of working class girls. As one advocate for such an initiative put it in the 1850s: 'our object is to improve the servants of the rich and the wives of the poor' (Austin, 1857, quoted in Alexander, 1976, p. 62). This pressure was to become more intense towards the end of the century as new, better paid and more prestigious jobs involving a lesser degree of personal scrutiny became available for unmarried women. The ensuing 'servant problem', which was more prevalent in city areas, and was compounded by the entry of younger girls into compulsory schooling, was to contribute to the focus upon domestic science in the curriculum of girls after the 1880s.

The employment of large numbers of increasingly expensive servants as an essential feature of respectable Victorian homes was also to have indirect effects upon the education of middle class girls. The growing cost for middle class men of running a domestic establishment commensurate with their status, and their reluctance therefore to embark on marriage (Banks and Banks, 1965), was a factor which contributed to the pressure from unmarried middle class women for an adequate education which would enable them to support themselves. (In 1851 it was estimated that there were one million unmarried adult women in the population. A causal factor as significant as the unwillingness of men to marry was the large-scale emigration of men to the United States and the colonies which had left half a million 'redundant' women of marriageable age in Britain, primarily from the 'upper and educated sections of society' (Greg, 1862, quoted in Hollis, 1979, p. 38). Yet another consequence of the employment of large numbers of servants was that married women of the upper middle class were released from the more arduous aspects of domestic responsibility. Although the 'leisure' that this provided was often consumed in the intricate maintenance of social relations and social boundaries, it was also to allow many of these women to extend the frontiers of the private sphere beyond the confines of their own homes to a preoccupation with the domestic lives and education of the poor. This point will be returned to in the next section.

The domestic sphere was of course not only a site of paid employment for women of the working class. Large numbers of unmarried women from genteel families were employed as governesses,[3] virtually the only respectable form of paid occupation open to them. The employment of governesses, like that of domestic servants, enhanced the status of their middle class employers; though within these households the social position of governess was anomalous and often humiliating. They were appallingly paid, and as destitute 'ladies' were neither one of the family nor one of the servants.

> What is the position of governess? she has none. While engaged in a family ... she is infinitely less considered than the servants; she has no companionship whatsoever; ... the governess is condemned to solitude ... though her habits and manners are to *form* the habits and manners of the young, they are unfit for those already formed. (*English Woman's Journal*, 1860, quoted in Hollis, 1979, p. 90)

The social marginality and poverty of governesses were thus also factors which, when combined with a consciousness of their own limited training as teachers, were to contribute to the growing struggle of middle class women to gain for themselves an education which would enable them to be financially self-sufficient and socially and intellectually respected.

However as I have already indicated, in the middle of the century employment outside the domestic sphere was not only considered inappropriate for ladies of the middle class, it was increasingly thought of as immoral for women of the working class as well. The home, whether of their fathers, husbands or employers, was becoming enshrined as the proper place for all women to spend their time. Towards the end of the first half of the century the hitherto broad scope of paid labour for working class women (and children) was gradually though unevenly being reduced, partially as a consequence of protective legislation. The separation of the workplace from the home, which prevented women from engaging in waged work at the same time as caring for the house and children, and the exclusion of women from many new areas of employment as they opened up, were further factors which contributed to the gradual curtailment of their work outside the home. Contemporary census returns are unreliable sources of women's participation in the labour market since so much remunerative work done by women was casual (particularly in London) and home-based (Alexander, 1976). Yet bearing these limitations in mind, official figures indicate a very substantial change in the pattern of women's paid work in the second half of the nineteenth century. According to these, one in four married women with husbands alive were in employment in 1851; by 1911, nine out of ten of such women were engaged solely in housewifery (Oakley, 1976, p. 44). This recomposition of the working class family, which produced the working class 'housewife', was further confirmed by the introduction of compulsory elementary education, which effectively withdrew the labour of older children from the domestic sphere. Many women probably welcomed a reduction of their strenuous and ill-paid labour outside the home and the opportunity to concentrate on domestic tasks, but for others the curtailment of paid employment for themselves and for their children entailed yet greater hardship and was resisted.

What is evident overall is that in the context of concerns about unsupervised 'marauding' street children, infant mortality, insanitary housing, inadequate domestic skills, neglect of husbands ('the employment of married women . . . is undoubtedly an evil . . . because it disables them from making their husbands' homes comfortable', Greg, 1862, quoted in Hollis, 1979, p. 55), there was in the second half of the century an increasing recognition of the contribution to social order which could be made by working class women in their capacity as homemaker. Women and girls were in the course of those years to be selected both as a focal point and as a point of access to their class for a series of philanthropic, medical and educational initiatives designed in large part to improve the values, health and behaviour of the poor (Donzelot, 1979).

Philanthropy, the urban and the domestic

During the eighteenth century charitable visiting to the homes of the poor had begun to take on a new importance as a consequence of increasing social dislocation. In that period it had become established as a means of maintaining pastoral contacts, alleviating distress and reinforcing traditional relations of hierarchy and obligation, and was particularly prevalent among Evangelicals who chose this as a way of practising religious principles (Hall, 1979; Summers, 1979). Anne Summers has argued that in the early part of the nineteenth century it became in addition a way of recruiting domestic labour for the rapidly expanding households of the middle classes (ibid.). The responsibility for visiting fell predominantly upon women, who were considered uniquely suited to the task. Interestingly, even the most vehement of the early Victorian propagandists for the notion of separate spheres supported the idea that ladies should engage in philanthropic visiting. It was hoped that through the tactful deployment of their moral influence and domestic knowledge, deferential social bonds between the classes could be maintained.

However the expansion of the cities and the increasing physical segregation of the rich from the poor within the mid-nineteenth century metropolis disrupted these traditional forms of personal contact. Fears that the consequence of this social separation might be to increase the 'demoralisation' of the urban poor, and thus the threat of insurrection, provoked an upsurge in charitable handouts. Yet in the new context these gifts no longer had the capacity to elicit obligation and cooperation (Jones, 1976). Indeed, charity itself grew to be seen as part of the problem and was held responsible for the perceived lack of thrift and self-reliance of the poor: 'the mass misery of the great cities arose from spasmodic, indiscriminate and unconditional doles' (B. Webb, 1926, quoted in Hollis, 1979, p. 226). The underlying problem was understood in terms of the moral deficiency of the individual and the family. Poverty was seen by most philanthropists 'not as a structural or economic problem for society, but a moral one. It was a function . . . of personal failure; as such it would . . . be solved through the reform and help of individuals' (Summers, 1979, p. 52). This analysis of urban 'demoralisation' and the recognition of the inadequacy of traditional 'indiscriminate' charity precipitated new approaches within philanthropy. In 1869 the Charitable Organisation Society (COS) was established in London with the objective of recreating personal contacts with the poor and coordinating the allocation of charitable funds to ensure that payments were made only to the 'deserving'. In this way virtues of thrift, self-sufficiency and industry would be promoted and further demands for payment would be less likely. Intrinsic to the new method of allocation and character-building was the classification of need and merit, and as a consequence the surveillance and rendering of advice to the individual within the domestic context.[4]

Women were absolutely central to these philanthropic initiatives, both as their objects and their perpetrators. Donzelot (1979) has pointed out that in the shift in philanthropic activity in France (which paralleled that of England) from charitable handouts to an emphasis on savings, autonomy and advice,

> it was necessary to change the criteria for granting aid; the order of priorities had to reflect this concern to reinforce family autonomy. Children came before the elderly, for 'beyond childhood there was the whole period of maturity . . .'. And women before men, for by aiding them one was also aiding their children. (p. 66)

It was via women and children that the moral, hygienic and budgeting norms were to be diffused into the families of the working class.[5] A central component of this philanthropic intervention was subsequently to be the institutionalisation of free compulsory education; this both withdrew children from the domain of 'deficient' parental influence while simultaneously feeding back into the family the new norms acquired in the context of the school. (I shall return to this in greater detail in the next section.) Donzelot goes on to suggest that the singling out of women and children in this way represented a curtailment of patriarchal authority in the working class domestic sphere. This is an assertion which seems impossible to substantiate (and has been criticised as 'incipiently anti-feminist', Barrett and McIntosh, 1982, p. 104) in that it totally fails to take account of the growing economic power of working class men compared to their wives within the family. During this period working class women and children were gradually being excluded from the labour market and were being forced into financial dependency in increasing numbers, a phenomenon which received considerable support from many working class men. As Henry Broadhurst stated at the 1877 Trades Union Congress:

> It was [the] duty [of] men and husbands to use their utmost efforts to bring about a condition of things, where their wives would be in their proper sphere at home, instead of being dragged into competition for livelihood against the great and strong men of the world. (Quoted in Weeks, 1981, p. 68)

However it can be conceded that the imposition of compulsory education *did* curtail paternal appropriation of child labour (though this was compensated for among certain sectors of the working class by the securement of the family wage[6]) and that the focus of philanthropy on women and girls (which of course preceded COS) *did* raise the status of both middle and working class women by identifying them as potential carriers of domestic expertise.

This was both recognised and exploited by many of the middle class women active in the philanthropic project. Although many men supported their involvement there was also opposition, and contemporary comments indicate that middle class women found it necessary to justify their activity first in terms of the centrality of working class women to the desired transformation of the 'morality' of the social order, and secondly in terms of their own suitability as catalysts of this purpose. Thus:

> It is for woman, in her functions of mother, housewife and teacher, to effect those urgently needed changes in infant management, domestic economy, education and the general habits of her own sex.... It is for her to teach and apply the laws of health in her own sphere, where men cannot act.... (Powers, 1859, quoted in Hollis, 1979, p. 239)

And:

> We care for the evils affecting women most of all because they react upon the whole of society, and abstract from the common good. . . . (J. Butler, 1869, quoted in Hollis, 1979, p. 223)

And:

> I am convinced that *women* should have a greater share in it. No Boards of Guardians . . . can be expected to manage girls' schools as they ought to be, neither can male inspectors alone inspect them. Results would be far different if the influence of women of feeling were largely introduced. (L. Twining, 1880, quoted in Wilson, 1977, p. 53)

And:

> We might almost say that the welfare of the work girl is at the root of . . . the question, How are we to improve the lives of our working classes?. . . if we raise the work girl, if we can make her conscious of her own great responsibilities . . . we shall then give her an influence over her sweetheart, her husband and her sons. (M. Stanley, 1890, quoted in Dyhouse, 1981, p. 106)

It has been suggested that philanthropic activists, particularly those associated with COS who were drawn mainly from urban professional groups, were able through their specific forms of charitable practice to elevate themselves to the level of the 'urban gentry' in relation to the poor (Jones, 1976). However this observation fails to take into account the specific and contradictory position of the vast numbers of *women* who were involved in philanthropic projects of one kind or another. It has been estimated that towards the end of the nineteenth century there were 20,000 women who were paid officials of charitable societies, and a further 500,000 who were voluntary workers; in addition there were 200 women on school boards and over 800 who were guardians of poor law unions (Hollis, 1979, pp. 226–8). Although many of these women, forerunners of today's social workers, may have exercised 'tremendous despotism' as Octavia Hill admitted having done (Malpass, 1982), their interests and concerns were not identical to those of the men of their class. It cannot be assumed that they were engaged *only* in dispensing middle class morality and socialising the poor.

In the latter part of the nineteenth century philanthropy was a means for many women of the middle class of extending the terrain of the domestic sphere so that it grew to encompass domestic issues in the wider society. Although in some ways this affirmed the notion of their 'essential' womanliness, it also fractured the Victorian domestic ideal by offering women new areas of influence and power which required both time and commitment, and which must inevitably have resulted in withdrawing from their husbands some of the service and attention to which they had become accustomed. In addition, through the gradual professionalisation of philanthropy, the establishment of training courses, the founding of girls' clubs (see Dyhouse, 1981) and of settlement houses in poor areas, the formation of a Union of Women Workers, and much more, women philanthropists acquired a new social visibility. As a contemporary participant put it, 'the public has learnt a new respect for the capacity of women' (quoted in Hollis, 1979, p. 257). However it is essential to emphasise that the energy of these women was not directed only towards the enhancement of their own public status. Many were also completely dedicated to achieving social reforms which would improve the living circumstances of the poor, in spite of the fact that in some instances these reforms were not in their own interest as members of the middle class. The campaigns to improve and regulate the pay and conditions of domestic servants are an example of this, as the following indicates:

> There are many reasons for the great disinclination which girls have for domestic service . . . [it] is incessant hard work at all hours of the day and sometimes of the night also. It is at best but a kind of slavery. . . . One feasible suggestion of an improvement is a system . . . under which servants could go home at night. Heads of household might then have to wait upon themselves a little more than they now do . . . but girls of the working class . . . are just as much entitled to freedom of choice as any other persons are and we must not try to 'bump' people, especially women, into what we think are their places. (Paterson, 1869, quoted in Hollis, 1979, p. 64)

The explicitly feminist note on which this excerpt ends is also an example of the commitment demonstrated by many women involved

The urban, the domestic and education for girls / 173

in philanthropy to other women regardless of their social position. This was particularly exemplified in the 1870s and 1880s campaign to repeal the Contagious Diseases Acts[7] within which Josephine Butler was particularly prominent. Butler, a member of the mid-nineteenth century Langham Circle of feminists which included many women active in philanthropy and education, criticised the acts on the grounds that it was women whose lives were effectively circumscribed by them; it was women rather than men who were detained and subjected to humiliating personal physical examination, described by her as 'instrumental rape'. Butler insisted on placing the plight of prostitutes within a broader analysis of the political economy of women and in pointing to the similarity of the position of *all* women in relation to men regardless of their class. There is no doubt that many women of the middle class active in the campaign to repeal the Contagious Diseases Acts (as well as in other philanthropic projects) often 'expressed an identity of interest ... with their "fallen sisters" ' (Walkowitz, 1980, p. 7). They also formed alliances with working class men (ibid.). These expressions of solidarity with the poor and the vociferous defence of prostitutes against their largely middle and upper class clientele simply cannot be understood as a manifestation of *class* interest or as part of the attempt of 'the new professional gentry ... to place itself upon equal terms with the traditional aristocracy and to visit ... its newfound status upon the poor' (Jones, 1976, p. 270).

Nevertheless, middle class women's involvement in the philanthropic initiatives of the latter part of the nineteenth century was to have paradoxical consequences. In spite of the fact that many of the women were closely connected to the expanding feminist movement, that many were motivated by a humanitarian concern to alleviate suffering rather than a desire to assert the social values of their class, that some supported more liberal measures and the intervention of the state in order to solve the problems of unemployment rather than the policies advocated by COS, and that their influence on social policy was often progressive, ultimately philanthropy was probably to have more far-reaching and more positive effects upon its women activists of the middle class than upon the poor to whom they administered. The doctrine of 'separate spheres' — the ideological separation of private from public life — was towards the end of the century to have been subverted by philanthropy,[8] but in ways which were quite class specific. As I have already pointed out, the employment of large numbers of servants by wealthier families and the explosive nature of the urban context enabled middle class women to extend their sphere of influence beyond the confines of their own homes. They gained a measure of public visibility and authority precisely through their intervention into the 'private' sphere of working class women and through their public exercise of domestic expertise, while all the time maintaining unimpaired their traditional authority within their own private spheres. In contrast, however, the elevation of the importance of the domestic resulted for working class women in the gradual *curtailment* of their public activities while simultaneously *undermining* the 'privacy' of their domestic sphere.

Changes in the education of girls

As has already been indicated, some of the earliest pressures for a broader and more serious education for middle class women arose from a need to improve the training of governesses and teachers in small private schools for girls. This had proved to be so lamentably inadequate that many could not compete in formal examinations with working class girls who were training to become elementary school teachers in the pupil-teacher apprenticeship scheme established in the 1840s. 'It was increasingly felt that working class education was better than that for the middle classes and it should not be' (David, 1980, p. 108). In spite of a number of developments in the mid-nineteenth century, this view of the general standard of education for middle class girls was echoed by the Taunton Commission which in 1865 reported on girls' endowed schools and criticised 'the want of thoroughness and foundation; want of system; slovenliness and showy superficiality; ... undue time given to accomplishments ... very small amount of professional skill ... (quoted in Hollis, 1979, pp. 140–1).

However, education for middle class women did not simply signify a reassertion of social hierarchy or a more rigorous acquisition of knowledge. In a context in which over one-third of women were not married, in which many middle class women were forced to suffer the indignity of financial dependence upon fathers and brothers, and in which the financial position of married women (prevented by law from owning property) was similarly circumscribed, education grew to be perceived by some women as the means of access to paid work in the public sphere and thus to the severance of economic dependence and inequality. It was argued that 'Women want work both for the health of their minds and their bodies. They want it often because ... they will have children and others dependent on them — *for all the reasons men want work*' (Bodichon, 1857, quoted in Spender, 1982, p. 297).

Not only was the demand for education by middle class women distinctly radical in that it was perceived as a vehicle for their emancipation and thus challenged prevailing assumptions about the appropriate behaviour of ladies, it was also linked through the individuals who participated in the campaign to a number of other radical causes of the mid- and late-nineteenth century.[9] The women and men (many from non-conformist professional families) who were active in the struggle to improve educational provision for girls were often personal friends of those involved in the promotion of social reform in other fields. Several were to participate in the campaign to change legislation regarding married women's property, the Contagious Diseases Acts repeal movement, attempts to open occupations to women, the movement for women's suffrage, as well as radical initiatives within philanthropy.

In the middle of the century, the discontent with existing standards of education provoked some women active in these circles to establish (with the support of some men and in the face of considerable opposition and scepticism from other members of their class) a few institutions at both secondary and university level which provided a more scholarly education for middle class girls and young women. In these institutions few concessions were made to domesticity or accomplishments; girls were provided with a curriculum which was far more demanding than hitherto.[10] Within this new movement to improve the education of middle class girls, there were however significant differences of approach. Sarah Delamont (1978a) has identified two distinct strands: the 'uncompromising' and the 'separatists'.

Among the most important of the 'uncompromising' pioneers of girls' education were Frances Buss, founder of North London Collegiate School, and Emily Davies, founder of Girton College, Cambridge. This strand was initially to be the more influential of the two in that a far larger number of schools were to be patterned according to the principles established by Buss and her followers in the Girls' Public Day School Company, providers of endowed high schools throughout the country for young ladies from the middle classes. These women argued, in the tradition of the enlightenment, that differences between men and women were a product of the environment[11] and not natural, that there must be 'but one true theory of education for men and women alike'. (Tod, 1874, quoted in Dyhouse 1981, p. 141). Moreover, in order to be taken seriously, girls must have exactly the same curriculum and examinations as boys, regardless of the inappropriateness of the predominance of classics within these. Davies was a particularly unremitting opponent of modifications to the curriculum, which were proposed by some in order to take into account the specific experience and expectations of women. Her position was that

> Only by following to the letter the educational courses laid down for men could women claim to be measured with men. Any diversion from this iron rule . . . would be interpreted by a skeptical public . . . as a sop to women's inferior intellects. (McWilliams-Tullberg, 1980, p. 126)

The 'separatists', among whom were Dorothea Beale and Anne Clough, forerunners in the education of girls of the *upper* middle class at both public boarding schools and university level, argued that the existing emphasis on classics in the curriculum and examinations of boys of that class was not the most apposite for girls, whose future would be different; they proposed a more varied curriculum and special examinations. Underlying their programme was the conviction that men and women were fundamentally different, and although they insisted that women should be well educated, this was to prepare them better for tasks suited to the exercise of womanly influence. However to assume therefore that these women were not feminists is to simplify the issue and project upon it the criteria of late twentieth century feminism. Walkowitz (1980)[12] and Banks (1981) among others have drawn attention to the range of positions (as well as their contradictory nature) which were taken up by feminists in the nineteenth century. Important among these, and one which undoubtedly contributed to the gains made by women during this period, was that which stressed the value and defended the autonomy of women's unique proficiency within 'their' sphere. Thus the expertise promoted by the separatists in education was precisely that which was exploited by many women philanthropists and which ironically enabled them to make inroads into public life.

During the latter part of the nineteenth century there was a very substantial expansion in the provision of secondary education for middle class girls along the lines fought for by those feminists active in the 1850s, and endorsed by the Taunton Commission in 1865.

Indeed in the 1890s the Bryce Commission concluded that 'there has probably been more change in the condition of Secondary Education for girls than in any other department of education' (quoted in Lawson and Silver, 1973, p. 343). At the same time increasing numbers of places were made available to women in higher education. Nevertheless, although there is no doubt that in terms of educational standards women had by the end of the century made enormous progress and had in many instances achieved for middle class young girls a curriculum and examinations which were virtually identical to those of their brothers, the long-term gains are harder to assess. Opposition to their objectives was widespread and took a variety of forms. Educational institutions were constantly under pressure to compromise by demonstrating their respectability and suitability for young ladies in order to maintain the financial, political and moral support of the public (Delamont, 1978a). Conventional femininity and modesty were placed at a premium within these institutions. It was felt that too great a visibility of 'strong-minded' women and too open an alliance with the women's suffrage movement might jeopardise the educational cause, and for this reason Emily Davies withdrew her active support from the suffrage campaign (McWilliams-Tullberg, 1980). Tremendous opposition was also manifested in the numbers of astonishing medical theories which were developed during that period and which purported to demonstrate significant physiological and mental differences between men and women. It was alleged that too much intellectual work could have dangerous consequences for the health of adolescent girls and young women; indeed in extreme cases cerebral exercise could lead to sterility, inability to breastfeed and even death (Dyhouse, 1981; Duffin, 1978; Griffiths and Saraga, 1979). (Unsurprisingly no such concerns were expressed about the frail constitutions of young women of the working class.) Resistance to women's participation in higher education was often particularly strong. In 1897 Cambridge undergraduates celebrated the university's continuing refusal to grant women the title of their degrees with 'a night of riotous bonfires, fire-works and fun' (McWilliams-Tullberg, 1980, p. 141).[13]

Overall the attempts to create educational opportunities for middle class women were opposed far more virulently than was the involvement of middle class women in philanthropy. It is possible that the relation of education to domesticity appeared more tenuous and thus placed in question the femininity and respectability of women educators in a way in which charitable visiting and the deployment of domestic advice did not. Equal education for women represented an encroachment upon a male terrain; its object was to prepare women to compete for jobs and become financially independent of men rather than to minister to the poor on a voluntary basis. As Barbara Bodichon pointed out in 1857, 'there is a prejudice against women accepting money for work' (quoted in Spender, 1982, p. 297). Thus it is ironic, yet not surprising in such a context, that women's achievements in the field of education managed to open to them on the whole one paid occupation only — that of teaching (McWilliams-Tullberg, 1980). Education was not then the vehicle for emancipation for middle class women that it was hoped and feared it would be, in that it usually led directly back into the confines of the secondary school classroom. However teaching did offer the possibility of financial independence and, as with philanthropy, the involvement of middle class women in it helped expand the conceptual boundaries of the bourgeois domestic domain. The school can be considered to occupy a midway point — the interface — between the private and the public spheres; as such teaching cannot be considered *merely* an extension of women's traditional sphere of influence. Like philanthropy, it also constituted a point of entry into public life.

The education of working class girls

The education of working class girls was quite different. An expansion of educational provision for children of poor families was not only demanded from within their class — by its recipients — it was also imposed as part of a wider response to the social dislocation of the nineteenth century. As with the philanthropic enterprise, the concern with the education of the poor was not uniform in nature. Undoubtedly much was motivated by a benevolent determination to eradicate ignorance and improve the quality of working class life. However after the middle of the century, compulsory education (as well as being considered a necessary sequel to the 1867 Franchise Act, Simon, 1974) grew also to be perceived as a solution to the urban problem: to demoralisation and the threat of insurrection. Compulsory schooling was to be a means of clearing the streets of the many thousands of vagrant and rebellious children neither at school or work whose growing numbers increasingly preoccupied the Victorian imagination. Simultaneously it was to be a means of socialising them (with iron discipline) into habits of obedience and thrift and of disseminating through them moral order into the homes of the poor.

As was pointed out in the section on philanthropy, girls were considered quite crucial to this enterprise of diffusing bourgeois norms. In the early part of the century the education of working class girls, where it existed, was not a vehicle for the transmission of domestic skills to the degree it was to become after the introduction of compulsory schooling. Although provision had varied from school to school and region to region, on the whole boys and girls in schools for the poor had received a similar education, with an emphasis on obedience, piety, the 3 Rs, and with extra needlework for girls.[14] As the curriculum for working class children in general broadened and became more vocational, as domesticity became equated with moral order, and as the demand for trained servants expanded, so domestic economy became a central component in the education of urban working class girls. Carol Dyhouse (1981) has documented the impact of Education Department legislation on the curriculum of Board schools after the 1870 Education Act. Under pressure from such groups as the National Association for the Promotion of Housewifery, domestic economy for girls was made into one of the compulsory 'specific subjects' for which government grants were paid. As a consequence the numbers of girls studying domestic economy rose between 1874 and 1882 from 844 to 59,812. Similar massive increases took place over the following years as a result of the payment of grants for cookery and laundry work (ibid., p. 89). By 1900 the London School Board had set up 168 'cookery centres' designed to train girls from 470 local schools (ibid., p. 90). However this emphasis on domestic subjects was not accepted without a considerable amount of resistance, both from a few middle class feminists (ibid., p. 170) and in particular from women who felt that their daughters' time would be more fruitfully employed assisting in the home. One of the London School Board women superintendents complained that 'prejudice against [cookery instruction] was almost insuperable, parents put every possible obstacle in the way of their children attending classes' (quoted in ibid., p. 90).

On the front line of this educational enterprise to domesticate the children of the urban poor were the elementary schoolteachers. It was they who were responsible for imparting the requisite moral values and maintaining discipline on a day-to-day basis. As Gerald Grace (1978) has pointed out, their position was crucial and contradictory. Before the middle of the century teachers of the poor were on the whole drawn from the working class. In order to ensure that they became effective civilisers rather than inciters of discontent, it was essential that their training be rigorous in the transmission of appropriate moral values as well as closely monitored. To guard against the employment of individuals who might have an improper influence, attempts were made to recruit more members of the 'respectable' middle classes.

> The education of trained masters and mistresses is very superficial ... they are very often ... full of airs and have no moral influence over their scholars. I think this is not so much the fault of the training colleges. ... Pupil teachers being taken generally from the very lowest class of society, they are destitute of that mass of information which children of respectable parents imbibe without knowing it. ... It seems to me very desirable that young people of a higher grade should be encouraged to enter on the work of popular education. (Evidence to the Newcastle Commission, 1861, quoted in Hollis, 1979, p. 92)

Although this kind of appeal coincided with the growing demand of women from the middle class for paid employment, it was eventually girls from the *lower* middle class, as Frances Widdowson (1980) has pointed out, who entered elementary teaching in increasing numbers (and who were to contribute to the enhancement of its professional status). With the advent of compulsory education and the expansion of demand for teachers, recruitment was increasingly directed at women from this class, both because as women they were cheaper than men, and (as the above quote shows) because they came from a respectable background and thus already possessed the required moral attributes suited to what Grace has described as the 'missionary' enterprise. By the end of the century, women constituted 60 per cent of teachers in elementary schools (Lawson and Silver, 1973).[15] Interestingly, Widdowson has noted that during this period ladies from more genteel backgrounds were advised to enter elementary teaching (if at all) in rural areas, in that this more closely 'corresponded with the accepted conventions of the solid middle-class domestic ideology of the 19th century' (1980, p. 31), and the domestic-urban dualism to which I referred earlier. On the whole however, late nineteenth century attempts to recruit 'ladies' into elementary teaching were unsuccessful both because they were unattracted by the low status of the work and because their more protected and liberal educational experience in middle class schools was considered as unsuitable preparation for it (ibid.).

It was thus women from the artisan and lower middle class who came increasingly to dominate the occupational group. One consequence of this was that modifications were made in the courses offered by training colleges. The heavy concentration on domestic skills, the emphasis on moral instruction and surveillance, and the extremely narrow academic preparation of the early years, considered appropriate for girls from the working class, were slowly abandoned in favour of a rather more liberal education which began to resemble that of girls from a higher social standing (ibid.). In spite of these changes, it was still women from the lower middle class whose arduous task it most often was to discipline working class children and to administer the regime designed to improve their morals, manners and domestic skills (though in this capacity they were supervised by male headteachers and a male inspectorate). The personal contact between women of the more prosperous middle class and the poor was on the whole confined to philanthropic activities and social work (which were likely to be voluntary). Yet in both instances it was overwhelmingly *women* who were agents in the project of disseminating bourgeois moral values and household skills to the wives and children of the urban working class. As I have already pointed out, paradoxically it was precisely the process of domesticating the poor which enabled women of the middle class to extend their own spheres of influence. It was also these activities, rather than the pursuit of better education for themselves, which appear to have received least opposition from the men of their class.

Motherhood, physical deterioration and setbacks

I have drawn attention to some of the changes which took place in women's education and the domestic sphere during the latter part of the nineteenth century and to the complex relationship between the advances which occurred for middle class women and the consolidation of domesticity for women of the working class. However it is important to point out that the gains made by middle class women were in many instances short-lived. As Carol Dyhouse has argued, 'the history of the women's movement since the late nineteenth century serves in many ways to demonstrate the resilience and ideological resourcefulness of a society or culture threatened by feminism: there is no simple tale of steady progress' (1981, p. 61). The early twentieth century saw the introduction of a special emphasis on mothering. This new ideology of motherhood was to encompass *all* women. Although in its expression it was to take forms which varied according to the social position of the women concerned, its overall effect was to transcend class and to contribute to a narrowing of the gap between the domestic experience and education of both poor and rich women.

Anna Davin has pointed to the growing importance of population as a national resource at the turn of the century. This was a period in which imperialist objectives appeared to be threatened by the diminishing vitality of the British race. Concerns were exacerbated in 1900 when one-third of men recruited to fight the Boer War were found physically 'deficient' for this purpose. At the same time Britain's industrial superiority in the world was being challenged by the United States, Germany and Japan. It was this context which provoked a wave of anxiety about high rates of infant mortality, the extremely poor health of large sectors of the population, and the decline of the birth rate, particularly among the middle classes (Davin, 1978). Urbanisation was again to be a crucial component in the crisis. It was the city environment which was held largely responsible for the decline in the nation's fitness and for the production of the 'physical degenerate'. 'The casual residuum once more became the topic of anxious debate, provoked this time not by fears of revolution but by intimations of impending imperial decline' (Jones, 1976, p. 330). As a consequence, state intervention into matters of social reform was considered increasingly warranted. Yet although the urban maintained its symbolic resonance as a causal factor in contemporary understandings of the issue, the *solution* to the problem of public health and declining national power was perceived to reside in the quality of mothering and in the family. Again it was the private sphere upon which attention was to be focused. However in contrast to the nineteenth century, when moral inadequacy and the paid work of wives outside the home tended to be blamed for domestic incompetence, the problem of the early twentieth century was defined in terms of 'fecklessness' and of ignorance among poor women in the skills of mothering (Davin, 1978). Once again the issues of poverty, bad housing and insanitary conditions, so pervasive in the urban environment, were relegated to second place.

Eugenicist ideas about the degeneration of the race and the importance of heredity and selective breeding, although initiated in the latter part of the nineteenth century, were given a new impetus in this context. It was these theories which fuelled the opposition to middle class women's increasing participation in the public sphere. Thus those women who pursued higher education, who chose to restrict the number of children they gave birth to, or worse still, who chose to remain unmarried, were accused of 'shirking' their responsibilities to the nation. As women from 'superior stock' they were considered particularly crucial to the promotion of racial progress and national efficiency. Since it was argued that intellectual work impaired women's reproductive processes, higher education for women was indeed a danger to 'Britain's proud position among the nations of the world' (quoted in ibid., p. 20): 'Many of the most cultivated and able families of the English speaking race will have become extinct, through the prime error of supposing that an education which is good for men must also be good for women' (quoted in Duffin, 1978, p. 82).

Unsurprisingly, these concerns for Britain's international position were to find expression in contemporary proposals for education. A parliamentary committee set up in order to investigate the 'physical deterioration' of the nation, pointed in its report in 1904 to the appalling conditions of urban living for the working class, and proposed ' "Some great scheme of social education" which would aim "to raise the standards of domestic competence" and would underline the importance of proper ideals of home life among young girls destined to become wives and mothers of future generations' (Dyhouse, 1981, p. 92). In this it was typical of a number of publications and official reports of the period [ibid.]. The consensus was that elementary schooling for girls had hitherto concentrated too much on reading and writing, and insufficiently on nutrition, hygiene and in particular on preparation for maternity; this was in spite of the developments in the teaching of domestic economy which had taken place in the last decades of the nineteenth century. The next few years saw a tremendous expansion in the provision of training for motherhood and domesticity for working class girls, in the belief that this would improve the health of the nation. It was recommended that domestic subjects should take precedence over others in the school curriculum which were considered irrelevant — like maths — and that such instruction should not be confined to girls in elementary schools but should be provided for all ages. Helena Bosanquet, active in philanthropy from the days of COS, wrote in 1904 on the subject of physical degeneration:

Begin with the girls in school, and give them systematic and compulsory instruction in the elementary laws of health and feeding, and care of children, and the wise spending of money. Go on with the young women in evening classes and girls' clubs; and continue with the mothers wherever you can get at them. (quoted in Davin, 1978, p. 26).

Overall these developments in the education of working class girls in the first years of the twentieth century represented a consolidation and institutionalisation of what had gone before, rather than a reorientation. The ideology of motherhood confirmed and entrenched the key position of women and girls as the points of access to the working class family, and as the relayers of the standards of behaviour which were considered necessary in order to combat the problems of the urban environment.[16]

The impact of the new emphasis on motherhood upon the education of middle class girls was more complex. Among the advocates of a good education for middle class girls during the latter part of the nineteenth century, it had been those who were uncompromising in their demands for a curriculum identical to that of middle class boys who had been able to achieve most success through their capture of large numbers of girls' day schools. However in the context of the early twentieth century focus upon motherhood, the views of these educationalists became far more contentious and divisions between them arose. A number of headmistresses of previously 'uncompromising' schools became supporters of eugenicist principles, and they endorsed the notion that many educated women were evading their responsibilities to the nation and acting selfishly in their pursuit of intellectual work (Dyhouse, 1981). It was increasingly felt that 'the old "blue stocking" type, who prided herself on not knowing how to sew or mend, and who thought cooking menial and beneath her, no longer appeals to anyone' (Gilliland, 1911, quoted in Dyhouse, 1981, p. 163); domestic 'science' and 'arts' should be elevated to be a compulsory feature of the curriculum for all secondary school girls, and should if necessary replace traditional science, maths and classics. It was argued that a serious and 'scientific' study of domestic economy was not demeaning; on the contrary, it would raise the status of the housewife and mother.[17]

However there was also considerable opposition to this line, particularly from the Girls' Public Day School Trust which was willing to forgo government grants rather than submit to pressure from the Board of

Education to introduce housewifery into the curriculum. Its members argued that to do so would be to undermine the educational objectives of the schools (Dyhouse, 1981). (None the less, concessions were made later by the introduction of household management for girls over 17 (David, 1980) and as educational provision grew increasingly to be linked to adult occupations over the following years, so further concessions were made.) Claims that domestic training constituted a science worthy of university study were ridiculed by some contemporary feminists and dismissed as 'pretentious', 'a travesty of science' and 'a degradation of university standards and an insult to women' (quoted in Dyhouse, 1981, p. 168).

It must not be assumed however that positive and negative responses to the issue of domestic education in the secondary school curriculum of middle class girls signalled in a simple fashion a division between feminists and anti-feminists.[18] Within feminism of the late nineteenth and early twentieth centuries there were, as today, a range of political and theoretical positions. It has already been pointed out that the 'uncompromising' believed that differences between men and women were largely environmental in origin and that the school curriculum for boys and girls should therefore be identical; this position can easily be located within the framework of late twentieth century feminism. Less easy to reconcile with the ideas of today (though not impossible,[19]) are the views of the 'separatists'; often rooted in religious and, in some instances, eugenicist principles (Gordon, 1977), these claimed that women were essentially different from men — indeed even superior — and that their special attributes should be exercised in order to improve the city and society at large. So, for example, women engaged in urban settlement work had 'not only a right, but a duty, to bring [their] womanly qualities to bear upon the city and ultimately upon the world so that it too, like the 19th century home, would become clean and orderly, and pure' (Banks, 1981, p. 94). It was thus this second strand which enabled some feminists to make their mark upon the public sphere; this they accomplished through exploiting their 'natural' propensity to be morally superior, to mother and to understand the intricacies of domestic management during periods of national anxiety about the city and the nation's health. By stressing the 'naturalness' of women's domain this approach was in many ways successful; it proved less threatening and therefore defused opposition at a time when the support of men was particularly crucial if women were to be granted the vote. It was also on occasion quite radical. A substantial number of women of this conviction, who were also socialists, were involved both in Britain and the United States in the rapidly expanding urban settlement movement of this period which was concerned to ameliorate the conditions of working class women and children in their communities.[20] The new valuation of motherhood was also to be used some years later to justify demands for improved maternity and infant welfare.

Ultimately, however, the discourse of motherhood and scientific housekeeping, although permitting certain gains, constituted a new form of regulation which served to define more narrowly than for some time the special sphere of women. It was in a most particular way to affect those women of the middle class for whom mothering and housework had scarcely been an occupation in the latter part of the nineteenth century. The early twentieth century invocation of motherhood and housewifery served to inhibit the relegation of child care and domestic supervision to servants whom it was felt would in all probability be ignorant of the requisite scientific knowledge. As motherhood grew in social importance, so child rearing became defined as a more exacting task which required the expertise of the initiated. Another extremely important factor in this reconstitution of the private sphere for middle class women was the marked decline in the availability of servants at the turn of the century. Thus, overall, this period saw a reduction in the gap between the education and domestic experience of women of different classes. The ideology of motherhood, of 'natural' difference between the sexes, and the emergence of scientific theories to support these, exalted as part of a response both to the crisis of the city and to the demand of women for the vote, were effectively to narrow the sphere of *both* middle and working class women.

By drawing attention to the increasing similarity in the pattern of middle class and working class women's confinement to the home, it is important not to minimise the significance of material differences in standards of living. However differences between women do not in a simple fashion reflect the class positions and relations of their husbands. Distinctions between women have their own historical fluctuations which are related to the degree of opposition to their participation in the world of men as well as to factors of the kind I have discussed, such as the threat of disorder and ill-health, the availability of employment and servants, and demographic change, all aspects of the development of capitalism and the urban context of the nineteenth and early twentieth century. Deeply implicated in this complex positioning and in the specific consolidation of the role of housewife/mother during the twentieth century are notions of natural difference and the importance of good mothering to social order. These have continued to pervade family discourse right up to the present time. They exist in numerous government educational and welfare policy statements, and reappear at particular moments of crisis, like the present, in which inner city riots have been blamed upon bad mothering, and high rates of unemployment have been associated with women's assertion that they have a right to work. A reiteration of the invocation of natural difference in order to defend privilege is classically exemplified in the statement made by Tory Minister for Social Services, Patrick Jenkin:

> Quite frankly I don't think mothers have the same right to work as fathers. If the good lord had intended us to have equal rights to go out to work, he wouldn't have created man and woman. These are biological facts . . . . (*Man Alive* (*sic*), television interview, November 1979)

Until recently these have been the prevailing views within education authorities. It is only in the last few years, as a consequence of pressure from the most recent wave of feminists, that notions of natural difference and the emphasis on domesticity in the curriculum of girls have begun to be called into question by a few educational policy makers.[21]

Acknowledgments

Very many thanks for valuable comments on an earlier draft of this article to Lucy Bland, Gerald Grace, Diana Leonard, Adam Mills, Angela McRobbie, Michelle Stanworth and Barbara Taylor.

Notes

1. More than twice as large as the proportion of children in the population today.
2. In which the husband represented the head (Davidoff *et al.*, 1976).
3. In 1851 there were an estimated 250,000 (Delamont, 1978a).
4. See Donzelot (1979) for a further discussion of the shift in philanthropy from the gift of charity to the rendering of advice.

5 This period saw an increasing number of state interventions into the lives of the poor on medical and sanitary grounds. Walkowitz (1980, p. 71) points out that 'the mid-century sanitary movement ... created a close identification of public order and public health.'

6 For a discussion of the family wage, see Land (1980). The economic dependence of wives upon their husbands could in practice only be realised within the labour aristocracy; nevertheless as an ideal it was widespread and percolated down to all but the most destitute.

7 The Contagious Diseases Acts were sanitary measures introduced during the 1860s in an attempt to control prostitutes who were perceived by many as the source of venereal disease as well as of a more general moral and physical pollution.

8 This point has been emphasised by Paul Hirst (1981) in his discussion of Donzelot (1979).

9 Several were members of the Langham Circle (see page 173).

10 In the view of one recent historian who was critical of this educational development, 'The curriculum and organisation of these schools ... undoubtedly suffered [sic] from their connection with the feminist movement' (Peterson, 1971, p. 159)!

11 As did for example Harriet Taylor and John Stuart Mill (Mill, 1869). For a discussion of Taylor's influence on Mill, see Spender (1982).

12 See also Wood (1982).

13 Full degrees and University membership were not awarded to women until 1948.

14 Working class schools were frequently mixed, unlike those of the middle classes, and older girls were often recruited to help care for younger children.

15 By 1914 the figures had risen to 75 per cent (Widdowson, 1980).

16 The part played by boys as well as girls in this capacity was commented upon by the London School Board inspectors in 1903: 'The results achieved by the Board have not been confined to the children. The influence of the schools has had a very wholesome and civilizing effect upon parents in the poorer quarters of London' (quoted in Rubinstein, 1977, p. 257).

17 In the United States at this time home economics was similarly becoming a subject which both confined women and established them as experts in a field of national importance. In fact Ehrenreich and English (1979) have pointed out that the alleged salience of the study of home economics was used during this period by some feminists to justify their access to higher education.

18 See Banks (1981) for a further discussion of this.

19 The views of many of the women involved in the Greenham Common peace movement of today can be compared with those of the nineteenth and early twentieth century 'separatists' in that they believe women to be essentially less violent than men, and thus better placed to fight for peace.

20 See for example the work of Jane Addams (1910) in Chicago.

21 For example by the Inner London Education Authority; see article by Frances Morrell in this volume.

Bibliography

Addams, J. (1910), *The Spirit of Youth and the City Streets*, New York, Macmillan.

Alexander, S. (1976), 'Women's work in nineteenth-century London; a study of the years 1820—50', in J. Mitchell and A. Oakley (eds), *The Rights and Wrongs of Women*, Harmondsworth, Penguin.

Banks, O. (1981), *Faces of Feminism*, Oxford, Martin Robertson.

Banks, J.A. and O. (1965), *Feminism and Family Planning in Victorian England*, Liverpool University Press.

Barrett, M. and McIntosh, M. (1982), *The Anti-social Family*, London, Verso.

Bennett, F., Campbell, B. and Coward, R. (1981), 'Feminists — the degenerates of the social?', in *Politics and Power* 3, London, Routledge & Kegan Paul.

Burnett, J. (1977), *Useful Toil*, Harmondsworth, Penguin.

David, M. (1980), *The State, the Family and Education*, London, Routledge & Kegan Paul.

Davidoff, L., L'Esperance, J. and Newby, H. (1976), 'Landscape with figures: home and community in English society', in J. Mitchell and A. Oakley (eds), *The Rights and Wrongs of Women*, Harmondsworth, Penguin.

Davin, A. (1978), 'Imperialism and motherhood', in *History Workshop*, issue 5.

Delamont, S. (1978a), 'The contradictions of ladies' education', in S. Delamont and L. Duffin (eds) *The Nineteenth Century Woman*, London, Croom Helm.

Delamont, S. (1978b), 'The domestic ideology and women's education', in S. Delamont and L. Duffin (eds), *The Nineteenth Century Woman*, London, Croom Helm.

Donzelot, J. (1979), *The Policing of Families*, London, Hutchinson.

Douglas, M. (1966), *Purity and Danger*, London, Routledge & Kegan Paul.

Duffin, L. (1978), 'Prisoners of progress: women and evolution', in S. Delamont and L. Duffin (eds), *The Nineteenth Century Woman*, London, Croom Helm.

Dyhouse, C. (1981), *Girls Growing Up in Late Victorian and Edwardian England*, London, Routledge & Kegan Paul.
Ehrenreich, B. and English, D. (1979), *For Her Own Good: 150 Years of the Experts Advice to Women*, London, Pluto.
Gordon, L. (1977), *Women's Body, Women's Right*, Harmondsworth, Penguin.
Grace, G. (1978), *Teachers, Ideology and Control*, London, Routledge & Kegan Paul.
Griffiths, D. and Saraga, E. (1979), 'Sex differences and cognitive ability: a sterile field of enquiry', in O. Hartnett, G. Boden and M. Fuller (eds), *Sex-role Stereotyping*, London, Tavistock.
Hall, C. (1979), 'The early formation of Victorian domestic ideology', in S. Burman (ed.), *Fit Work for Women*, London, Croom Helm.
Hirst, P. (1981), 'The genesis of the social', in *Politics and Power* 3, London, Routledge & Kegan Paul.
Hodges, J. and Hussain, A. (1979), 'Review article: Jacques Donzelot' in *Ideology and Consciousness*, no. 5.
Hollis, P. (1979), *Women in Public: The Women's Movement 1850–1900*, London, George Allen and Unwin.
Jones, G.S. (1976), *Outcast London*, Harmondsworth, Penguin.
Land, H. (1980), 'The family wage', *Feminist Review* 6.
Lawson, J. and Silver, H. (1973), *A Social History of Education in England*, London, Methuen.
Malpass, P. (1982), 'Octavia Hill', *New Society*, 4 November.
Marks, P. (1976), 'Femininity in the classroom: an account of changing attitudes', in J. Mitchell and A. Oakley (eds), *The Rights and Wrongs of Women*, Harmondsworth, Penguin.
McWilliams-Tullberg, R. (1980), 'Women and degrees at Cambridge University, 1862–1897', in M. Vicinus (ed.), *A Widening Sphere: Changing Roles of Victorian Women*, London, Methuen.
Mill, J.S; (1869), *The Subjection of Women*, reprinted 1974, Oxford University Press.
Oakley, A. (1976), *Housewife*, Harmondsworth, Penguin.
Peterson, A.D.C. (1971), *A Hundred Years of Education*, London, Duckworth.
Rose, N. (1979), 'The psychological complex: mental measurement and social administration', *Ideology and Consciousness*, no. 5.
Rubinstein, D. (1977), 'Socialization and the London School Board 1870–1904: aims, methods and public opinion', in P. McCann (ed.), *Popular Education and Socialization in the Nineteenth Century*, London, Methuen.
Ruskin, J. (1902), 'Of queen's gardens' in *Sesame and Lilies*, New York, Homewood.
Sennet, R. (1977), *The Fall of Public Man*, Cambridge University Press.
Silver, P. and Silver, H. (1974), *The Education of the Poor*, London, Routledge & Kegan Paul.
Simon, B. (1974), *Education and the Labour Movement 1870–1920*, London, Lawrence & Wishart.

Spender, D. (1982), *Women of Ideas*, London, Routledge & Kegan Paul.
Summers, A. (1979). 'A home from home — women's philanthropic work in the nineteenth century', in S. Burman (ed.), *Fit Work for Women*, London, Croom Helm.
Walkowitz, J. (1980), *Prostitution and Victorian Society*, Cambridge University Press.
Walvin, J. (1982), *A Child's World*, Harmondsworth, Penguin.
Weeks, J. (1981), *Sex, Politics and Society*, New York, Longman.
Widdowson, F. (1980), *Going up into the Next Class: Women and Elementary Teacher Training 1840–1914*, London, WRRC Publications.
Williams, R. (1975), *The Country and the City*, Harmondsworth, Penguin.
Wilson, E. (1977), *Women and the Welfare State*, London, Tavistock.
Wood, N. (1982), 'Prostitution and feminism in nineteenth century Britain', *m/f* no. 7.

Part III

Contemporary policy and practice

7
Policy for schools in inner London
Frances Morrell

Introduction

The Inner London Education Authority (ILEA) has been attacked for over-providing resources for education and for not fully realising the goal of equality of educational opportunity. It is clearly the belief of those who mount such attacks that the constant reiteration of a falsehood will in the course of time assume the status of a truth in the consciousness of parents, teachers and even educationists. The politics and ideology of urban education have been for too long marked by such distortions.

There is a need, as Dr Gerald Grace rightly says in his Introduction to this book, for systematic and careful study of urban schooling to be encouraged. This paper is written as a contribution to such study and with the intention of setting the record straight about the educational standards and policies of the ILEA. I welcome the opportunity to do this and I will attempt it in three parts:

1 by clarifying the social, cultural and economic context within which inner London teachers and schools have to operate;

2 by reviewing the educational achievements of inner London pupils as they are represented in external examination results;

3 by outlining the educational policies endorsed by the Authority for further advance in the future, recognising that while the average attainment of London children is measurably improving, the relative attainment by class, gender and race remains constant. The key educational challenge is to recognise that equality of educational opportunity

means a systematic policy of positive action to help children in these categories.

It is necessary in my view to consider these three elements together if any balanced and informed view of the ILEA is to emerge. The tendency of many commentators to concentrate upon (2) without reference to the issues in (1) is clearly the source of much misinformation about schooling in inner London.

1 The social, cultural and economic context of inner London schooling

The nature and extent of the educational needs of the school population in inner London is unique in this country. This fact was underlined in the recent HMI Report on Educational Provision in the ILEA (1980) where the Inspectorate stated:

> The pupil population of inner London contains a large number of disadvantaged children. In addition, about 40% are from ethnic minority groups and one in ten of all pupils speaks a mother tongue which is not English. Significant parts of the area suffer from urban decay and some have changing populations. The ILEA is faced with a combination of problems to an extent probably unmatched elsewhere in England and Wales.[1]

The force of this statement is confirmed when Department of the Environment indices of deprivation are examined (Table 7.1) or when the 1981 Census figures are inspected (Table 7.2)[2]

It is important to recognise that the educational work of the ILEA and of its teachers and schools has to proceed in the face of such social and economic disadvantage among its pupils and that in addition to this, a sensitive and flexible response has to be made to a whole range of cultural and ethnic traditions which characterise a varied and cosmopolitan school population. There can be no exaggeration in saying that taken together these factors make for a very considerable educational challenge and it must obviously follow that any evaluation of educational achievements has to be interpreted in the light of this challenge. The practice adopted in some quarters of commenting upon educational results abstracted from their social, cultural and economic context is clearly not only unscholarly but also deliberately misleading.

Table 7.1: Most deprived local authorities in the country on DOE scoring (1981)

Indices

	Economic	Social	Housing	Basic
1	*Hackney*	*Hackney*	*Hackney*	*Hackney*
2	*Tower Hamlets*	*Lambeth*	Newham	Newham
3	Newham	*Tower Hamlets*	*Lambeth*	*Tower Hamlets*
4	*Lambeth*	Newham	*Hammersmith*	*Lambeth*
5	Manchester	*Hammersmith*	*Tower Hamlets*	*Hammersmith*
6	*Islington*	*Islington*	Haringey	Haringey
7	Liverpool	*Southwark*	Brent	*Islington*
8	*Hammersmith*	Haringey	*Islington*	Brent
9	Wolverhampton	*Wandsworth*	*Wandsworth*	*Wandsworth*
10	Haringey	Manchester	*Camden*	*Southwark*
ILEA	5/10	7/10	7/10	7/10

Table 7.2: 1981 Census: Density of population in certain urban areas

LEA	People per hectare
ILEA	81.4
Brent and Haringey } Ealing and Newham }	59.3
Liverpool	46.6
Manchester	40.3
Birmingham	38.8
Sheffield	14.7

2 Educational achievements of inner London pupils

A great deal of attention focuses upon educational achievements as represented in external examination passes. This is understandable in so far as such passes provide one visible measure for assessing what schools and pupils have accomplished. This should not blind us, however, to a whole range of educational achievements which are shown in more subtle, more intangible and less measurable ways. Many inner London schools, as the reports of inspectors testify, stimulate qualities of creativity, of artistic expression, of articulateness, of initiative, cooperation and social concern among their pupils. These qualities, not always easily assessed through the formal examination system, are nevertheless part of the achievements of inner London schools and should not be overlooked. When we turn to a review of educational achievement as expressed in external examination results, it is clear that in the face of the disadvantages already outlined and in the face of considerable institutional fluidity arising out of many factors, these results are commendable. The previous Education Officer, Mr Peter Newsam, remarked in the report *School Examination Results in the ILEA 1979 and 1980* that

> if examination results are to be taken as the test, the suggestion that standards in ILEA secondary schools have fallen, though frequently made, is unsubstantiated. The results have remained notably stable . . . stable results indicate that the secondary school system has maintained its performance over a period when pupils' education from primary school onwards was affected by the high turnover of teaching staff in the early and mid 1970s.
> Furthermore, the ending of selection and the onset of falling rolls have meant that over half the Authority's secondary schools are still affected by some form of reorganisation and will be for several years to come.

This view has been reiterated by the present Education Officer, Mr William Stubbs, in his report to the Schools Sub-committee.

This report (*GCE and CSE Examination Results in ILEA Schools: Summer 1982*, 24 June 1983) shows continued stability in the face of much social, economic and institutional change. I think I can do no better than to quote directly the relevant extracts from this report:

The Secondary System 1977–82
2. The fifth-year pupils were the first group to be admitted to ILEA secondary schools after the ending of selection in 1977. This is of great importance. The National Children's Bureau, as part of their National Child Development Study, examined the examination achievements of boys and girls in different types of school.
They reported 'One of the most consistent and striking findings was of a tendency for pupils in schools undergoing reorganisation while they were there to have lower exam attainment'. Every child in inner London secondary school fifth forms in 1981–82 was in a

school undergoing comprehensive reorganisation for her/his entire secondary school career and yet, as the R & S report shows, success rates did not, overall, decline.'

The Examinations
4. For the Authority as a whole, the results were broadly similar to the previous year's which, as I reported to committee last year (ILEA 2252), had continued improvements that schools had been achieving over a period of years. The problems which the 1982 candidates faced during their school careers had been no less real than their predecessors: they too had experienced considerable turnover in staff for much of their school careers as reported above, they were the first non-selective cohort in ILEA secondary schools, which, in addition, have had to adjust to falling rolls which have also necessitated reorganisations; an increasing number of them come from families which do not use English as their first language; and a very high proportion of them suffer from some social or economic disadvantage . . . .

Notwithstanding all this, standards have been maintained: in 1978 9.8 per cent of pupils gained 5 or more 'O' levels/CSE Grade 1 (i.e., 'O' level equivalent); in 1982 the proportion was 9.9 per cent; in 1978 18.4 per cent gained at least one CSE Grade 1; by 1982 the proportion had increased to 21.7%. 60.7% of 'A' level candidates gained one or more passes in 1978 and 60.9% in 1982: the figures for two 'A' levels or more were 35.5% and 35.9% respectively. All in all, this is a most worthy achievement . . . .

In summary, the analysis shows
6. (a) that the proportion of pupils entering CSE in 1982 was the highest since the introduction of the examination and that the proportion of pupils obtaining at least one Grade 1 ('O' level equivalent) was also the highest ever;
 (b) that the proportion of pupils entering 'O' level and those gaining at least one Grade A, B or C had each fallen by 1% whilst those gaining 5 or more 'O' levels graded A, B or C had fallen by 0.7%;
 (c) that the combined 'O' level and CSE results — and a high proportion of pupils enter a combination of the two examinations — showed little difference from previous years.

Mr Stubbs is right in my view to refer to these results as 'a most worthy achievement' but this is not to say that the Authority is complacent about the position. On the contrary, it is the intention of the Authority to attack even more vigorously some of the roots of educational underachievement which are related to class, race and gender disadvantage and it is to a consideration of these policies that I now turn.

3 Policies for the future

This chapter has so far dealt with an analysis of the current situation. The next, more difficult, task is to point the way forward and to identify policies that are likely to *change* the current patterns of achievement within inner city schools. Before outlining new policies, however, it is important to stress two facts: that Inner London faces unique problems amongst LEAs; but that it has, at the same time, unrivalled human resources to overcome these problems.

That ILEA's situation is unique is obvious through study of its statistics; 320,000 school pupils, 200,000 students, 24,000 teachers and lecturers and over 225,000 part-time adult students out of a population of over two million people living in high density in 114 square miles, speaking at least 131 different languages.

The human resources available to cope with this cosmospolitan richness are also impressive: a tradition of progressive education that stretches back to the early members of the LCC; a capable administrative machine; a highly respected inspectorate; a learning resources branch that includes an educational television service; a research and statistics branch unique amongst LEAs and a committed teaching and non-teaching service.

Traditional policies

The traditional ILEA policies have always been well-motivated and generous. Thus elected members of ILEA have, with their officers, paid attention to the special educational needs of many children both in ordinary and special schools; adopted annual and quinquennial reviews for schools; the ILEA Inspectorate has studied and produced reports on the curriculum of both primary and secondary schools, as well as a range of detailed guidelines on selected subjects; a network of school support centres covering the whole Authority has also been established and corporal punishment has been abolished; the procedures for dealing with suspensions and expulsions have been reviewed and revised.

By providing generous pupil-teacher ratios, advisory teachers, librarians and media resources officers it was hoped to raise the educational standards of all pupils. Similarly, by investing resources in computers — for special schools as well as for primary and secondary schools — we were seeking to enhance learning. An increase in provision for the under-fives will provide more children with a sound start to their schooling. Parental involvement is also to be encouraged, not only at the pre-school and infant level, but also with older pupils. For example, the Hackney parent-pact on reading will involve parents actively in their children's learning. Cooperation will also be aided by the regular publication of a parents' newspaper as well as by the established parents' consultative meetings.

The policy of *positive discrimination,* whereby schools receive certain resources according to their level of social disadvantage, is to be continued. A major review of the Educational Priority Indices revealed that the chances of learning failure were directly related to the number of disadvantages experienced by pupils.[3]

An initiative for secondary pupils who have not achieved is also to be the subject of a new pilot scheme. The well-established *bridging courses*, providing an FE link for disaffected school pupils, and *access courses*, enabling motivated students who lack formal qualifications to earn a place in higher education, are also to be continued.

We have also supported an initiative on study skills and have established a summer school of exciting sixth form special courses. Many of these are organised in university and polytechnic departments and offer our sixth formers the opportunity to work closely with acknowledged experts in a variety of different fields across the whole range of academic subjects.

For young people today, even if well qualified, the difficulties of getting employment are considerable. We have, therefore, provided the careers service both with extra personnel and with computer schemes so that relevant information can be easily assessed. Special courses for the young unemployed have been set up. These can be taken at school and at college by students allowed to study for twenty-one hours or less. We have also established Tertiary Education Boards to ensure that the very best use is made of resources for the teaching and learning of the 16–19 group. Similarly, we are currently reviewing the whole of the further and higher education sector. In this context we are investigating the value of creche facilities for young parents who wish to study.

As one of the pioneering Authorities to establish educational maintenance allowances, we believe learning must not be restricted to those whose families can afford to support them. In the same way we have reduced the fees of adult classes and given special reductions to those who are unemployed or are over retirement age. Finally, we have encouraged a series of experiments into community schools so that the benefits of a single management structure including schools, college, youth and adult facilities can be evaluated.

All these policies are laudable and continue work started, in some cases, many years ago. However, it is obvious that these policies are not enough. The analyses reported earlier in this chapter demonstrated that, whatever the generosity of the Authority, normal methods and procedures have not provided an equal opportunity for all. Because of the current economic situation, it is now clear that unless more radical steps are taken on behalf of specific groups even the benefits of the current system will be at risk.

New initiatives

One of our first actions in 1981 as the newly elected members of ILEA was to hold a seminar on achievement in schools for all heads and representative teachers of our schools. In this seminar we reviewed the evidence on differences in achievement between pupils of different class background, between pupils of different ethnic groups, and between girls and boys.[4] Since then we have held three day conferences and consulted widely, not only with the teachers' associations and trade unions but also with parents and community groups.

We have modified our policies as a result of these consultations and are now moving forward on three fronts.

(i) *Class differences in learning*

We have set up a committee to examine the curriculum of secondary schools under the chair of Dr David Hargreaves of the Oxford University Department of Education. In addition to the many visits to schools by members of the Committee, evidence has been requested and three research studies focused on pupils, parents and teachers have been commissioned. We hope this will provide a real opportunity for a thorough investigation of the curriculum offered in our secondary schools. The members of the Committee include parents and representatives from industry and the trade unions as well as professional educators. It is our aim, also, to set up a working party to look at primary education with a special regard to the performance of pupils from working class family backgrounds. It is hoped that the results of a longitudinal research study of a sample of the Authority's schools, now in its third year, will illuminate this issue.

There is also the vital question of assessment to consider. Whilst recognising the difficulties of the current public examinations for many inner city pupils, the Authority has, of course, little opportunity to influence changes to the system. (The new examinations council is made up solely by nominees of the Secretary of State.) However, the Authority will continue to draw attention to the injustices of the present system and particularly to the difficulties facing pupils with a working class background. We will look critically at any proposed changes. Within our own schools we will encourage the development of various types of new assessments. We have initiated experiments with *pupil profiles* and hope to develop, at least in mathematics and science, a series of *graded assessments* which are based on published criteria, relatively short-term, and on which it is possible for high proportions of pupils to achieve success. We believe it may be possible to develop such assessments with fewer of the problems of validity and reliability that so affect the current system of examinations. A portfolio of results for these assessments, from profiles, and from ordinary working assignments can be built up by each pupil (the 'London Portfolio').[5]

Whilst the current system of examinations exists, however, we wish our pupils to perform as well as possible and so we have established Easter revision centres for fifth-year pupils. We hope that these will be of special value to pupils whose circumstances make studying in the home difficult.

For the working class child the experience of attending a school in which she or he realises that other children are more in accord with the ethos of the school and their parents on easier terms with the teachers can be very painful. Although the realisation of 'difference' may take time, once admitted it cannot but influence the attitude of the child. Although we know from autobiographies that for some exceptional individuals this self-awareness may provide a spur to motivation, for many it is more likely to lead to what Carol Dweck, an American psychologist who has studied differences in learning, has termed 'learned helplessness'.[6] Thus the pupil from a working class background may learn to conform to the negative stereotype that may be held by the school.

Curiously, the one powerful group in society that usually represents the interests of working class people — the manual workers trade unions — has not, in general, greatly involved itself in education. This needs to happen as the interest of such a pressure group adds a permanence that is otherwise missing. I hope that our ILEA initiatives may provide the opportunity for constructive debate and encourage the trade unions to take more interest in the education of the children of their members.

(ii) *Gender differences in learning*

With regard to gender differences, we have established a caucus of women political members serviced by women officers, the number of whom has increased, and have commissioned a series of investigations into the career patterns of women teachers.[7] Although the imbalance of female and male *secondary headteachers* within the ILEA is comparatively slight, in primary and special schools and in permanent full time staff of adult education institutions, it is much more marked. We will do all we can to correct this imbalance by encouraging job sharing and developing suitable in-service courses for women who have, for a variety of reasons, interrupted their careers.

In order to encourage this work we have established specialised officers posts within the Equal Opportunities Unit to take responsibility for women. The ILEA Inspectorate has produced a detailed report on equal opportunities for girls and boys.[8] One new inspector for equal opportunities has also been recently appointed as has a specialist women's officer for the youth service. Further action may follow once the research that we have commissioned on girls in the youth service has been reported.

All schools in the service recently took part in a survey of anti-sexist initiatives and we were delighted at how many heads and teachers are responding to the Authority's lead.[9] Clearly there is more to be done but equally clearly sexism, and the limitations it imposes on the education of both girls and boys, is on the agenda of most of our schools. One direct way in which the Authority has been able to help has been to encourage our Learning Resources Branch to produce good non-sexist learning material. We are also contributing to the support of a resource centre being established by the Women's Education Group.

(iii) *Minority ethnic groups and differences in learning*

The ILEA anti-racist statement was presented at the recent day conference on multi-ethnic education. We are sending this statement to all institutions in the education service with the instruction to develop, additionally, their own policy statement. We are determined that within the education service, racism in all its manifestations will be challenged and dismantled. At present we are in discussion with trade unions representing our employees as to how the grievance procedure and the staff code may be revised to take account of racist offences.

We have also developed a series of papers on multi-ethnic education giving guidance on organisation and the curriculum as well as providing a background context for the initiatives.[10] Our thinking on race has been much influenced by a document produced by Berkshire LEA.[11] This seeks to replace notions of integration and of diversity by an emphasis on equality. Such an approach maintains: that black people must be fairly represented at all levels of management and government; that all established practices and procedures must be examined to ensure that they do not work to the advantage of white and the disadvantage of black people; and that there must be mutual respect and appreciation between all sectors of the community.

A number of initiatives in mother tongue teaching have been supported and we have recently increased the number of specialist language teachers. This is important for we believe the benefit to the child of learning his or her own mother tongue language to be considerable. At the same time we have increased the number of teachers of English as a second language for we also recognise the crucial need for all our pupils to have a full command of the English language.

We have established specialist posts for ethnic minority matters within the Equal Opportunity Unit. We have also developed the Multi-Ethnic Inspectors' team of advisory teachers. Liaison officer posts have been established in all divisions under a senior Education Liaison Officer. Resource coordinators have also been appointed. Our catering branch now has two specialist officers to advise on ethnic food and cooking methods.

We have also encouraged the Learning Resources Branch to continue its work developing material suitable for a multicultural society and have increased the aid given to the independent Afro-Caribbean Education Resource Group. Lastly, we support a number of supplementary schools and independent mother-tongue teaching classes.

Common themes

These policies have been designed to help particular groups. It will, however, be abundantly clear that help will actually be much more far-reaching. Initiatives to help pupils from working class homes will, if they improve the education on offer, help all pupils. Measures taken to help girls will undoubtedly also help boys. Ensuring the curriculum and organisation of schools is suitable for our multicultural society will help all pupils.

The fact that our initiatives have a common base is important. Underlying our approach are a number of principles. First, that we wish to give power to people who do not, in the normal way, have access to it. Thus working class parents, women and people from minority ethnic backgrounds are frequently absent from the groups within our society that wield power: from Parliament, the judiciary, the civil service, local government, the HM Inspectorate, the universities, examination boards and even from school governing bodies.

The second principle is that within the education service, equal opportunities must be provided. We do not believe that by accepting the status quo disadvantaged groups will improve their position. This is why we have created an Equal Opportunity Unit with the task of ensuring that such groups do, in reality, have a fair chance of appointment and promotion.

The third principle concerns sexism, racism and classism. We will challenge these wherever they arise. We are also aware that such actions are sometimes not intentional and we are concerned that the unintentional consequences of actions — the hidden curriculum — that may lead to lower expectations, less favourable treatment or more negative feedback to any of these groups, also be examined.

The final principle is to do with special needs. Where these exist we welcome the opportunity to provide the resources needed to help. The revision courses and the educational maintenance allowances that we have provided, the special curriculum enhancements to girls' schools and the mother-tongue teaching schemes are all examples of our concern.

There are those who will argue that our policies may lower educational standards. They are wrong. The establishment of truly equal opportunities within a comprehensive system of education can have only one effect: a raising of standards across the board. It is impossible to help disadvantaged groups without helping all pupils.

Effectiveness

All these initiatives must be made to work. It is essential that policies be delivered. To this end we are determined to use the Inspectorate and the Authority's Research and Statistics Branch to evaluate progress. At the same time we are asking all educational institutions to report back to the various sub-committees on the progress that has been achieved. In this way accountability of the education service to the elected representatives and through them to the community will be achieved.

It may well be asked if all these actions stand any chance of achieving what so far has eluded urban education. Clearly, it would be excessively naive to think that such a radical change could be brought about in so short a period of time. It is, after all, only two years since the local elections brought a new administration to the ILEA. However, it would also be unfair to disregard the efforts of so many people over the last two years. The slow and sometimes painful processes of *consultation* have taken place. *Policies* have been thrashed out between members of the Authority and with their officers. *Ideas* have been generated and debated. We have now set out a detailed timetable for Authority-wide discussion, school-based analysis of curriculum and organisation, and reporting back to the Education Committee.

Whether these policies ultimately bear fruit will depend on the work of all within the education service, and how readily they respond to these challenges.

It must be made clear that the Authority is determined on these questions. Equal opportunity initiatives are not an extra. They must be seen as a central concern, as part of the normal processes of education for all our pupils.

At the same time, however, it would be quite wrong for an Authority dedicated to equal opportunity to take advantage of the good will of its employees. Many ILEA teachers are under stress, not only from the demanding job they do, but also from the amalgamations and school closures that falling rolls have made necessary. Even though no employees have been made redundant, a number have had to move schools. For individuals, the experience of such a move or that of competing unsuccessfully for their own job can be very painful, as some teachers in amalgamated schools have found.

The Authority is sympathetic to these employees and will endeavour to turn this sympathy into positive actions by investigating, through the current discussions, ways of improving conditions of work.

This commitment to employees is important, for the Authority cannot, by itself, implement its policies. This can only be done by the thousands of teaching and non-teaching staff in the Authority's educational institutions. It is in their hands that the success of policies rests — policies which have been fully thought out on the basis of wide consultation. It is in all classrooms and in every interaction between pupils and teachers that equal opportunity must change from a policy into a reality.

Notes

1 Department of Education and Science (1980), *Report by the HMI on Educational Provision by the ILEA*, DES.
2 Figures supplied by Dr Peter Mortimore, Director of ILEA Research and Statistics Branch.
3 Sammons, P., Kysel, F. and Mortimore, P. (1983), 'Educational priority indices: a new perspective', *British Educational Research Journal* 9 (1), pp. 27–40.
4 Mortimore, P. (1982), *Achievement in schools*, seminar given at the Royal Festival Hall on 22 October 1981, ILEA Research and Statistics Branch.
5 Worby, H. and Bird, M. (1982), *Record Keeping and Profiles Guidance for Schools*, ILEA Research and Statistics Branch. ILEA (1982), *Secondary education further developments*. (ILEA 2524). *Report to Schools Sub-Committee 25 November 1982.*
6 Dweck, C. (1977), 'Learned helplessness and negative evaluation', *Educator* 19 (2).
7 Martini, R. (1982), *Female and Male Teaching Staff in the ILEA: Equal Opportunity*, ILEA Research and Statistics Branch.
8 ILEA (1982), *Equal opportunities for girls and boys: a report by the ILEA Inspectorate*.

9 Coulter, A. (1983), *Anti-sexist Initiatives in ILEA Schools,* ILEA Research and Statistics Board.
10 ILEA (1983), papers presented to a conference on multi-ethnic education held at Quinton Kynaston school, 30 April 1983.
11 Advisory Committee for Multicultural Education (Berkshire) (1982), *Education for equality: a paper for discussion in Berkshire.*

8
Education in New York City: public schools for whom?

Dale Mann

New York has a thousand city-run public schools where 44,000 teachers meet 905,000 students in hopes of facilitating teaching and learning by all. The public schools' democratic premise — 'by all' — is so familiar that it seems a given; the institution is so large its continuation is taken for granted. Both are mistakes. Major policy changes being considered in the United States — for example, tax credits for private school tuition and/or vouchers to parents redeemable at any school of their choosing — would sharply tilt the values served by the public schools.

Public school policy in New York has always been a volatile mix of objective circumstances and subjective attitudes. While student enrollment declined, the cost of staffing went up. The enrollment of 964,000 in 1980 dropped to 904,225 in 1981 but the Board of Education asked the city for a $440 million increase from the prior year's $3.1 billion. Fewer children in the public schools has meant fewer adults equipped with what Aristotle called 'parental overfondness' to pressure the city and protect the schools. Then there are the common but mistaken beliefs that test scores for urban children do nothing but decline and that urban schools are so bureaucratically impregnable as to be beyond salvation. If the salvation of the public schools is at stake, and it is, there is the matter of just who will be saved. In 1958, public school enrollment was almost exactly that of 1980 (969,000 and 964,000 respectively). In 1958, 67 per cent of the enrollment was white; in 1980, 31 per cent was white, 39 per cent black and 30 per cent Hispanic.[1]

The objective factors are fewer students, higher costs, a smaller adult constituency, and a growing proportion of black and Hispanic students. The subjective factors are declining outcomes, despair over the prospects for improvement, and racism. When social reform programs of the 1960s seemed not to work, the question was 'give up or try harder.' The 1980s theme, 'If it's not broken, don't fix it' is less relevant than the choice between fixing the *public* schools or building another layer of schools for another part of the public. New York could easily end up with a residual group of 'public schools' that would be like what the city maintains for pre-schoolers, i.e. a segregated warehouse for the children of the poor with no prospect for improvement, precisely because it deals only with a clientele felt to be 'undeserving.'

Thus, the choice before New York is between (a) an expensive investment to improve the public school system, or (b) allowing an alternative system, largely for the middle class, to be added on top of the wreckage of the formerly public school system that would then enroll only the poor. Such a two-tiered system, while familiar to other countries and while already partly visible in New York, would none the less seriously compromise the equal educational opportunity aspirations of this country. Not only does that aspiration suit the city, the alternatives are more rigid stratification, less opportunity, more anger, and less justice.

The mythology of public education in America had always trumpeted schools as the engines of social and economic mobility. The revisionist critics of the 1960s destroyed that comfortable illusion and accelerated the erosion of public support. The challenge ahead is to run a race we may already have lost: the improvement of a public school system to the point where it will command broad support across all social classes and racial groups. Many people, including teachers, think that the city's schools are unmanageable and they point to reading scores. But in recent years, children have been tested under increasingly secure conditions with items selected from a consistent test pool. In 1979, 40 per cent of the school's enrollment had read as well as other children in the United States at the same grade level. In 1980, the figure reading on grade level had climbed to 47 per cent. In 1981, 51.2 per cent were reading on or above grade level expectations and in 1982, 51.7 per cent of all those tested achieved at that heartening level. Moreover, reading achievement has been going up faster for black and Hispanic children than for white children.

Another reason for qualified optimism about New York's schools is the rise in the College Entrance Examination Board's scholastic aptitude tests (SATs), the verbal and mathematic standardized exams which most of the nation's colleges use to evaluate student applicants. Nationally,

SAT scores rose by two points in 1982, the first increase in more than two decades. But New York City SAT scores have risen 11 points on the verbal and eight points on the math test during the past two years. Moreover, New York City's rise is probably due to a dramatic improvement among minority SAT student test-takers. Across the country, minority scores, though on the rise, still lag approximately 100 points below white scores. Yet in New York where almost 60 per cent of all students taking the SATs are minority students, the gap between the city average and the national average is only 40 points. Clearly, those New York City minority students who complete high school and apply to college are achieving verbal and math scores much higher than their peers across the country.

Some educators like to denigrate test scores (they don't measure the 'whole child,' they measure the 'wrong' thing) but such scores remain the best *child-related proxy* for the outcomes of the system. Variations in test scores can come from changing the tests, changing the composition of the group being tested, or changing the performance of children by teaching them. New York's test has remained stable and gains have come despite increased participation by groups who might have been expected to lower median achievement. Nationally, there is a growing body of evidence that suggests when teachers teach, children learn, and *mirabile dictu* the more teachers teach the more children learn![2] The chancellor of the New York City schools from 1979 to 1983, Frank Macchiarola, insisted on the educability of all children and required increases in the time teachers spend teaching. Yet the reputation of the public schools has fallen so low that many people have to struggle very hard before evidence of improvement can penetrate their prejudicial conviction that the children of the poor — children who are in the United States disproportionately non-white — cannot be taught. The evidence justifies trying harder and credits the effect of recent reforms, but it also highlights the 'schools for whom' question.

Below the city-wide averages, New York really is two school systems. The students above and below grade level are not at all evenly distributed across the city. At least 50 per cent of all students read at or above grade level in the two most predominantly white areas of the city (the boroughs of Queens and Staten Island). Governance in New York's elementary and junior high schools (children aged 6 to 13) is mainly done through thirty-two community school districts, each enrolling about 30,000 children. If the outcome measure is achievement scores,

Education in New York City: public schools for whom?

New York schools continue to work far better for children in white districts than in others. The critical point is the interaction between reading achievement and race and social class. Black children, Hispanic children, and the children of the poor are heavily overrepresented in the bottom achievement groups. For the children who are below grade level, 35 per cent are one to two years behind, and 27 per cent are more than two years behind.[3]

The 'public schools for whom' question gets raised even without race or social class. Take for example, the average per pupil costs to instruct children of different ages.

Table 8.1 Enrollment, budget, and direct instruction distributions 1979–1980

	Elementary	Junior high	High school	Special ed.
Per cent of October enrollment *	44	20	30	4
Per cent of total budget *	39	21	26	14
Average per pupil cost for direct instruction only **	$1,815	$2,258	$1,707	$4,929

Sources: * Board of Education of the City of New York, 'A functional analysis of the 1979/1980 New York City Board of Education budget' (June 1980), *Instructional/Organizational Budget for Public School Pupils: 1979–1980*, p. 17.
** Ibid., Exhibit 7, 'per pupil cost by organizational level, 1979–1980,' p. 13.

Why does the area with the greatest potential, elementary education, bear the heaviest disparity in the pupil/resource ratio? It is even more difficult to justify the resource disparity for special education (children with severe handicapping conditions) to a parent whose high school daughter is enrolled in a regular program but *also* has a desperate need for expensive remediation. Since 1974, total enrollment has dropped 12 per cent but special education enrollment has increased 200 per cent mainly because of mandates from the national government and the courts.

Public schools for whom? The choices of school officials inevitably provide something for one group that cannot then be made available to another and parents, taxpayers and voters have become very aware of the consequences. Spending twice as much on the schooling of a child diagnosed as minimally brain damaged does not in any sense equalize that child's educational opportunity. None the less, as the subsidy to such children and others with handicapping conditions has grown, it has also become more visible and far more contentious despite the meagerness of its redistributive effect.

The necessary hypocrisy of leadership requires that the question 'schools for whom' be answered, 'For everyone.' But if there is not enough to go around, helping some means not helping others. Should always scarce resources be concentrated on improving schools for the poor or for the middle class? A little of both is unlikely to help either. Fortunately for school leaders, two factors ease the pinch. First, in the aggregate, the children of the middle class learn anyway and succeed anyway. Parental teaching, peer learning, and cultural reinforcement amplify the school's contributions, and the vocational success for graduates is more determined by connections than credentials, by discrimination than diplomas. Second, the schools have historically been a middle class institution — at least in their aspirations — and that legacy translates into bureaucratic momentum. In many policy areas, doing nothing serves middle class interests while substantial investments are necessary effectively to help the poor. This creates the opportunity for selective inattention to benefit the middle class in ways once proposed as a national policy of 'benign neglect' for the poor.

But while most of the contribution to educational achievement for most children comes from sources other than the classroom, that is not true for the children of the poor who have fewer non-school learning opportunities. The modal public school student in the city is now a fourth grader, living several miles from the central business district, black, and attending a school with other black and Hispanic children. That fourth grader currently reads not much below a level expected of most fourth graders (although the gap between expected and actual performance will increase for larger proportions of the student body as grade levels increase). That student *depends* on better schooling. New York's two major initiatives are a new student promotion policy and a comprehensive, direct project for school improvement.

Making schools better?: (1) promotional gates

Making schools better gets its push from disappointment with schools and their graduates' abilities. Clothing manufacturers do not pretend to have foolproof production processes: they protect their reputations by taking the labels off 'seconds' before selling them at a discount. Similarly, one can appear to 'improve' the schools by disavowing those who have not met certain achievement or competency standards.

Consider the high schools. They are under attack (and so are their graduates) because of employers' complaints about illiteracy and work habits and because of law suits by nominal graduates who cannot read their diplomas. Although obstacles to learning are psychological, economic and social as well as pedagogical, legislators continue to pretend that there are schooling solutions to socio-political problems. The lust to 'legislate learning'[4] can be seen in the imposition by the state's governing board of 'regents' competency tests' in reading, writing, and mathematics with a mandated skill below which diplomas are to be denied otherwise qualified students. The failure rates for these high school-level competency tests are certain to embarrass large numbers of youngsters and to diminish further the reputation of the city's high schools. Some have argued that nothing less than a massive demonstration of incompetence will gain attention to the desperate situation of many students. Blaming the victims and shaming the professionals some feel will cause improvement.

Whatever the effect, few believe that the solution lies at the high school level. One of education's incontrovertible propositions is the high premium returned on early teaching. Young children are more receptive to learning and early achievements compound later successes. Thus, the high school problem gets answered if at all at the elementary level. If high school diplomas are to have any meaning (and if children are to have advance warning and a reasonable chance to meet standards), then the process leading there has to be strengthened as well. The Micchiarole regime committed itself to the proposition that 'all children can learn,' a simple premise that became volatile when coupled with a student performance evaluation system (the 'promotional gates') that clarifies how difficult it is for some children to learn, or for some teachers to teach. In the past, promotions contingent on performance meant that some children were held back, labeled as failures, retaught the same things the same way that did not work originally, and thus placed increasingly at odds with their own potential, their classmates, teachers and the system. To avoid that damage, New York's *de facto* policy had been one of the 'social promotions,' passing students up the grades with their age-mates hoping to catch later what was not learned earlier. In 1980, the last year of these 'social promotions,' 93 per cent of all students in regular elementary classes were promoted to the next grade.

But catch-up did not work and eventually the utility of all diplomas was corrupted since large numbers of marginally competent youngsters were graduated into a demanding, skeptical, even hostile world of work. Thus, the promotional gates policy implemented in 1981–2 attempted: (1) to re-establish the connection between grade levels and competencies; (2) to keep the faith with students and parents who want their efforts to have vocational consequences; and (3) to assure employers that the schools were sorting out 'unqualified' job applicants.

Enforcing promotion standards also required, in fairness to the children who could not meet the standard, that they be retaught but in ways different from what had not previously worked. Equipping each grade level with a different 'back-up' curriculum was too expensive. Therefore, in 1981–2 'promotional gates' were introduced at the fourth and seventh grade levels with the intention of protecting the later integrity of the high school diploma and identifying those who need special help early enough for it to make a difference. The strategy required that in order to ascend to the fifth or eighth grades, fourth grade students could not be more than a year below grade level and seventh graders not more than a year and a half behind.

But what was to be tested? Academic freedom, the culture of school professionalism, and the power of the teachers union meant that what children were actually taught was determined by 44,000 teachers behind that many closed classroom doors. Before minimum competencies could be established for students, the system had to insure a minimum prior coverage of related topics by teachers. Creating that codified, city-wide statement of the scope and sequence of New York City's elementary curriculum took more than a decade.

What has happened? In the first year of the 'promotional gates' policy more than one-fifth of all the children tested failed to get through.[5] Initially, 25,000 students (21.6 per cent of all fourth and seventh graders) were told that they were being held back and were offered a chance to enroll in a remedial summer school and retake the test. In fact, the improved test performance of 4,672 children allowed them to rejoin their previous classes before the new school year began.

Almost 20,000 others repeated their previous grades but this time, the central board put them in smaller classes (15 to 20 students rather than 30-plus), with more time on instructional tasks, with one of a small set of 'proven' curricula, and with specially trained teachers.

Seventy per cent of those held back subsequently tested well enough to be promoted. The Board asserted that, 'Gates students were able to attain end-of-year promotional criteria in greater proportions than students in a comparison group.'[6] The comparison group, otherwise similar students from a previous year who had not been held back and had not had the especially organized Gates instruction, were promoted at the same rates but did not do as well on their subsequent academic performance as those who were held back and retaught.

There is a continuing controversy about the measurement aspects of this. The test publisher says that the measurement error is plus or minus eight points for any child (enough randomly to close or open the promotional gate for thousands of children). The Board cites statistically significant differences in its findings although that derives as much from the size of the sample as the meaning of the intervention. Virtually everyone has profound doubts about the adequacy of Gates instruction for these demonstrably needy children.

The resolve of the city's policy makers is strained further by the fates of those children who do not pass the test for the second and third years. Thirty per cent of those enrolled did fail the first year and were indeed retained again ('double-holdovers'). The group represents 5 per cent of all fourth and seventh graders in the city. Moreover, 2,800 students have been retained in the seventh grade for the *third* time and about 2,000 of this group are unlikely to test well enough to move on. This group will now be allowed to attend (but not matriculate in) high schools, they will receive basic skills (reading and math), remedial instruction in separate classes, but they will join their age-mates for other classes. Enforcing standards causes pain to those who do not measure up, but the promotional gates policy is a step in the right direction. It is not a good policy, but it is a preferable one. It is not, however, the only path to better schooling.

Making schools better? (2) The School Improvement Project

The neo-conservative assessment of public schooling in the United States can be summarized by one of its most influential proponents, James S. Coleman:

> Schools bring little influence to bear on a child's achievement
> that is independent of his background and general
> social context; this very lack of independent effect means
> that the inequalities imposed on children by their home,
> neighborhood and peer environment are carried along to become
> the inequalities with which they confront adult life at the end
> of school. For equality of educational opportunity must imply a
> strong effect of schools that is independent of the child's
> immediate social environment, and that strong independent
> effect is not present in American schools.[7]

In the School Improvement Project (SIP), begun in 1978, New York chose to challenge two of the central tenets of the neo-conservative dogma — that poor children could not be helped in public schools and that those schools themselves could not be improved. How much learning can a principal expect of a child who comes up the steps, alone because his mother is in full-time paid employment, angry because he was a captive spectator at a screaming match among adults, confused because only one parent is in the home, and unmotivated because of the absence of models to emulate (i.e. parents who read)? If a child is otherwise reasonably intact, but none the less poor, is there something that will help that child learn in that school and despite that poverty? Does there exist an instructionally effective school that can ameliorate the learning-related difficulties ordinarily associated with low social class standing? Much of the analysis has been influenced by the late Ronald Edmonds who tried to bring the instructionally effective school to New York City. Edmonds argued that an instructionally effective school would (at its maximum), teach 'poor children at least as well as it teaches middle-class children' or, 'an effective school [will] bring the children of the poor to those minimal masteries of basic school skills that now describe minimally successful pupil performance for the children of the middle class.'[8]

The School Improvement Project was begun to convince the city's educators — especially those working with the bottom one-third achieving children — that the schools they already controlled could make a difference with the children who were already there. One critical part of that was illuminating the contribution that 'within-school factors' (things accessible to school people right now) make to the achievement of poor children. Teachers cannot, for example, go into the students' homes each weekday evening and turn the TV off but they do already control the 'within-school factor' of how much of their day they devote how intensely to instructing.

A second and contentious aspect of the project was that schools could be improved within existing resources. American teachers have become accustomed to extra pay for extra effort. Many advocates of school improvement would like to see more money for schools; the unique aspect of this school improvement project was its emphasis on the more effective arrangement and deployment of what was already present in the schools.

Edmonds's analysis had tried to isolate those factors thought to characterize schools that successfully teach poor children: (1) *administrative style* (especially strong leadership); (2) *teacher expectations* that they and their students can do well; (3) an *instructional emphasis* on basic skills acquisition; (4) a safe *school climate* conducive to learning; and (5) an *ongoing system to assess pupil progress* and drive subsequent teaching and learning. Over the project's three-year history, nineteen elementary schools have taken part, virtually all of which volunteered to join the effort. They all began with a needs assessment, self-study activity, the formation of a planning committee which was to represent all the school's constituencies, and the formulation of a sequenced set of objectives and activities. Initially, schools were helped and sometimes led through those activities by a liaison staff member assigned to the school from the central board. Staff help was designed to wither away from nearly full-time help at the beginning to one day a week in the third and last year of project assistance to the schools.

Two sorts of outcomes are available with respect to these schools. The children's achievement scores are the most critical since not only are children the ultimate purpose of the school, they are the measure of the adults' outcomes. Second, there are a number of process outcomes that describe the staff, parent and organizational reactions to the program.

Between 1980 and 1981, the number of elementary school pupils, city-wide, reading at or above grade level increased by 4 per cent, from 47 to 51 per cent. Participating schools in the School Improvement Project went up an average of 5.8 per cent. All but one of the project schools showed gains, with a maximum increase of 12 per cent for one school. And, the longer the school had been in the project the greater the gain: first year schools gained an average of 4.6 per cent; second year schools, an average of 7.2 per cent.[9]

The long path to better student achievement twists through personal factors (New York's teaching staff averages more than a decade on the job, virtually all are settled in mid-career), organizational factors (especially the size of the bureaucracy and the unionization of the teachers) and professional factors (beliefs about what works and what is possible). Administration is almost always action-at-a-distance and if children are to be helped, that must come from the manipulation of the adult and organizational components of the system. The central Board of Education's evaluation of the program[10] maintains that more schools more successfully dealt with the instructional emphasis and pupil evaluation components than with the factors of administrative style or teacher expectations. In fact, one entire group of schools (those in the first cohort) never addressed the question of teacher expectations. On some evidence the range of classroom practices which yield success for children is being narrowed.[11] But curriculum changes in the project schools show a wide diversity, even a scatter of approaches raising the question of Hawthorne effects rather than any more concrete improvement deriving from a mature technology. Moreover, school achievement is such a recalcitrant target that is is unlikely to yield to two of the five factors without the other three. The lack of improvement in the administrator and teacher expectation areas is even more troublesome. The socio-political survival of these improvement efforts depends heavily on the good offices of the principal and changing the artifactual part of the curriculum without also changing teacher process variables does not bode well for the future.

Like all of education, New York's public schools depend on the state of the art and science teaching. The process of school improvement cannot be more successful than the 'products' through which schooling proceeds. To the extent that we have what economists call production function relationships — desirable outcomes that result reliably from combining known inputs — then the prospects for substantial reform are brightened. The wide variation in the substance of the school improvement plans is partly linked to the state of the art but it also signals what many teachers believe — that no one knows how, within existing resources, to improve the schooling of poor children.

And that is related to a second major difficulty with New York's school improvement effort — the concentration on schools that volunteer. The experience of the volunteers is unlikely to be very compelling to the hundreds of schools in the city with demonstrably greater and probably quite different processual and substantive needs for reform. The map of New York City could be lit like a pinball machine with all the discrete innovations underway at any given time. In three years,

1979–81, the Board of Education piloted 781 innovative programs.[12] Both the Ford Foundation and the federal government have long since concluded that light-house 'demonstrations' do not, by themselves, lead to replication, especially not among the lowest achieving group of schools.

From the beginning the project was hard pressed because it directly challenged defeatist conclusions and minimalist standards, because it rejected the prevailing social science wisdom, and because its own 'bootstrap' logic ran counter to a tradition of 'extra pay for extra effort.' No one expects New York's public schools to have dramatically more money, regardless of the nobility of the cause. To be credible, SIP had to demonstrate that New York schools could be improved on their own resources without large, outside grants. And 'improvement' had to carry all the way through to changes in pupil outcomes, especially test scores.

Despite its shortcomings, SIP is too important a test of propositions too central to the survival of the schools to be abandoned. In any effort to make schools better, there is no substitute for thinking ahead (planning) and there is no way around, over, or through the people who do the work of schooling (the process of involving teachers). Neither are there short cuts. Equality of educational opportunity – building toward a situation in which all children have the same opportunity to learn the same things – is the central premise of a *public* school system. In that regard, SIP has been a properly courageous attempt that deserves to be both modified and continued. It also deserves to be extended in a revised version to the high schools where nothing of its sort yet exists.

SIP is one example of the project or program-mediated approach to school improvement. We have for too long assumed that improvement is best packaged as a project and imposed by an outsider. Teachers, adults in mid-career, are then supposed to be so dazzled by the better mousetrap that they will abandon those practices which, until that moment, were their own best professional solution to a difficult problem (how to teach) and instead substitute that better idea. If schools are to be improved, New York needs to invent new ways to increase professional investment. Principals in their schools and teachers in their classrooms are the final arbiters of school policy – federal legislation, court mandates, chancellor's regulations to the contrary not yet withstanding.

Improving school management

If its $3 billion-plus operating budget were instead income, New York's Board of Education would rank as the country's eightieth largest business, right after Republic Steel. Convened as a staff meeting, the Board's 70,000 employees would overrun the 60,000 seating capacity of a New York City football stadium; 19,000 teach elementary school; 11,000 teach junior high school; 14,000 teach high school. The Board of Education has more instructional employees (58,000) than the Chrysler Corporation has total hourly employees (54,000) and, while Chrysler's operations are concentrated in only forty American plants, the Board oversees more than a thousand schools. Sixteen thousand employees serve 514,000 lunches and almost a hundred thousand breakfasts each school day.[13] Twenty-three cents of every city expenditure dollar was spent by the Board of Education. The Board provides schooling to children from twenty-seven separate language groups. By virtue of its mammoth size, one would expect a lot of regulations, standard operating procedures, and bureaucracy and in that regard, the Board does not disappoint.

But sophistication in the management of the instructional process itself is another thing. Most production engineers, faced with the process where inputs are variable and technology is weak and uncertain would recommend against trying to routinize and centralize production, especially if it had to be done in a thousand different locations. Instead they would recommend substantial autonomy at the production sites in order to accommodate local variety and in the hopes of improving the process through naturally occurring experiments.

A contemporary management system that capitalized on the leadership potential of principals would have four features:

1. a set of *goals* agreed to by the relevant parties;
2. enough delegated *power* to implement activities in pursuit of the goals;
3. a goal achievement *assessment system*; and
4. a *reward structure* reflecting differential performance.

Those features do not exist and indeed, under current arrangements, principals can quite reasonably object that they should not be held accountable (4 above) for achieving (3) what they cannot control (2). So why try? (1). For some purposes, New York's schools are rampantly decentralized or 'loosely coupled.' But for most purposes the reality is less hands off than handcuffs. The New York State Education Code dubs the principal 'the responsible head of the school' but that is an empty slogan unless responsibility is matched by appropriate authority. Vast areas of the central bureaucracy define their work as stopping principals from doing foolish if not downright bad things. In pursuit of its teachers' interest, the United Federation of Teachers has reduced the power of building principals. The local community boards (there are thirty-two) frequently blame school administrators for what isn't done and punish them by further diminishing their discretion. How might we realize a better system?

The first component, goal setting, is not an easy process given the competing demands and limited resources of schools. But New York school administrators have had a lot of experience, bad and good, with the mechanisms of participation. The existing curriculum of every school represents a 'solution' to the complicated problems of goal setting: the point is not a wholesale replacement but an appropriate modification and one that expects more not only of children but also of teachers.

The real test comes with the second component, 'power'. The single greatest contribution to the ability of school principals to manage their buildings is also the most controversial — control of the budget and the dollar, material, and personnel resources allocated in the budget. In New York's system, the administrator closest to the child has the least budget power. The Central Board disburses money to community districts by a formula that includes (a) a weighted per student capita factor; (b) a 'breakage factor' that governs the point over the agreed upon class size at which a new class must be formed to accommodate teachers' coverage of pupils; (c) teacher preparation periods and the number of children with handicapping conditions; (d) reading retardation; and (e) a nominal discretionary amount to the community districts generally derived from funds for compensatory education. Eighty-five per cent of a district's allocation is determined by the first factor, enrollment. The central Board requires the districts to spend their totals within predetermined categories; there is for example, a module for 'administration,' for 'instruction,' and for 'facilities.'

Each community superintendent then forms a budget for the district's schools. In reality, both the principal and the superintendent know how the various factors apply to their schools and districts (they are the source of the data from which the Board begins its calculations).

At the district level, there are two sources of flexibility, the small discretionary fund and the differing salary costs of teachers because of longevity. However, the variation above or below that for which a given school is eligible is never more than one or two teachers.

The principal then returns to the school with the budget allotments in one hand and the contract in the other to make up a program of teaching and learning for the children. The United Federation of Teachers contract specifies class size, a sensitive factor of adult working conditions but one unrelated to student outcomes within the ranges ordinarily encountered in public schools. For any given teacher, a weekly program composed of 'A basic maximum of 25 teaching periods, five preparation periods, and five administrative periods for teachers with homeroom classes shall be established before any other type of program for administrative purposes in which teachers teach less than 25 periods is arranged.'[14] And,

1 There should be no more than three consecutive assignments . . . .
2 There should be no more than four consecutive working assignments including building assignments per day.
3 The number of different rooms in which assignments occur should be held to the absolute minimum administratively possible.
4 The number of lesson preparations should be kept to the minimum consistent with the nature of the subject, the size of the department . . . and special requests of the teachers . . . .[15]

Moreover, the contract's 'Relief from non-teaching chores' section stipulates:

Except for the minimum number of teachers necessary to supervise school sites and to protect pupil health and safety, teachers will be relieved of cafeteria, patrol, bus and study hall service . . . scoring city-wide standardized achievement tests, and of preparing absentee post cards and truant slips.[16]

Having satisfied those constraints, a good principal will still try to match teacher characteristics with student characteristics. Teachers vary in the component instructional activities or in the style of teaching that they do well; there are complementary variations in the learning styles of students.[17] But the 'Teacher assignments' clauses of the contract require that, 'With regard to requests as to grade level of special assignment (such as Corrective Reading Teachers, or Intellectually Gifted Classes), teachers with the highest seniority in the school should be given preference if qualifications for the position are the same.'[18]

The current system sends teachers to school buildings according to the number of children enrolled and once there, deploys them in patterns fixed by contract and regulations. Thus, a principal 'organizes' classes, and schedules the school's activities but largely as a matter of clerical routine. If class size may only vary within narrow limits, how can special needs be accommodated? If teachers may only teach 'within license' how can new classroom teaching patterns or new curricular emphasis be established? The current procedures for resource allocation at the building level have more to do with adult working conditions than children's learning conditions.

By contrast, school site budgeting might give large fractions of the cost of running a school over to people at the building level who then decide how best to invest those resources within a framework of district-wide policies, agreed-upon general goals and other constraints including contracts and regulations. Table 8.2 presents some of the general dimensions of five New York schools of various sizes and grade levels.

Only one school has less than a million dollar budget; most are far more substantial operations at least as measured by staff size and dollar cost. The barriers to more effective management are clearest for our sample high school (although the same constraints apply to all schools). The particular school cost $25 million to build and is one of the newest in the system. Its current enrollment is 2,995, a number the principal regards with apprehension. State law requires one librarian for every 1000 students. It is easy to imagine an enrollment increase of six students, all of whom might be legally defined as 'pupils with special education needs' (PSEN). At the 3001st student, the principal would have to employ another librarian not required with one less student but, since the enrollment increase came from PSEN students, a category covered by reimbursable funds but not by local tax-levy funds, the principal would not receive any extra money to meet his legal obligation!

Or take the case of the secretaries. The number of secretaries is a contractual matter based on the school's enrollment. Much of what the secretaries do could be done as well by less costly aides yet the principal is forbidden that economy. Similarly, the contract requires that cafeteria supervision be done by teachers whose teaching load is

Table 8.2: Budget dimensions of five sample schools by size and level

Categories	Small elementary (K–6)	Large elementary (K–6)	Small junior high (6–8)	Large junior high (7–9)	Large high school (9–12)
No. of students	767	2,053	695	1,257	1,995
Teachers	$570,000 (28)	$1,762,694 (78)	$907,310 (40)	$1,304,000 (64)	$2,308,000 (115)
Supervision	$ 32,668 (1)	$ 121,741 (4)	$ 95,022 (3)	$ 140,290 (5)	$ 295,000 (11)
Clerical	$ 14,184 (1)	$ 56,364 (4)	$ 29,600 (2)	$ 43,131 (3)	$ 130,000 (10)
Para-professionals	$ 42,730 (5)	$ 5,761**		$ 51,275 (6)	
Counselors			$ 25,800 (1)	$ 49,226 (2)	$ 46,400 (2)
Aides	$ 31,696 (7)	$ 61,746**	$ 52,486**	$ 36,224 (8)	$ 31,600**
Guards			$ 9,869		$ 40,000 (4)
Other than personnel			$ 2,587		$ 31,000
Totals	$691,778 (42)	$1,958,306 (86)	$1,122,674 (46)	$1,624,147 (88)	$2,882,000 (142)

* Dollar amounts are Fiscal 1980. Figures in parentheses are numbers of staff.
** Total for hourly rates: numbers of staff unavailable.

thereby reduced from five to three periods. That supervision could be done as competently at far less cost by an aide. Because the money coming into the school was nearly totally obligated, this particular principal sought to support some of the students' extra-curricular activities by selling pretzels. The kids liked the pretzels and the money from the sales supported half the school clubs until someone discovered *and enforced* a federal regulation prohibiting competition when the school's cafeteria was open! The result of all these constraints and indignities is a $2.8 million operation with $8,000 of discretionary authority (the balance of the 'supplies and postage' account once those expenses are paid).

The principal can make a difference in the achievement of children by rearranging, reallocating and otherwise leading the school but the current system makes that unnecessarily difficult. Principals need greater control over resources, including teachers. School site budgeting can be developed within the framework of some straightforward guidelines. First, discretionary dollar amounts have to be large enough to make a difference. It should be clear that the receipts from cookie sales will not impact achievement, but at the same time, it is unreasonable to expect total autonomy over the total budget. Until New York gains some experience with the procedure, the amount of discretionary budget authority will have to be a Goldilocks proposition – neither too much, nor too little, but just right. One aspect ought to be negotiable – school site budgeting ought to be done at no extra cost.

Second, school site budgeting procedures will have to conform to existing superordinate policies and contractual obligations although we ought certainly to expect and encourage some unique bargains to be struck where local circumstances indicate. In general, the process of conforming building specific allocation to other constraints should occur through the involvement of key participants at the building level. The guideline here is not one of participatory democracy with every group or faction having a veto over the school's program. In the recent past we have misinterpreted the American political tradition by substituting 'consensus' for 'consent.' Consensus – that all should agree – assumes that differences among groups are so trivial that they should be suppressed into a single homogeneous opinion. Not only is that an insult to legitimately differing interests, its pursuit is so time-consuming that little if anything gets done. Rather, the American tradition rests on the 'consent of the governed,' the temporary suspension of disagreement while the polity acts.

In a trades union city, the unions are always a special case. The situation is not unlike that between principals and community school boards. If a school board directs and enforces the use of a reading curriculum the principal believes to be inadequate, we ought not to be surprised that that principal will seek to escape the consequences of the failure of the curriculum. Principals must try to steer their schools with a lot of other hands on the wheel. A high school principal has separate contracts for the teaching staff, the administrators, the secretaries, the para-professionals, the aides, the guards, the food service workers, and the custodians (who have three separate contractual arrangements). It is not unfair to say that that goes with the turf (school principals are all volunteers) although the turf does need rearranging. No public official is autonomous. The Board as a whole negotiates thirty-nine separate unit contracts, the unions have many *legitimate* interests in the school, they have the political clout to express these interests, and they are not going to disappear. The contract is a real constraint and so are federal and state regulations. But they are not insuperable; different principals view the same requirements quite differently; and in fact much of the folklore of the city's administrators has to do with ways to bend regulations, fudge requirements, and otherwise create the freedom necessary to lead.

School site budgeting will not be enthusiastically embraced by New York school principals. When principals have no real authority they are comfortably insulated from accountability. One reason administrators were historically willing to trade the prerogatives of leadership for the perquisites of organized labor (school administrators now have a union of their own) is that their management prerogatives were meager at best. Where the resource allocation process is nothing more than the multiplication of demand factors and the assignment of teachers according to someone else's rules, managerial life is simple if futile. Indeed, a common response from principals to the prospect of discretion over resource allocation is that 'they'd better give me another clerk,' which misses the point rather completely. Discretion at the building level is not part of the standard operating procedure for big city schools. Principals will need first to be convinced that they really have some autonomy and then be trained to use it. With school site budgeting, the final components of a better management system also fall into place.

The third characteristic was a 'goal achievement assessment system.' Here we need to be careful to give credit where it is due, we need to be sure that the goals being achieved are a function of the school's contribution and not of exogenous factors such as family background. Student achievement on standardized tests should be a primary measure of the school's output yet it is not related solely to what schools do. One conceptualization of the inputs to the schooling process is as follows:

1 *student characteristics* (e.g. IQ, gender, age, personality, aspiration);
2 *family background characteristics* (e.g., ethnicity, socioeconomic status, wealth, family size);
3 *teacher characteristics* (e.g., training, experience, age, gender); and
4 *school characteristics* (e.g., physical plant, per pupil expenditure, curriculum).[19]

It is significant that only the last two of those four factors are directly under the control of the school and that even within those two, the principal faces varying degrees of intransigency. Yet recall the premise of a democratic public school — that *all* children should be helped to learn. The leadership task is to find ways to organize and apply within-school factors so that they make a difference for children regardless of the child's biosocial characteristics. Given the state of our present pedagogical art, it is all too easy to predict next year's achievement scores for a given school from knowledge of its social class characteristics. But exactly that knowledge provides a baseline against which a school should set goals, measure progress, and evaluate outcomes.

Finally, there is the matter of a 'reward structure.' Should administrators be accountable for whether or not their schools meet their goals? High school principals with maximum experience are now paid $43,000 per year: elementary principals with maximum experience, $37,000. Adding or subtracting to that amount according to goal achievements seems altogether unreasonable, politically impossible, and probably unnecessary. New York principals are after all very good at a very demanding job. Their salaries are adequate compensation; the additional opportunities and professional satisfactions of operating a school site budget ought to elicit significant participation from a large, initial group of principals. Keying subsequent promotions to previous performance would be an additional incentive and one that departs from current practice. In general, career mobility in American educational administration has little if anything to do with whether the students under one's aegis learned anything. Instead access to the superintendency, for example, is related to having been a superintendent — good bad, or indifferent.[20] That is a sad reflection of how little we expect of schools and the people who run them.

There is now in the United States an enormous literature on program implementation all of which identifies the service delivery, school building level as the key to improvement. The studies of successful schools for children from low-income families are unanimous and adamant in identifying the principal as the *sine qua non* of more powerful schooling. Yet New York has not begun to incorporate that understanding in practice. School site budgeting can locate responsibility for schooling outcomes where it logically belongs and it can match that responsibility with concomitant discretion. And finally, school site budgeting can be expected to yield more local responsiveness to the enormous diversity of learning-related needs among New York neighborhoods than can currently be expected.

Conclusions

The recent premise of New York's school leaders that all children can learn is linked to a challenge to the system's teachers and administrators to find ways to make that happen. The net effect has been to emphasize the public service obligations of adults in a public school system. The 'schools for whom' question is a constant strain that recurs in virtually every policy area and that threatens to fracture an already fragile coalition of support. The response at the top of the system has been to create larger interests out of those competing tensions. That places the emphasis where it should be, on a single, comprehensive and democratic school system.

Unfortunately that is less an operational reality than a target for the future. Making schools better is the critical proposition. Making urban schools work within available resources is realism. Making them work for those who lack alternatives is equity. One part of that is the promotional gate policy, especially with respect to the concomitant 'second chance' resources that would be available to those who fail.

The School Improvement Project is even more important because it strikes to the center of schooling, i.e. the teacher and what the teacher believes is possible with and for poor children. The city desperately needs clear demonstrations of public schools that help poor children learn the same things at the same rates as do other children. We should not be discouraged that SIP has not made quick gains. The process deserves continued support, and modification, and extension to the secondary level.

Third, the management ability and accountability of building principals ought to be enhanced through the development of school site budgeting procedures that visit significant discretion over resources on delivery level leaders.

It is important to understand that schooling in New York can be improved. The overriding task is to make the outcomes of schooling more abundant. We must find ways to improve the schools and to make that improvement carry all the way through to the achievement of students. The next four years will be unusually perilous for the public schools. Because of private and religious school options, public schools have never had the sort of service monopoly that, for example, the Fire Department and the public utilities of the city enjoy. But neither have they had the sort of competition that is in prospect either from a tax credit for private school tuition or from a revived voucher plan that would give parents a chit equivalent to the current per pupil expenditure to be redeemed at any school of their choice. In that kind of world, the survival of the public schools will be contingent on our ability to have improved them, a process that will have to be greatly accelerated, now.

Notes

1 'Mayor's Management Report, Supplement,' 17 September 1980. At the same time, the percentage white for the city as a whole has dropped from 1960's 85 per cent to an estimated 65 per cent in 1979. New York City continues to attract large numbers of children from other countries. Seven per cent of the schools' enrollment (more than 60,000 children) had been in New York for less than one year in 1982. See, New York City Schools, 'Pupil reading achievement: a summary of the April 1982 citywide reading test results, Grades 2 through 9,' n.d.

2 For example, see Ralph A. Hanson and Richard E. Schutz, 'A new look at schooling effects from programmatic research and development', in Dale Mann (ed.), *Making Change Happen?*, New York, Teachers College Press, 1979; and Carolyn Denham

and Ann Lieberman (eds), *Time To Learn*, Washington, DC, National Institute of Education, May 1980.
3. Foundation for Child Development, *State of the Child, New York City: II*, New York, 1980.
4. Arthur E. Wise, *Legislated Learning: The Bureaucratization of the American Classroom*, Berkeley, University of California Press, 1979.
5. This discussion is based on New York City Public Schools, Office of Educational Evaluation, 'A final evaluation of the 1981–82 promotional gates program,' December 1982.
6. Ibid., p. iv.
7. James Coleman et al., *Equal Educational Opportunity Survey*, Washington, DC, Government Printing Office, 1966.
8. Ronald Edmonds, 'Effective schools for the urban poor,' *Educational Leadership*, 1979, vol. 37, pp. 15 and 16.
9. New York City Board of Education, Office of Educational evaluation, 'A preliminary report on student reading achievement in S.I.P. and L.S.D.P. schools, 1980–81,' mimeo, n.d.
10. The following discussion is taken from: New York City Public Schools, 'School Improvement Project, third annual process evaluation: 1981–82,' Office of Educational Evaluation, n.d.
11. Cf. Dale Mann, 'A Delphi analysis of the instructionally effective school,' Washington, DC, National Institute of Education, April 1983.
12. 'Mayor's Management Report, Supplement,' 17 September 1980, page 230.
13. Ibid.
14. 'Agreement between the Board of Education of the City School District of the City of New York and the United Federation of Teachers . . .' (September 1980–2), Article 7A2 b, p. 16.
15. Ibid.
16. Ibid.
17. Donald M. Medley, 'Teacher competence and teacher effectiveness: a review of the process-product research,' Washington, DC, American Association of Colleges for Teacher Education, 1977.
18. 'Agreement between the Board of Education of the City School District of the City of New York and the United Federation of Teachers . . .', op. cit.
19. R. Gary Bridge, Charles M. Judd, Peter R. Moock, *The Determinants of Educational Outcomes: The Impact of*

Families, Peers, Teachers, and Schools, Cambridge, Mass., Ballinger, 1979, p. 10.

20 See James C. March and James G. March, 'Almost random careers: the Wisconsin school superintendency, 1940–1972,' *Administrative Science Quarterly*, vol. 22, no. 3, September 1977.

9
Contradictions and constraints in an inner city infant school
Jan Lee

The 1960s were characterised by an increasing concern with the 'crisis' of the inner city and various strategies were developed to deal with the urban 'problems'. In Britain and America, one response to the crisis of the inner city school was in the nature of compensatory educational programmes. In Britain, this took the form of educational priority areas at the primary level of education. The Plowden Report (1967) signalled an upsurge of interest in primary school education and its pedagogies, which combined with the EPA intervention with its emphasis on positive discrimination in the early years of schooling in deprived urban areas to influence the development of the pedagogical forms that were generally claimed as being 'progressive'.[1] However, by the mid-1970s there were signs of a 'backlash' against this trend, evident in the *Black Papers*,[2] Callaghan's Ruskin Speech (1976) and the renewed emphasis on a 'core curriculum', curriculum evaluation, assessment and the 'needs' of industry or latterly unemployment. This reaction at the primary stage of education was fuelled by the Bennett study (1976) and the Tyndale affair (1976). However, in all the debate about progressive methods, little account has been taken of the teachers' position in these developments, or how the progressive ideology had been incorporated into teachers' practice. The original research (Lee, 1980) on which this article is based was primarily, therefore, an examination of teacher ideology and practice in one particular 'progressive', inner city, infant school,[3] in an attempt to discern the way in which the teachers themselves defined the progressive pedagogy, its aims and practice; and further, to discern how they, within the context of the inner city, differentially responded to the progressive 'trend' and the effect which this had on their pedagogical practice. The wider concern of the study was with an attempt to discern at the substantive level and within a socio-historical perspective some indications of the interaction of structural and situational features on teacher ideology within a particular reified form of schooling and to discern the possibilities and the limitations of change within this educational context.

The constraints of space do not allow for a detailed exposition of the research.[4] I have attempted, therefore, to present some of the data from the perspective of its contribution to the notion of 'urban contributions'. Castells (1977) argues that the collective needs (i.e. housing, amenities, health, etc.) increase with the development of society, both for economic reasons and as a result of class struggle in which workers attempt to improve their living standards. This he regards as providing the basis for fundamental contradictions. Firstly, he argues that '. . . public consumption that is to say housing, public amenities, transport etc. thus becomes simultaneously an indispensable element for the functioning of a system and a permanent objective of workers' demands and a deficit sector of the capitalist economy.' This then gives rise to a second fundamental contradiction, 'namely that between the individual way of appropriating higher living standards ("doing your own thing") and the objectively collective way of managing the process'. This inevitably requires massive intervention of the state in 'the treatment and administration of urban problems', (Castells, 1977, p. 43). In this way the 'urban crisis' can be seen as a manifestation of what Castells calls 'a civilisation in crisis'. From this analysis it could be argued that urban contradictions are of crucial importance in a process of social change and that education is one of the possible sites for contradiction and class struggle. Castells is convinced that it is 'urban protest movements' which are the 'real instigators of change and innovation' and not the planning institutions. This necessitates investigation of urban protest movements at two levels. Firstly 'we must look at the extent to which change in the kinds of public demands for amenities are reflected in the urban organisation.' Secondly, 'we should try to understand how new social contradictions emerging in the industrial capitalist societies are articulated with economic and political contradictions embedded in their social structure' (Castells, 1977, p. 45). It is intended, therefore, to attempt to see in what ways the data exemplifies, highlights or modifies this notion of urban contradictions in the context of the inner city school. As Stuart Hall (1977, p. 17) states, 'The point where power and the urban school intersect is also the point where the struggle for power is in the cities, and thus the fate of a class will be decided.'

The need for 'alternative' historical accounts

Historical accounts of nineteenth century education, particularly in relation to infant schools and/or the progressive pedagogy, tend towards unilinear accounts or overarching explanations that seldom acknowledge or accommodate the struggles, opposition or forms of resistance that might have affected the outcomes of educational policy or practice or indeed the very form of schooling. In evaluating the outcomes of nineteenth century and twentieth century educational progress and policies, historians have too often assumed that outcomes were what was intended and only what was intended.

Equally, too often the assumption is made that the accounts of educationists and government policy makers were an accurate reflection of the process of schooling. As in sociology, small-scale research at the level of the school and/or classroom can help to provide a more complex picture of the educational process and the interactions between the 'super structure' and 'base'. Much of the sociology of education has been concerned implicitly or otherwise with the view of education as little more than a tool of social control. Historical accounts and their uncritical use or omission by sociologists aids the unquestioning acceptance of 'commonsense notions' which in itself contributes to the acceptance and perpetuation of the hegemonic order. If the educational system is to be perceived as the site of contradictory pressures or demands in relation to the urban working class then there is a need for historical accounts of working class consciousness, traditions, culture, involvement in the education system, etc. Incidents such as the working class schoolboy strikes of 1889 and 1911 are ill served by historians and by history itself. Lynch (1974) argues that it is this failure to produce evidence which is crucial to both socio-historical inquiry and to traditions of working class consciousness, because not only is the historian limited in what he can find out about such aspects of working class life but the working class tradition is itself enfeebled by its past actions and arguments rarely existing in accessible form.

'Thus when the past comes to be conceptualised and made a meaningful source for present action, working class consciousness is handicapped in opposing versions of history that seek to legitimise contemporary ideological conceptions of social and political realities' (ibid, p. 148). The recent demands of black groups and women's groups for accounts of their 'hidden history' is an apt comment on the ideological function of most historical accounts.

Historians such as B. Simon, H. Silver and R. Johnson have attempted to detail the ways in which working class demands, particularly through the Chartist movement, affected the provision of mass schooling. Small-scale studies, such as those by Simon Frith (1977) render as problematic the present reified form of schooling by outlining the way in which the rational organisation of children in an institution based on teachers and formal curriculum is only one *form* of schooling that was available. His concern is with how the rational schooling developed as a form of socialisation with the problems this created and solved for the relationship between educators and educated. These studies highlight the development of potentially conflicting roles for education, e.g. instructional and moral. Absenteeism and examples of confrontations between working class parents and teachers over the *form* of schooling in the nineteenth century indicates that there were not shared criteria of what schooling was for. It could be argued then that national education was not simply a matter of providing an elementary education to a class that was otherwise intellectually and morally destitute: 'it was rather a matter of providing a particular *form* of education to a class which had (however unsystematically) alternative *forms* of learning available' (ibid., p. 85). It would seem extremely important to an understanding of the reification of education that these struggles and contradictions over the form and control of education are made explicit. In many ways these set the wider parameters and the nature of the constraints within which educational developments or potential for change are contained. Equally, it should be noted that the actual experience of education for some of the working class had in some cases been accompanied by significant economic and social gains. It was these largely skilled labour groups who gained most from education and formed the backbone of the trade union movement and local labour parties. In the twentieth century the latter groups were instrumental in the development of secondary and comprehensive education. But whilst the *content* of education may have been challenged perhaps with some effect for the working class elite, the *control* of education by the ideological apparatus of the state has not been significantly challenged and this too must set limits for the possibilities of change. There must, however, be a constant problem of legitimating that authority at the classroom level at least. It would appear that there are contradictions inherent in the educational process, not only related to relative class positions, but to the realisation of education's twin aims: that of improving the intellectual capacity of the child to serve the 'national need' and that of preventing radical change (the maintenance of social hegemony). Nowhere is this contradiction more evident than in the schooling of the urban working class.[5]

Apparent continuities and changes in the educational process need then to be analysed not just in terms of a one-dimensional effect of state control on education but also of the way in which popular resistance allied to wider social issues may promote or modify policy decisions. More important is the effect, if any, of all this, on the continuing classroom struggle.

The progressive pedagogy and the infant school

The infant school is a largely neglected area of inquiry both historically and sociologically. Historical accounts that do exist tend to regard the development of the infant school as being inevitably linked with the development of a progressive pedagogy. This liberal ideological position apart, describing the course of development, does not explain the mechanics of transition. Explanations as to how and why the progressive pedagogy has come to be, in theory, the official ideology of the infant school involve largely attribution to two factors: (1) the influence of progressive educationists and scientific theory; and (2) a limited view of social changes and state intervention[6] seen largely in terms of their effects on family life and aims of schooling. These linear explanations of the development of an educational process implicitly accept the autonomy in practice of the infant educational system, and the explicit aims of infant education as being to develop the cognitive and affective skills of the child. These and other ideologically consensual views of education are manifest in the ideology of the teachers in this study along with its resultant effects on perception and the failure of the urban working class in the education system. Conflicts about educational methods and the persistent failure of the education system to provide equality of opportunity are seen by some historians as the result of inadequate understanding of the underlying educational theories.[7] The present research attempted to extrapolate the way in which the structural constraints of the classroom and the educational system limited the practical expression of the theoretical commitment.

Small-scale historical studies again highlight 'areas of neglect' that by their neglect also serve to perpetuate a prevailing ideology. Discrete historical studies of individual school records indicate that many schools, even in the days of the supposedly harsh monitorial system, demonstrated child-centred and humane approaches to urban working class children and school affairs and a relatively strong school-community liaison. Silver (1977) claims that there was a record of humanity, efficiency and in many ways innovation that stretched from the 1820s to the twentieth century. Silver notes that although there have been abundant statements about the intentions of the founders of the monitorial system, about its stated methods, etc., there has been almost no information about the detailed operation of monitorial schools, even though the monitorial system dominated English popular education for half a century. Silver argues that this is because studies of the history of educational innovation have used 'definitions of the term which exclude any consideration of the monitorial system, refuse to handle it with more progressive innovations' (ibid., p. 58). He claims therefore that the very definition of terms like 'innovation', 'progressive' and 'reform' that historians have used have ensured certain kinds of neglect and this has certainly influenced the sociologists' perception too.[8] So what was 'typical' about the urban schools of the nineteenth century and how can one discern between statements of intention, motive and policy on the one hand and the classroom reality on the other? Much of what we regard as 'typical' in relation to urban schools in the nineteenth century has been provided from historical data of the educationists and policy makers. As the present research demonstrated the reality of classroom practice does not necessarily reflect the former. R.J.W. Selleck (1972) attempts to provide a more complex analysis of the development of the progressive movement in education. He attempts to understand the interplay of theory, ideology, social climate and educational practice and the ways in which this facilitated or modified the progressives' cause. If the Plowden Report (1967) is seen as 'institutionalising' many of the early progressives' theories it would indicate that many intervening factors have continued to operate against the implementation or achievement of a progressive practice. It could be argued that the predominance of issues related to the progressive pedagogy both between the wars and in the 1960s were related to wider socio-economic and political developments and the need to once more consolidate concessions made to the working class in the cause of the war effort. The need to set the school in its historical context can enable a clearer exposition of the relevant issues of the period to be made, rather than inferring assumed twentieth century educational motives on to nineteenth century educational process and practice, as does Whitbread (1973).

In this way the history of infant education in England might then be seen as characterised by diverse strands of educational thought, and where the progressive pedagogy has historically been evident as one of those strands its predominance in certain periods and the form which it takes, is tempered by the socio-political climate, etc. Equally, a more valid use of L. Howdle's (1968) notions of the 'custodial', 'instructional' and 'developmental' functions of education, may be to use them as a kind of conceptual framework with which to examine the educational process, rather than as an explanation of the dominant tradition as identifying more-or-less discrete stages in the development of infant education. It is possible then to identify how these three traditions have always been present in the educational process and the extent to which they are still present, as exemplified in this research. Also, in attempting to understand why English infant education developed as a discrete stage, its abiding concern with the religious/moral function needs to be assessed and the continuation of this tradition and its possible interrelation with changing conceptions of childhood and the child.[9]

An essential corollary of this analysis of the wider social structure is an examination of the way in which the classroom teacher and the schooling process mediate and accommodate 'new' practices and pedagogies. Selleck (1972) notes the importance of the 'nature of the teaching profession' as a further ideological problem in implementing progressive practices at the classroom level at the beginning of the twentieth century. This 'nature' is defined by the educational culture of the teaching, which, through its ideas, attitudes, values, habits and procedures, provides the teacher with ways of acting and helps to determine her professional identity. It is this 'teacher ideology' that formed a major part of the present research and which clearly exemplifies limitations and constraints as regards the radical potential of the progressive pedagogy in challenging the effectiveness and provision of the present form of schooling for the urban working class. The eventual adoption of the Dalton Plan into classroom practice in 1939 can be seen as an indication of the contradictions felt by the teachers at that time. The Dalton Plan offered a progressive methodology — a set of procedures, ways of organising a classroom and conducting a discussion — but this could be adapted without discarding old methods and expectations. '(The Dalton Plan) offered security at a time when the educational culture of the English primary school was uncertain and unstable' (Selleck, 1972, p. 153). It could be argued that very similar conditions applied in the 1960s. The present research and other recent studies would certainly question the extent to which the Plowden principles were or could be effected in the classroom practice of infant schools. The professionalisation of teaching has entailed conflict provoked by the 'social distance' of teacher from taught. The scant details that do exist of nineteenth century teachers of the urban working class demonstrate the preoccupation with their 'day to day survival and work production' which resulted in the majority being largely concerned with the 'nature of the pupils and the homes they had to deal with, rather than the nature of the society in which they operated' (Grace, 1978, p. 38). These attitudes were clearly demonstrated by the teachers in the present study. It is these continuities that imply resistance and residual attitudes in the educational system that support the notion of the relative autonomy of educational ideology (see Lee, 1980, pp. 60 and 61) and the resultant complex interrelation of this with the requisites of the state and the wider social structure.

The changing relations between the three main social classes in nineteenth century Britain are an important factor in the interpretation of educational changes at that time and since. Bernstein (1975) regards the more recent development in the progressive pedagogy as being related to the development and conflicts between the 'new middle class' and the old. Bowles and Gintis note that a structural weakness in the schooling system was realised in the late nineteenth century, 'the most striking feature of which was the incompatibility between the democratic ideology of the common school and the social reality of the class structure' (Bowles and Gintis, 1976, p. 186). It would seem that these contradictions were significant during the 1960s and 1970s and that the predominance of progressive ideology at that time may have been regarded as a means of attempting to eradicate or merely obscure these class inequalities. That many are now claiming and demonstrating that progressive innovations have been scarcely more than progressive rhetoric does not necessarily entail that this was the *intention* of government or educationalists' policy. The structure of the class system, the occupational structure and the economic constraints need to be considered in relation to the ideology and practice of the classroom teacher in order to try and understand how these factors interact and affect the maintenance of order despite contradictions and forces for change.

A critical analysis of the historical data on the infant school and the progressive movement can be interpreted as demonstrating (albeit implicitly) a resultant number of contradictions within the infant school system and practice. There are contradictions between the developmental and instructional function of infant schooling, contradictions between these and the custodial, moral and preparatory traditions in the development of infant schooling, contradictions between the constraints of the family and the constraints of the occupational system, contradictions in being seen as a discrete stage in the educational process and yet accorded low status and priority and therefore vulnerable to the demands of the junior and secondary stages, contradictions between theory and practice, contradictions between the motives of the 'providers' and the needs of the 'provided', etc. It is hoped that this limited attempt to inquire into teacher ideology and practice will demonstrate some aspects of the contradictions that would appear from this socio-historical analysis to be inherent in the particular structure and form of infant education that has developed and in its functions *vis-à-vis* the urban working class.

Canal Street School

The infant school in which the research was conducted was a purpose built, open-plan design building set in the midst of local borough and formerly GLC controlled council estates in an inner city area of southeast London. The majority of the accommodation is in the form of flats some of which were built in the 1960s and are therefore typified by the 'walkways' and 'green areas' of that era. The area is noted locally for conflict and violence.[10] The catchment area of the school is therefore uniformly working class and the existence of a relatively large black community in the area is perhaps exemplified in that Martin Webster saw fit to stand as the National Front candidate in a recent parliamentary by-election.

The school was characterised by relatively explicit conflict over pedagogy and practice. The head and several, mainly younger, members of staff were committed to a progressive ideology; the deputy head and other generally older members of staff were opposed to this and could be regarded as more traditional in their outlook.[11] However, despite this internal conflict, it is possible to demonstrate the way in which in general teacher ideology and pedagogical strategies (developed in response to the inherent contradictions in the education system) accommodated the urban contradictions manifest in the schooling of the working class. Arguably, the most important aspects of teacher ideology in relation to urban contradictions are those of class and race. The interaction of teacher ideology and the reality of urban contradictions in the schooling process are partially resolved by pedagogical strategies such as the 'cult of the individual', the autonomy of infant education, the importance of play and the nature of childhood, etc. It is at this level that the progressive ideology could be seen to have a radical potential but that the conflict of situational and structural constraints distorted these realisations.

Class and politics

The teachers' views on class were in part attributable to their general socio-political views, which were remarkable by their apparent lacunae, rather than any expressed similarities. It would seem from the teachers' response that they either regarded the nature of society as having universal properties that were 'commonsense' to all and therefore needed no explanation; or that the 'realm of the political' was far removed from the educational sphere and almost by definition superior but separate. Repeatedly, the educationist context and/or their own social class background appeared to be the source and the limit of the teachers' views. Consequently, no theory of the organisation, functioning or general nature of society was proffered. Instead, specific problems such as 'vandalism', 'greed', 'housing' and 'poor education' were identified as 'problems' of society; but they are in reality the teachers' perception of their experiences working in a working class inner city school. There was no attempt to extend or generalise their understanding of the problem. For example, one teacher (a 'progressive') often expressed considerable sympathy for the 'lot' of the parents. When asked why she thought that areas such as that surrounding the school existed, she replied:

> It's the housing .... If his job's dreadful or he's not getting paid a lot etc. There are so many factors but bad housing is one helluva factor for our kids. No facilities. A dead life, vacuum. There are parents on this estate who don't leave it. They shop here, live here, go to the launderette here, their children go to school here.

An expication of the problems, but no explanation as to why they exist. So whilst there were differences between the traditional and progressive teachers as to the identification of the 'problems' and their proposed solutions, they were all based on 'apolitical' or 'neutral' assumptions about society. Closer questioning about the home lives and occupations of the children's families revealed scant understanding of those factors in relation to the occupational and economic organisation of society. For example:

> *I*: 'Do you know what work the parents do from this area?'
> *Head*: 'It varies. . . . The sort of jobs the fathers do are very mixed really. We have got a couple of taxi drivers; at one stage we seemed to have quite a lot of lorry drivers — that seems to be less now. Bus conductors, railway workers. *Very, very mixed. Difficult to generalise about that, I think.*' [My emphasis]

Whilst the actual jobs that the parents do may be 'mixed', the obvious generalisation is that the majority are unskilled, manual jobs. Also, one could speculate that there is a correlation between the movement off the estate of the 'better' or 'better off' families that the teachers so frequently referred to as being indicated by the decrease in lorry drivers. The changing composition on the estate as regards race could also be deduced from this, since some occupations, such as taxi driving and lorry driving are noticeable by their 'whiteness', whereas black people have historically been employed in public transport and other lower-paid occupations.

Acknowledgment of inequality in society by the progressive teachers, combined with an acceptance of the 'status quo', is resolved through the cult of the individual. This seemed to be a necessary 'coping' strategy evolved partly in order to resolve conflicts within the progressive pedagogy both theoretically and at the substantive level. Evidence of teachers being at the interface of the reality of working class existence and a capitalist society whose organisation necessitates the continuity of the hierarchical structure was often implicit in the teachers' statements. For example the head sees the teachers' job as being:

> much more to do with the individual people and individual families and trying to help support them as best they can, and a large part of that, of course, is helping them to understand and cope with the

sort of system they are facing. And it seems to me that *politics are about generalisations and generalisations do not apply.* [My emphasis]

This statement implicitly contains political assumptions about that system. This conservatism further ensures that the response to the system is 'adjustment' by the parents rather than 'adjustment' of the system. Furthermore, the classless view of society that the teachers purportedly hold militates against notions of social conflict and the root causes of the problems are therefore explained variously in terms of the 'old' notions of moral depravity (by the traditional teachers) or the more liberal notions of 'cultural deprivation' (the progressive teachers).

Another striking similarity in the teachers' attitudes in relation to their world views is their professed 'classless' view of society. The teachers were unanimous in their denial of the existence or the value of notions of class, despite frequently using such terms during the interviews. Most had refused or omitted to answer the question on class in the questionnaire and there had been heated discussion in the staff room as to the point of such a question. Most teachers emphasised that their criterion for evaluation was based on an assessment of the individual. 'People work. There are just different people and their parents are people with different problems.' However, all the teachers did in fact utilise class notions and concepts both explicitly and implicitly. Two areas presented themselves as of particular importance: (i) The distinction, albeit implicit, that is made between the 'deserving' and 'non-deserving' poor or the 'respectable' and 'rough' working class; and (ii) the class values that are implicit in the teachers' ideas about how they would like the children prepared for school, and a latent consciousness as to the attitudes that are necessary for success or failure in the educational system.

Firstly, the distinction between the 'deserving' and the 'feckless' poor was implied by all the teachers, despite crucial differences that existed between the traditional and progressive teachers on other issues related to the children and their families. Teacher C's (traditional) reference to her own background and in particular her mother's experience illustrates how she regards society as not rewarding the 'deserving' poor: 'She [her mother] made sure that four children had a decent education and went without herself in lots of different ways and now she's on the breadline. That, to me, is all wrong.' Her values appear to have been consciously influenced to a very large extent by her socialisation in the home and family. 'But my standards come from my home and not my school,' she says, and it is apparent that she regards these standards as 'normal' and something that all children should be taught. Her views are perhaps most clearly expressed in the following quotation:

> I see in this school a lot of problem families where the parents never ask for anything and have that determination to hold themselves and keep above water and do the best they can even if it is in poor circumstances. But there are others who think 'why' should I bother?' Able-bodied men and women who don't go to work and just sit and expect to be provided for.

Teacher B (traditional) also held the view that people were depending too much on the state, in particular the Welfare State. She stated, sarcastically, that schools could no longer do without involvement in social services, 'not the way things are now. Parents expect it. They come in and ask us for it.' She felt that the response of the schools to the prospect of vast unemployment in the future should be 'a course in make do and mend' because these parents just sit back and wait for somebody to put it into their laps. *They* can do it; *they* can look after my kids; *they* can give me money; *they* can buy shoes. Nobody has ever said to them, 'Have you tried to do anything yourself?'

Despite the teachers' acknowledgment of the increasing number of single parent families and unemployed people on the estate, they all laid the blame on mismanagement. Teacher A (progressive) epitomises this view: 'I've seen parents give them [their children] 10p to shut up and let them stuff themselves with sweets instead of saving that 10p, even if you're poor, to cook them an egg. It's a strange mentality.' There was ample evidence to suggest a continuity with the Victorian morality of 'self-help', etc. However, the teachers do not consciously see this as a moral or socialising role of the school. Equally, they are unaware of the class bias of the notion of 'bad management'. A person is only considered a bad manager if their income is so low that the 'bad management' requires them to seek support of some kind. The existence of material poverty amongst the families is denied: 'It's not that they haven't enough money coming in, it's just that they can't manage. They have their priorities wrong: mum and dad have their cigarettes and beer, etc., to the cost of the children's clothing.' The teachers identified more with the 'respectable' and 'deserving' parents and this was implied in their constant references to the 'exodus' from the estate of the 'better' families. One of the characterisations of the 'poorer' families is that they have 'a history of being moved around'.

The implicit class bias in the teachers' views is particularly apparent in their response to questions about how parents do and should prepare their children for school. All the teachers stressed the importance of parental involvement with the children and the need for books, etc., in the home, for talking to the children, taking them out, and doing things with them (like reading stories to them and making things together). They were concerned about the children not knowing nursery rhymes and that they 'haven't played with sand, water, etc., made dough, pastry or helped mum cooking.' The teachers felt that television played too great a role in their children's lives. The head felt that many parents did not want to be bothered with their children after school and so one reaction is that 'they are told to sit quietly and watch television.'

These views of what teachers see the children as lacking when they come to school appeared to influence greatly their views about the children's homes as well: this despite the fact that most of the teachers seldom visited (and some had *never* visited) the children's homes.[12] Moreover, they constantly emphasised their feeling of social distance from the environment. 'I would *hate* to have young children and live here' (Teacher C). 'I wouldn't live here, not in a million years' (Teacher D). Teacher B felt that the home life of the children was 'not a very nice one; television and rough play. Unsupervised.' Others felt that there were no 'shared family activities' or that it was 'pretty dull outside of school'. Although it was acknowledged that some children had plenty of toys at home (because some parents had queried why the children needed to play with toys at school!) it was argued that the children did not know how to *play* with the toys: 'that's why we have toys in school. It's to teach them how to play.' The latter implies a culturally bound notion of what is to be considered 'play'. The same applies to the progressive teachers' notion of independence. Many of these parents were working and the children were often 'left to their own devices' or were 'latch-key' children. Consequently many appeared to the researcher to be independent, capable, even precocious. The progressive teachers and the head in particular, felt that the children should be encouraged to be as independent as possible before coming to school. That they did not appear to acknowledge these characteristics among the working class poor suggests that their definition of 'independent' was class-culturally bound. For example, the head described what he regarded as 'being encouraged to take on independence'. 'As many opportunities being made of making decisions for themselves. Something quite small, about what colour socks they are going to wear that day', whereas on other occasions he talked about the children who were allocated to the Nurture Group, as requiring a highly directive approach 'because by and large we feel they are the children who are not yet at the stage where they can cope with the amount of choice and the amount of autonomy which is expected from the rest of the school.' It could be argued that these children were perhaps regarded as 'behavioural problems' because they exercised too *much* choice and autonomy, or a different manifestation of choice, etc. In doing so they challenged the boundaries of choice and autonomy that are implicit in any formal situation.

The progressive teachers then would appear to have limited consciousness about the working class and their failure in the educational system. They regard the cause of variations in educational achievement as due to environmental features or family background, but having denied the existence of wider structural features (and implicitly heredity) they inevitably resolve the contradictions through the concept of 'individualism'. This limited consciousness would appear to be fuelled further by three other aspects of teacher ideology: (i) the autonomy of education; (ii) the status of infant teachers; and (iii) teacher professionalism.

Bernstein (1975), in discussing the 'invisible' pedagogy, argues that 'the infant school teacher will not necessarily have high status, as the competences she is transmitting are, in principle, possible also for the mother.' This status is compounded by the fact that the vast majority of infant teachers are women, and are seen to be perpetuating their roles as wives and mothers: a status or class position they hold in common with the mothers of the children. However, as Weber claims, 'class distinctions are linked in the most varied ways with status distinctions' (1970, p. 395). It would be argued here, contrary to R. King (1978), that the status distinctions of the teachers do not cut across the class distinctions but are part of the teachers' consciousness in their claim for professional status.[13] It could be argued, then, that it is precisely because infant teachers are not far removed from the class position of their clients that they have emphasised their professional status particularly in terms of the division between mental and manual labour and their distance from the parents and their environment, etc. Teacher A saw professionalism as 'a safety-guard . . . we're fed up with being the underdogs — particularly infant teachers.' Teacher C states, 'I say that we have to have had a "calling"; a special commitment that you wouldn't (I assume) if you were a dustman.' Other statements demonstrate continuation with the 'missionary' ideology of the nineteenth century. It would be claimed then that the teachers are falsely conscious as regards the concept of class and moreover that their class interests are pursued under cover of the ideology of professionalism. This last point is expressed lucidly by Finn, Grant and Johnson (1977, p. 167):

> The ideology of professionalism has been used by the teaching organisations to either defend their middle class status, or to assimilate themselves into that class. Trapped between the developing power of monopoly capital and the advance of the working class, professionalism can be understood as a petit-bourgeois strategy for advancing and defending a relatively privileged position.

Race and the inner city

Racism, racial conflict and questions of racial equality and a multiracial society are issues that have received much public attention since the 1960s. The inner city, in particular, is characterised by a concentration of people from different racial/ethnic origins. Eighty per cent of the black population live in urban areas with half that number in Britain's ten largest cities.[14] The 'problems' of the inner city, such as bad housing/shortage of housing, unemployment, poor amenities, etc., have been diagnosed by some as the 'cause' of this racial conflict. The 'problem' of race is unmistakably manifest in the inner city, whatever the causes. Racial conflict was experienced in the first 'race riot' in 1958 (Notting Hill) but the interrelation of racial and inner city conflict was patently manifest in the riots of 1980 (Bristol) and 1981. There is a continuing confrontation with the National Front and the police.

Canal Street School reflects the multiracial context of most working class, inner city schools. However, unless the issue of race had been specifically raised by the interviewer, this fact would not have been gleaned from any of the explicit statements of the teachers, although some of the implications of their statements suggested racial bias. Neither was the multiracial context of the school apparent in the displays or the work of the children and teachers. The responses of the teachers to the question of racial issues at all levels and those of class and the inner city expressed the centrality of certain principles to the teachers' ideologies.

Firstly, the school is conceived of as kind of 'neutral' space that is separate from the wider society, so society is not seen to impinge to any great extent on the schools, and the schools are expected to have little effect on society. In many respects the teachers feel that the schools can and should hermetically seal off the children from the wider society. Teacher A states, 'I recognise that there is racism in this country. There isn't in this school I would have thought. There is on the estate.' Furthermore, their own views tend either to be derived from this narrow educationist context or to be influenced by it to a large extent. This has the effect of limiting their consciousness as regards both society and education. For example:

> *I*: 'Do black people have as much opportunity to move out of the area?'
> *Teacher C*: 'No, I don't think they do.'
> *I*: 'Why is this – is it economic or attitudes or . . .?'
> *Teacher C*: (pause) 'I don't know. Quite often the families themselves are bigger. They tend to have more children than working class whites, therefore it makes it more difficult.'

An important contradiction presents itself here since the teachers operate according to quite clearly defined views on the kinds of attitudes and behaviour that children should display in school and this seriously affects the teacher's typification of the child and arguably their chance of success in the educational system. Then to ignore or regard as irrelevant the varying class/cultural/racial differences in values and attitudes that will affect not least the child's self-identity, confidence, understanding of the power relationship between teacher and taught, etc., will tend to ensure that certain children's educational potential is never fully realised. (This will be looked at in more detail later.)

Secondly, there is the role in teacher ideology of the nature of the infant school as a discrete form of schooling and the implications for such concepts as 'childhood'. The teachers frequently referred to

Contradictions and constraints in an inner city infant school / 251

differences that they perceived of as emanating from working with infant age children. The head was conscious that as regards racial conflict, this was an issue that was forced upon the secondary schools, so that teachers could not ignore it, as they could at the infant stage. This study identified defining characteristics of infant education loosely based on psychological theories pertaining to child development, individualism, play as learning and childhood innocence, etc. Childhood innocence is particularly important in allowing the teachers to disregard any racist remarks/behaviour in school.[15] Equally, by regarding the educationist context as 'separate' from society coupled with this belief in the universal nature of childhood innocence, the teachers are able to acknowledge the varying performances/behaviour of the children whilst ignoring its origins.

Thirdly, the 'cult of the individual' plays a crucial role in all these processes. The teachers' apparent concern with individual development and education is seen as a strategy which cuts across the effects of the wider society. Many of the teachers indicated that they had never considered seriously the apparent failure or underachievement of working class or black children in the educational system. As Teacher C stated, 'I don't really think about it — they're children, so I probably don't associate them with being black or working class: they're just children and the area's quite rough.' The head did acknowledge the failure of working class and black children in the education system but his explanation was that it was due to 'wrong expectations; particularly the expectation that the most important thing for a working class child is to be able to read.' He felt that other things were more important: 'things to do with thinking for themselves, making decisions for themselves, exercising autonomy'. But, as already indicated, these latter concepts are utilised in a culturally specific way. The head's individualistic philosophy is evident in the following quotation: 'If we defined the principle on which we acted, [it] would be to say that we do not regard the children or treat the children differently from each other — we treat them as individuals.'

The apparently unconscious operation of concepts that are based on class/moral/political assumptions in the teachers' ideologies meant that the teachers did not feel intervention in the form of positive discrimination or confrontation was necessary in relation to the issue of race or class. The head felt that the solution *vis-à-vis* schooling was fairly simple: 'I mean, I suspect probably a lot of things that you can do are very simple things: like ensuring that pictures you have on display have black faces instead of white ones.' The emphasis on individualism militated against the teachers perceiving the pupils as belonging to any social category, such as class, race or locality. It also cuts across the communality and consociality of sectors of the working class and black groups. Historically, the working class and the black movement have resisted and attempted to effect their demands through forms of social solidarity. In particular, the present form of schooling ensures that it is the working class or black child who displays the correct individualistic responses that will succeed in the system, but forfeits community solidarity.

The progressive pedagogy

The rise of the progressive ideology to the forefront of educational thinking in the 1960s should be seen in its historical context. It is apparent that the industrial and technological expansion along with other socio-economic factors (see Lee, 1980 pp. 45–51) would have been influential in this process. Equally, the failure of the educational system *vis-à-vis* the working class was a situation that, as in the nineteenth century, the organised elite of the working class through the labour and trade union movement was demanding should be remedied through greater equality of opportunity. The progressive ideology, with its stress on the social and environmental background of the children, demands for greater parental involvement, and emphasis on the developmental approach to learning, could be seen as having the potential to satisfy these demands. At the level of classroom practice it could be seen to provide alternative methods of management and organisation that might resolve both increasing conflict between teachers and taught and economic problems of providing for a bulging inner city population resulting in overcrowded schools and classes. However, it would be argued that the *form* that the progressive pedagogy took in the majority of cases was shaped by situational and structural constraints and contradictions that have been identified as being inherent in the present-day schooling system.

Parental conflict and the observed differences between doctrine and outcome must suffice as examples. It was apparent from this study that there had been considerable conflict between the school and the parents over the 'new methods' of the school. The head was conscious that the parents' criticism was not so *direct* any more, but at one stage 'rarely a week passed without me interviewing a parent who was worried about their child's progress, or critical of what the school was doing.' He suspected that this may be because 'they've [parents] given up and get the feeling there is no point going back because they [teachers] will not do anything anyway and at least they [the children] are going on to the junior school where they teach them properly.' He was aware that the issues over which there was the greatest conflict were the standard of education attained (in the formal sense of the three Rs) and the discipline. It was evident that as rolls had fallen in the surrounding schools, the parents had 'voted with their feet' and taken the children to these schools. This had resulted in a drastic reduction in the school roll over the past five years, but an increase in the 'turnover' of children and with an increasing number of difficult or 'problem' children. Interestingly, one of the progressive teachers ascribed this conflict to 'class' differences that are consistently denied elsewhere. Despite showing considerable concern over the school's methods, etc., the teachers regard the majority of parents as being apathetic as regards their children's education. This is attributed to both the 'class barrier' and the preoccupation with 'home' problems. It would seem, however, that the progressive teachers only accepted parental interest if it could be seen to support the teacher and her practice. The progressive teachers' convinced resistance to parental pressure is epitomised in the statement: 'We are the way we are and if you want your children to come, thank you very much, but if you don't then please don't come.' This entrenched stand versus parental opinion was evident in Sharp and Green's study (1975) where it had led to a virtual breakdown in communication between the parents and the school at one point. It was also evident in the reaction of the Tyndale teachers. Consequently, the parents' eventual 'non-involvement' is interpreted as 'non-interest' as Teacher A explained: 'We invited them in *any* time they wanted to talk about whatever was worrying them; we very rarely got a good turn out. They didn't *want* to find out, and when they did they came back with exactly the same questions. They just didn't understand, *it was beyond them*' (My emphasis). It would seem that the teachers ignored the power relationships of a hierarchical society whilst at the same time implicitly acting upon them. The head's final justification for ignoring the parents' opposition was, 'But ultimately teachers are experts and they must decide what is best for the child . . . .' This claim would appear to be based on implicit moral values and 'professionalism' which becomes a kind of ideological justification for this perception of the power relationship between teachers and parents. As Karier (1974) argues: 'While repeatedly professing to serve the interests of the student and humanity, he [the teacher] more often served the interests of collective power.' The traditional teachers also experience parental pressure but their opposition seemed to be based on parents encroaching on what they regarded as their prerogative as teachers. Again, issues of professional ideology and the primacy of the educationist context are predominant.

Observed differences between 'doctrine and commitment'

A major concern of the study was an attempt to ascertain how the teachers themselves perceived and defined the progressive pedagogy in both philosophical and practical terms. This was then compared with class observation in order to try and identify ways in which 'intention' and 'outcome' might differ. The three main areas in which this could be identified were (i) in relation to 'outcome' as regards the three Rs or formal skills; (ii) aspects of the teacher relationship related to 'management'; and (iii) aspects of the teacher relationship related to assessment or typification of the children. The basic conflict *within* the school in relation to pedagogical practice was most acute over three issues: (i) the teaching of the basic skills or the three Rs which crudely polarised around the primacy of 'methods' or 'results'; (ii) the class organisation raised the conflict over directive or non-directive teaching; and (iii) discipline — basically whether it should be teacher-controlled or self-controlled. These conflicts were endemic to differences at a more general level of pedagogical belief or philosophy. These were manifest in (i) the nature of the teacher/child relationship; (ii) the nature of the learning process; and (iii) the aims of educational practice. It was in no way the intention of this study to compare the 'effectiveness' of these apparently differing methods, but to try and discern in what way the intention of the progressive pedagogy differed from its outcomes and in doing so to identify the way in which the institutional structure of education, aspects of teacher ideology, contradictions within the schooling process and the urban contradiction might be effective in promoting and/or perpetuating these discrepancies and dichotomies.

The progressive teachers expressed concern about the primacy or overemphasis on literacy skills. Again, it is the emphasis on methods rather than results, the emphasis being on interest and the use that the child saw in the skill, rather than it being an end in itself. From the teachers' expressed statements about their practice it would seem that, firstly, a great deal of care would have to be taken in providing stimulation and encouragement of interest in books, etc. Secondly, that teachers would have to interact very closely with the children to discern what the child was understanding or how his understanding could be expressed through any of the literacy skills. Thirdly, that the teachers would have to be available to observe the actions and conversations of children in order to extend their understanding or to enable them to realise it through formal skills. The teachers would then be more concerned to encourage and guide the children's learning based on the children's own knowledge or perceptions. Since the teachers were also attempting not to be too directive then their two crucial inputs must be (i) wide and stimulating provisioning, and (ii) constant and extended teacher observation and appropriate intervention. It is perhaps not surprising that the teachers' observed educational practice did not adhere to this ideal in many respects. In general, however, the progressive teachers were consistent in their attempt not to be too directive with the children. The kind and standard of the provisioning of resources did not appear adequate to stimulate the children to the extent required for the effective pursuance of the teachers' expressed methods. In particular, there was little evidence of any resources that would provide specific mathematical experiences. The 'book-corner' which was the cornerstone of the teachers' approach to reading was not attractively arranged or displayed. The children were not seen to make much use of the resources that were set up in the class areas, and neither they, nor the displays, were changed very frequently. The kind and amount of interaction between the teachers and children was constrained by the individual attention that is so crucial to the teachers' pedagogical belief and ideology. It did seem, however, that despite their assertions to the contrary, the progressive teachers are mainly involved in activities that they regard as relevant to the learning of basic concepts involved in the literacy skills. Moreover, it seems that they are limited to the extent to which they can be child-initiated or integrated with other activities because of the teachers' continuous involvement with individual children. The latter could conceivably have functioned effectively if the other children were totally involved in what the teacher regarded as 'useful' activities or if one of the other adults/ teachers had made themselves available to observe or interact with these self-directed groups. On the contrary, on very many occasions, relatively large numbers of children could be observed 'drifting' from one thing to another, seldom completing any activity, not always knowing how to use equipment or resources, and with many interesting conversations and expressed interest in books etc. going unnoticed. It is perhaps possible to perceive the strong emphasis by the head and the progressive teachers on the need for the children to be able to be independent, etc. Again, this is an instance of where the inadequacies of a pedagogy are interpreted as inadequacies in the children. It was also apparent that for the majority of children, the teachers failed to use the child's own knowledge and perceptions. This was particularly the case with the black children and the 'poor' working class. It could be argued that this is due, in part, to the notion of 'child-centredness' that the teachers operate. This imputes great significance and initiative to the child, but does not acknowledge the inherent inequality of the relationship between the teacher and child in the institutional form of schooling. They waited for the children to reveal what they knew, but without making the children aware that they might already have what the teacher regarded as 'useful knowledge'. Moreover the teachers *did* appear to have implicit notions of what they expected the child to reveal and this too had effects *vis-à-vis* the typification of the child. It is apparent how integral to this approach to learning is the teachers' commitment to a particular form of class organisation and management. It could be argued that it is the primacy of the teachers' adherence to certain methods of organisation and management that contradicts, conflicts and would render questionable the effectiveness of some of their approaches to learning, given the particular form of rational schooling and the contradictory role of the education system in a hierarchical society.

The teachers' assessments of the children would certainly lend weight to the impression that certain 'social' or 'affective' characteristics of the children were the effective basis of their typification.[16] The 'able' child is therefore regarded as 'very self-directive. Tries anything new. Very independent. Concentration span very long. Creative work lively and imaginative.' The least able are described thus: 'wanders from one thing to another, not appearing to get anything concrete from any experience. Concentration span *very short* — very vague.' Whilst it is apparent that these former attitudes are obviously what the progressive teacher wants to develop and regards as aspects of the 'good learner', it is not apparent in what way she is actually developing these attitudes, but moreover their potential development is denied some children. The distinguishing criterion would appear to be certain 'personality' or 'social' characteristics. Again, it would be suggested that the particular notion of child-centredness upon which the teachers operate encourages the belief that they are providing an environment in which all children have the potential to develop as 'good learners' but which in fact accords differential responses to certain mainly social characteristics.

It would seem that the progressive teachers in this study had, in their early experiments with various kinds of organisation, etc. (see Lee, 1980, pp. 259–265), realised that there was some conflict between the developmental approach they were aiming at and the kind of organisation that produced high attainment in the formal skills for certain children. Unlike Sharp and Green's teachers, however, they had consciously decided to emphasise the developmental approach which had resulted in their emphasis on means rather than ends. They consequently defined ends somewhat differently to traditional teachers, whilst still emphasising the need for children to acquire formal literacy skills. It could be argued that the discrepancy between their intention and outcomes is related to their failure to take into account sufficiently the hierarchical structure of society and the social structure of the classroom situation. Their emphasis on non-direction and on individualised learning process entailed considerable problems over management and order which further undermined the effectiveness of their methods as regards both developmental and formal skills. Their typification of the children rejected in many ways a rationalisation of this process. One unintended consequence of this process would seem to be the relative autonomy that many of the working class children gained from this. This resulted in what Lacey (1979) calls 'polarisation', becoming more evident in the classroom, since many of the working class children took the implicit structure of the progressive classroom at face value. The teachers remarked on the children's obsession with this 'primary concern with their peer group'. Peer group interaction is seen as both a consequence of, and a problem for, these progressive teachers when 'one of the problems in a school like this, is the absence of "normative models". We seem to have so few natural straightforward children that there are very few models for the children to use' (Head). They were critical of the children being so obsessed with '. . . personalities and people and other children.' This attitude denies the social and cultural basis of these children and also implies some notion of an 'ideal pupil' that the teachers are wanting the children to develop into.

Finally, it could perhaps be argued from the evidence of the research that some of the characteristics of the 'invisible' pedagogy that Bernstein (1975) outlines might be the result of an 'internal logic' within a particular commitment to a certain form of the progressive pedagogy operating within certain social and institutional parameters. In particular this could be seen to relate to the following characteristics outlined by Bernstein: 'where the child *apparently* regulates his own movements and social relationships'; 'where there is reduced emphasis upon the transmission and acquisition of specific skills' and 'where the criteria for evaluating the pedagogy are multiple and diffuse and not easily measured' (Bernstein, 1975, p. 116). Moreover, the amount and extent of the teachers' commitment to the other three characteristics outlined by Bernstein (i.e. 'where the control of the teacher over the child is implicit rather than explicit'; 'where ideally the teacher arranges the context which the child is expected to re-arrange and explore'; 'where within this arranged context the child *apparently* has wide powers over what he selects, over how he structures and over the time-scale of his activities' (ibid.)) may vary and differential emphasis on and between these three variables may produce different pedagogical forms. This relative autonomy of the teacher will largely depend on the 'ethos' of the school and in turn the relative autonomy of the school will be related to wider socio-historical influences.

The interrelation between ideology and practice

There was considerable similarity in the general views of *all* the teachers in the study in relation to society, class, race, etc. For the traditional teachers, these perspectives were not challenged by their experiences in the educationist context, rather they reinforced general attributes and attitudes, etc., which had been uncritically derived from their home/ family background and which had not been challenged either by their own schooling or teacher training.[17] The progressive teachers had experienced similar educational and professional backgrounds but there was partial 'penetration' as regards pedagogical practice. This entailed that the teachers questioned their own schooling/socialisation/training, to some extent and with varying emphases. It could be suggested that this partial penetration was a factor of both general social/moral changes, and a feature of personal experience in this context. This was reinforced by the relative autonomy and influence of the infant school at this historical conjuncture and which this particular head had exploited.

The progressive teachers therefore took up some of the challenges and contradictions of schooling in the inner city context. However, their 'critical consciousness' appeared to be limited to the educationist context and consequently the *direction* of the changes both in practice and philosophy was largely determined by their wider social and educational perspective. So the educationist context contains contradictory elements that enable, as well as limit, the possibility of change. D. Hargreaves (1980, p. 126) argues that, 'At the theoretical level the teachers' culture is a significant but inadequately formulated "intervening variable" between the macro and micro levels of sociological analysis.' Ideological notions of 'professionalism' and the dichotomy between theory and practice provide some justification for both the traditional and progressive teachers' perception of contradictions in the schooling process. The research demonstrated that the progressive teachers often expressed consciousness of relatively radical perspectives *vis-à-vis* the wider society but that these were never systematically developed or integrated. It could be argued that this is a factor of the professed 'apolitical' stance of teachers and which is further a characteristic of western 'democracy' where conservatism parades as the 'rationale' and 'norm' and where the ends of capitalism are served by the ideological and hegemonic notion of 'political neutrality'.

It can be seen then, that socio-political features of society can constrain and limit the teachers' perspectives, even when the actual classroom experience throws up challenges to this perspective. Thus, the progressive teachers, when faced with the manifestation of the conflict over the developmental/integrative function of education, initially took up the challenge (see Lee, 1980). Attempts at team teaching, for instance, facilitated teacher consciousness and critical assessment of their aims, etc. The organisational problems of team teaching meant that the teachers were more directly confronted with the problems of fulfilling the integrative function, at a time when the developmental function of education was receiving greater emphasis and 'made sense' at the level of classroom experience in the urban context. The 'management' crisis that team teaching also posed, being introduced at a time of large classes (a bureaucratic/economic response to the 'problem') posed such problems for the teachers in relation to their 'occupational interest', etc., that they had to attempt to resolve some of these issues. The historical and particular context of Canal Street School appears to have influenced the teachers into resolving the 'management' crisis by opting totally for the developmental function of education. This, in turn, had serious implications and consequences as regards the teachers' 'management' function and the acquisition of formal skills on the part of the children. These contradictions are likely to continue with similar consequences, if changes, choices, conflicts, etc. are contained within the institutional framework in which they originated.

The teachers' responses at the level of classroom practice would, therefore, seem to be a complex of active responses interacting with various 'high level' beliefs and responses, etc. The 'cult of the individual' has been seen to resolve several dilemmas for the progressive teacher. Their partial but increased awareness and sympathy towards the social background factors of the parents and pupils could have developed into a radical and critical consciousness. However, the apolitical and classless aspects of their ideological perspective limited the response to one that would enable both ideological perspectives to exist. Individualism resolved this and also facilitated the developmental and child-centred pedagogical beliefs. However, concomitantly it also increased the problem over the 'management' and integrative functions of schooling and could be seen to highlight contradictions in both the social relations *of* learning and *in* learning. The teachers appeared not to challenge the concepts of professionalism and 'autonomy' of education, etc. This combined with wider socialising influences would appear to have been partially resolved by their perception of the 'problems' as emanating from the social deprivation of the children. This social pathology perspective facilitates the emphasis on individual developmentalism whilst in some part it also provides a rationalisation of low academic standards and the typification of the children. At a general level this can be seen as a consequence of what Holly (1976, p. 7) terms 'the contradiction of a unitary social organisation of learning within a class-divided society'.

Conclusion: facing the contradictions — education and social change

It has been suggested that the particular progressive style and philosophy exemplified in this study could create greater opportunity for pupil opposition but that the teachers tended to define this in psychologically deviant terms. These particular progressive teachers appear to have initially confronted and attempted to resolve some of the most blatant contradictions within the schooling process as regards working class children. Their failure or inability to confront the wider educational and social issues has resulted in pedagogical practice where, as Holly asserts, 'The social *relationships* in school are friendly and informal but the social *relations* of learning remain pre-socialist' (ibid., p. 7). It could be argued that many of the characteristics of the progressive pedagogy could have a radical potential. For example allowing greater autonomy and promoting individual development *could* mean that the working class and black child's culture and identity are acknowledged in a way that allows for both high attainment and/or a challenge to the present form of schooling and greater consciousness as to the role of education in society. However, it would seem from this study that since the social relations of learning are not challenged the contradictions of the present process have been resolved in a way that results in much of the progressive pedagogy becoming an *implicit* rather than explicit form of social control. This is demonstrated in particular by two of the issues over which there was conflict *within* the school, i.e. discipline and didactic or exploratory methods. For example, whilst the traditional teachers used explicit modes of control, the progressive teachers preferred not to impose rules, etc. but to try and understand the 'emotional' or 'personal' problems of the child. However, it is apparent that the same ends are being pursued, i.e. the control of certain kinds of behaviour; and the power relationship remains the same.[18] Furthermore, the effects on behaviour of a class as a relatively artificial form of social grouping are ignored, and in the case of the progressive teachers is resolved through the philosophy of individualism and social pathology. The traditional teachers regarded disruptive behaviour more frequently as being the results of 'having no standards imposed at home'. In both cases, the underlying moral/socialisation assumptions are the same in that certain kinds of behaviour are perceived as incongruent with cognitive ability.

The conflict between the teachers over primacy of 'methods' or 'results' also suggests a false dichotomy as a result of conservative, educationist responses to some of the inherent contradictions in the present schooling process. The traditional teachers regard the failure of certain groups of children as being largely attributable to heredity and to some extent environment (parental expectations/attitudes etc.). The progressive teachers mainly see the root causes as being environmental. In both cases there are implicit assumptions about the kinds of attitudes, behaviour, language, knowledge, etc. that the children need to portray before their potential is realised through the formal schooling system. It could be argued that if the teachers were to take on seriously as a basic premise that *all* children have the potential to achieve academically and were to develop strategies/methods/practice that endeavoured to maximise this potential, then different institutional and structural constraints could be perceived. However, it would seem that a critical and political consciousness is necessary to both ensure the nature of the contradictions is realised and that the fundamental contradiction of the schooling of the working class in a rigid hierarchical social system is confronted not least in the educationist context. The theoretical separation of politics and education merely serves to perpetuate ideological consensus. The contradictions of the schooling process need to be confronted in a radical way through the fusion of education and politics in praxis.

The HMI report on the educational provision in the Toxteth area was at pains to point out the effect of social and economic conditions on the work of the schools. They are not optimistic:

None of the social or economic conditions appears to have
improved and some may well be deteriorating. On recent visits
HMI have the impression that tensions in Toxteth remain
high and the comments made by teachers and others have confirmed
this. (HMI, 1982, p. 14)

The effects of social and economic conditions on schools appears to be interpreted *in practice* as meaning that there is a direct causal relationship between environmental factors and cognitive ability; little account is taken of the way in which the form of schooling exacerbates or even creates the problems. The teachers' notions of 'autonomy of education', etc. prevent the critical assessment of the role of education in society. By constantly confining themselves to the educationist context, or more often the specific school context, the social control process by which certain social and economic conditions are translated into 'deviant' or 'low ability' outcomes is not acknowledged.

Individualism, in particular, played an important role in the teachers' philosophy in helping to resolve some contradictions at the expense of other issues. It would be argued that the priorities could be different if the contradictions were confronted with greater political, critical consciousness. Individualism can be seen as a divisive notion in a hierarchical class structure. The 'belief' in the primacy of the individual can be seen as an important ideological device in Western European societies where the 'freedom of the individual' is frequently hailed as the standard of Western democracy and adverse comparisons made with the apparently monolithic, totalitarian structures of Eastern European and/or communist societies. This notion of individualism would seem to have had an important effect on the development of the progressive pedagogy and could be seen to have a compromising or distorting effect on any potentially radical gains that were available with the expansion and changes of the 1960s. The concept of individualism would seem particularly alien to the traditions of the working class, where individualism might thrive but within a strong sense of community. Teachers would need to identify the way in which methods and practice could further communality and solidarity in the schooling of the urban working class to prevent the present process continuing where a few gain at the expense of the many — and only then if they demonstrate sufficient individuality. An oppositional attitude to the narrow educationist perspectives might facilitate the critical analysis of class-culturally specific notions such as 'play', 'nature of childhood' etc. A. Hargreaves distinguishes between 'adaptive strategies as largely exemplified in the pedagogical practice of the progressive teachers, and the possibility for more fundamental social and educational change'. He, too, identifies the crucial area which might provide the greatest potential for change, as the area in which teacher experience is connected to structural constraints: 'Change of such a magnitude demands the active involvement of teachers in particular and men and women in general, in the collective criticism of existing practices, structural arrangements and institutional goals' (Hargreaves, 1978, p. 95).

It could further be argued that the infant stage of the educational system theoretically contains the greatest potential for radical change to be realised. This is due partly to historical factors which have gradually relegated 'elementary' schooling to a relatively low status and import but which paradoxically allows greater autonomy or 'space' for the development of more radical strategies for the organisation and process of schooling and pedagogical practice. Conversely, this radical potential is at present less likely to be realised at the infant stage, partly as a function of low status, etc. which has tended to reduce its attraction for structurally minded teachers. However, if infant teachers were to identify with the parents, in relation to status and class, rather than trying to increase the social distance, the nature and direction of educational change might critically challenge the constraints of the present rational form of schooling. The radical realisation of this would eventually require that the *control* of education be challenged.

Finally, at a more theoretical level, the concept of the relative autonomy of ideology is an important factor in attempting to assess the intermediary processes between base and superstructure. Furthermore it would be argued that the relationship between superstructure and base might not be static but that it might vary in correspondence at different historical conjuncures. Accordingly, the greater the 'space' or the less direct the relationship, the more effective, potentially, is the role of the intervening ideologies. Radical historical accounts are therefore vital in enabling the discernment of historical conditions in which the 'space' offers the greatest potential for attempting to effect social change through the educational system.

The general perspective, then, would be that expressed by Sharp and Green:

> Under what historical conditions can men break through the structure of determinations? (Sharp and Green, 1975, p. 28)

Notes

1 A general definition of 'progressive' would be premised on the notion of child-centredness with classrooms as places where children move about freely, following their own interests and learning through discovery and informal cooperation with each other and the teacher.

2 See, for instance, G.H. Bantock, 'Progressivism and the content of education' in C.B. Cox and R. Boyson (eds), *Black Paper 1975*, London, Dent.

3 The choice of school was partly determined by the researcher's knowledge and experience of a large number of inner city infant schools throughout the ILEA but particularly in the South East Division in which the school is located. This school had a divisional reputation for its commitment to the development of the progressive pedagogy. Since the opening of the new building seven years previously, there had been almost continuous experimentation with different types of organisation (e.g. team teaching in different forms). The ideal progressive methods encouraged by the head and the progressive members of staff would fit the general description given in note 1 above.

4 This can be found in Jan Lee, 'Teacher ideology and the realisation of pedagogy: a study in a progressive inner-city

infant school', MA dissertation, King's College, London, 1980 (unpublished).

5 The 'Toxteth riots', violence against teachers in schools (as recently highlighted by the NUT) and large-scale absenteeism would be obvious indications of this factor.

6 For instance, N. Whitbread (1972) sees the government's intentions through the Revised Code of 1862 as a determination to produce mass literacy by efficient and economical methods rather than the development of 'rational human beings' (ibid., p. 49). She regards the Hadow Report (1933) as reflecting 'the great progress that had been made in infant education during the previous ten years or so' and as a synthesis of the developmental and instrumental approaches to learning. However, R.J.W. Selleck (1972) argues that the Hadow Report militated against these developments by making primary schools a preparatory stage in the hierarchical structure of secondary education.

7 See, for example, Whitbread (1973), pp. 128–9.

8 For example Sharp and Green (1975) regard the 'enlightenment of the progressive pedagogy as being in part a reaction 'against the excessively didactic authoritarian approach in, for example, the "payment by results" era' (p. 41).

9 L. Howdle (1968) claims that changes in concept and method in infant schools are related to changing conceptions of childhood and the child. The dominant concept of the child in the nineteenth century is seen as one of inherent sinfulness and the need for physical and ideological restraints on the child's independence of thought and action. This contrasts, theoretically, with the child-centredness of the progressive pedagogy.

10 For details see Lee (1980), p. 151.

11 The basic conflict in relation to pedagogical practice is more fully outlined later under the heading, Observed differences between 'Doctrine and Commitment'.

12 This is not to say that teachers *should* visit the homes of the children — but that they had quite definite views of home background which were not based on experience. Moreover given the emphasis on parental involvement in the 1960s (as promoted by developments in sociology of education and the Plowden Report, etc.) and the initiatives that were fostered by the ILEA in this area, it is an apt comment on the mismatch between policy and practice, even amongst the committed.

13 R. King's (1978) claim that teacher ideologies should be regarded as a function of their status group rather than 'a simple

derivative of their economic class' appears to be based on the observation in his research that 'other teachers occupy a similar class position but do not accept all aspects of the child-centred ideology' (ibid., p. 131).

14 'Britain's Black Population' (p. 5), by the Runnymede Trust and Radical Statistics Race Group: London, Heinemann Educational Books, 1980.

15 For example, Teacher D's response to the question of racism was, 'The children are a bit young. They *say* things but I don't think they mean them very often.' The majority of teachers, however, denied that the children were racially conscious or made racist remarks.

16 Nell Keddie (1971) also makes the observation that 'C stream pupils disrupt teachers' expectations and violate their norms of appropriate social, moral and intellectual pupil behaviour' (ibid., p. 134). Again, in the selection of appropriate teaching material for the different streams, she states, 'Throughout it is difficult to separate references to cognitive skills from imputed social and moral characteristics on the one hand and from characterisation of teaching material on the other' (ibid., p. 144).

17 This study would reaffirm Dale's (1977) conjecture that teacher training has little *conscious* effect on the teacher's cognitive style. The most positive statement that could be made is that one of the effects of teacher training is *not* to promote a critical, political or social consciousness in the teachers and that practical experience plays a more significant part in affecting teacher consciousness.

18 Similar criticism could be applied to Bernstein's work on class and language. It is questionable whether any higher-order conceptualisation is required from a child depending on whether the mother says, 'Shut up', or 'Dear, don't you think it would be nice to go and bang that saucepan outside in the garden so that the rabbit can listen to you?' The same end is required and the *power* relationship is the same, regardless of the 'subtlety' of the language.

Bibliography

Bantock, G.H. (1975), 'Progressivism and the content of education', in C.B. Cox and R. Boyson (eds), *Black Paper*, Dent, London.
Bennett, N. (1976), *Teaching Styles and Pupil Progress*, London, Open Books.
Bernstein, B. (1975), *Class Codes and Control, Volume III: Towards a Theory of Educational Transmissions*, London, Routledge & Kegan Paul.

Bowles, S. and Gintis, H. (1976), *Schooling in Capitalist America: Educational Reform and the Contradictions of Economic Life*, London, Routledge & Kegan Paul.

Castells, M. (1977), 'The class struggle and urban contradictions' in J. Cowley, A. Kaye, M. Mayo and M. Thompson (eds), *Community or Class Struggle*, Stage 1.

Dale, R. (1977), *The Structural Context of Teaching*, Course E202, Unit 5. Block 1, Milton Keynes, Open University Press.

Finn, D., Grant, N. and Johnson, R. (1977), 'Social democracy: education and the crisis', in *Working Papers in Cultural Studies 10: On Ideology*, CCCS, University of Birmingham.

Frith, S. (1977), 'Socialisation and rational schooling: elementary education in Leeds before 1870', in P. McCann (ed.), *Popular Education and Socialisation in the Nineteenth Century*, London, Methuen.

Grace, G. (1978), *Teachers, Ideology and Control. A Study in Urban Education*, London, Routledge & Kegan Paul.

Hall, S. (1977), 'Education and the crisis of the urban school', in J. Raynor and E. Harris (eds), *Schooling in the City*, London, Ward Lock Educational.

Hargreaves, A. (1978), 'The significance of classroom coping strategies', in L. Barton and R. Meighan (eds), *Schools, Pupils and Deviance*, Driffield, Nafferton Books.

Hargreaves, D. (1980), 'The occupational culture of teachers', in P. Woods (ed.), *Teacher Strategies: Explorations in the Sociology of the School*, London, Croom Helm.

Holly, D. (1976), 'Politics of learning', *Radical Education* no. 7 (Winter).

Howdle, L. (1968), 'An enquiry into the social factors affecting the orientations of English infant education since the early nineteenth century', MA, London, Institute of Education.

Karier, C.J. (1974), 'Ideology and evaluation in quest of meritocracy', in M.W. Apple, M.J. Subkoviak and H.S. Lufler (eds), 'Educational evaluation' (1974), pp. 279–330.

Keddie, N. (1971), 'Classroom knowledge', in M.F.D. Young (ed.), *Knowledge and Control*, London, Collier-Macmillan.

King, R. (1978), *All Things Bright and Beautiful? A Sociological Study of Infants' Classrooms*, Chichester, Wiley.

Lacey, C. (1979), 'Choice and constraint and the possibility of autonomous behaviour', in L. Barton and R. Meighan (eds), *School, Pupils and Deviance*, Driffield, Nafferton Books.

Lee, J. (1980), 'Teacher ideology and the realisation of pedagogy: a study in a progressive inner-city infant school', MA dissertation, King's College, London, 1980.

Lynch, G. (1974), 'Ideology and the social organisation of educational knowledge in England and Scotland 1840–1920', MA, Institute of Education, London.

Plowden Report (1967), Central Advisory Council for Education

(England), *Children and their Primary Schools*, London, HMSO.

Selleck, R.J.W. (1972), *English Primary Education and the Progressives 1914–1939*, London, Routledge & Kegan Paul.

Sharp, R. and Green, A. (1975), *Education and Social Control: A Study in Progressive Primary Education*, London, Routledge & Kegan Paul.

Silver, H. (1977), 'Aspects of neglect: the strange case of Victorian popular education', *Oxford Review of Education*, vol. 3, no. 1.

Weber, M. (1970), 'Class and market situation', in P. Worsley (ed.), *Modern Sociology: Introductory Readings*, Harmondsworth, Penguin.

Whitbread, N. (1972), *The Evolution of the Nursery Infant School: A History of Infant and Nursery Education in Britain 1800–1970*, London, Routledge & Kegan Paul.

10
Teachers for the inner city: change and continuity

Christopher Cook

In so far as a 'crisis in education' exists, one could reasonably claim that it is most visible in cities,[1] and that teachers in urban schools, more than others, bear the brunt of daily difficulties in practising their profession and of regular and hostile attacks from various quarters. How intending teachers might be prepared for working in such circumstances is a matter of some interest,[2] and this paper examines aspects of the ideology and practice of such preparation from the early days of organised teacher training until the present day.[3]

The development of a system of public elementary schools in nineteenth century England and Wales required, in due course, a supply of teachers in ever-increasing numbers to keep pace with growth in that system. That such teachers should be trained, and in a particular way, was a result of the way in which the school system was conceived and operated. Of the mixture of motives that inspired social reform in the context of relatively major changes brought about by industrialisation and the growth of centres of population, the desire to control the mass of the people, especially the urban working classes, was of great significance. That control might be substantially achieved by

> an enormously ambitious attempt to capture through educational means, the patterns of thought, sentiments and behaviour of the working class. Supervised by its trusty teacher, surrounded by its playground wall, the school was to raise a new race of working class people — respectful, cheerful, hard-working, loyal, pacific and religious. (Johnson, 1970, p. 119).

How best 'trusty teachers' might be prepared to tackle so formidable an agenda was a matter of concern to leading educationalists, and Kay-Shuttleworth, that 'architect of popular education' (Grace, 1978, p. 11), embarked upon a scheme of organised training in 1840. That the human agents of control should themselves be controlled was an explicit aim realised in the practices of his Battersea Normal School.[4] Convinced that this might be achieved by instilling a spirit of vocation in his students, which would both sustain their commitment and reconcile them to the drudgery involved, he sought:

> to inspire them with a large sympathy for their own class. To
> implant in their minds the thought that their chief honour would
> be to aid in rescuing that class from the misery of ignorance
> and its attendant vices. To wean them from the influence of that
> personal competition in a commercial society which leads to
> sordid aims. To place before them the unsatisfied want of the
> uneasy and distressed multitude, and to breathe into them
> the charity which seeks to heal its mental and moral diseases.
> (Kay-Shuttleworth, 1862, p. 309)

Kay-Shuttleworth had been impressed by continental exemplars and exhibited a 'partiality for the segregated life of the seminary as an important element in the training of teachers for the poor' (Rich, 1933, p. 60). Cast in the mould of 'social and cultural missionaries — a kind of secular priesthood dedicated to the work of civilization' (Grace, 1978, p. 11), the 'trusty teachers' underwent a strict preparation. The most Spartan of domestic arrangements, constant supervision, the absence of leisure and holidays, and the combination of mental and manual work with religious training characterised the institution established by Kay-Shuttleworth. Academic work was generally limited to the matter of the elementary school curriculum,[5] and by a 'laborious and frugal life, economy of management is reconciled with efficiency both of the moral and intellectual training of the School, and the master[6] goes out into the world humble, industrious and instructed' (Kay-Shuttleworth, 1862, pp. 404–5).

The training college at Battersea proved adequate for preparing teachers of the 'submissive and tractable though often dull children of the peasantry'[7] (ibid., p. 391–2). Careful attention was given to practical teaching; local village schools being used for practice purposes. However, Kay-Shuttleworth soon came to realise that truly urban schools presented greater difficulties. Only the exceptional teacher could cope with conditions so different from those experienced in a secluded training and which he left behind

> for the rude contact of a coarse, selfish and immoral populace
> whose gross appetites render the narrow streets in his
> neighbourhood scenes of impurity. He is at once brought
> face to face with an ignorant and corrupt multitude to whose
> children he is to prove a leader and guide . . . . His difficulties are
> formidable.' (ibid., pp. 392–3)

Kay-Shuttleworth had encountered urban conditions at first hand,[8] and his acknowledgment that urban schools were such as to require specially prepared teachers led him to place a high value on direct contact as an element of such preparation. In 1843 he proposed a 'Town Normal School' in 'the centre of a great manufacturing city' (ibid., p. 393), which would meet this need, an idea which was not taken up until later.[9]

Similar problems beset an exactly contemporary institution established in Chelsea, St Mark's College. Its founder, Rev. Derwent Coleridge, also shared a preference for missionary zeal but placed greater emphasis upon academic work. Latin was central to the curriculum, and religious activities and ritual were prominent.

Yet despite 'the special aim of the institution for elevating and ameliorating the lot of the labouring poor', (Rev. Moseley, HMI, quoted in Sturt, 1967, p. 142), conceived by Coleridge as a 'dull subsident mass in which lie buried the seeds of danger to the social state' (1862, p. 31), acquaintance with urban conditions and schools seems to have been relatively neglected. The matter of training to teach seems to have taken second place to Coleridge's more lofty ambitions:

> the better the schoolmaster is bred, the more highly he is
> trained, the more he is socially respected, the more ready he will
> be to combat the difficulties, to submit to the monotony, and
> to move with quiet dignity in the humbleness of his vocation.
> (Coleridge, 1862, p. 37)

In any case, to conceive of the typical teacher as 'country schoolmaster' who 'must stand as clergyman's assistant' (Coleridge, quoted in Sturt, 1967, p. 140),[10] points away from engagement with the realities of urban schools and reduces an appreciation of the salience of urban problems.

In some senses this is hardly surprising. Coleridge, like Kay-Shuttleworth, was a perceptive amateur social theorist. He grasped clearly that a solution to latent problems of unrest among the poor lay in schooling. His conception of the 'trusty teacher' was based upon the notion of a religiously and culturally inspired vocation to sustain the teacher in his difficult task, and attract honour and respectability to his position. He aimed 'to educate a class, not a caste, of elementary schoolmasters, men who would pursue their calling in freedom and hope'[11] (Coleridge, 1862, p. 15). In effect, Coleridge tried to create a new social status of teachers for the people, that would both set them apart from the poor, and reduce the possibility that they might cultivate too well 'the seeds of danger to the social state'. In terms of controlling the teachers, Coleridge, scholar and zealous High Churchman, fostered social elevation and refinement; Kay-Shuttleworth, able administrator and pragmatic social reformer, sought limitation of thought and action sustained by a religiously inspired spirit of self-sacrifice (Tropp, 1957, p. 13).

Various authorities concur as to the influence of these early pioneers on the subsequent form and content of the preparation of teachers, and with respect to the training of teachers for urban schools it is possible to discern a number of significant features that have endured.

In particular, the consequences of the desire to inculcate a 'missionary spirit' were profound. Given practical expression in the earliest colleges, it became a guiding principle as more colleges were established under denominational control. As Tropp notes, 'Every effort was made in the training colleges to bring the students into contact with religious and cultivated tutors and to fill them with missionary zeal and a deep sense of humility' (1957, p. 22). As future teachers,

> charged with the education of the unlettered proletariat,
> students needed to acquire not only the intellectual knowledge
> and the class management skills that would enable them to
> bring about conditions of mass literacy, but also the capacity to
> gentle the masses, modify excess and strengthen the social
> controls that would prevent literacy and the perception of better
> things from spilling over into social discontent and refractoriness.
> (Taylor, 1969, p. 273)

If the teachers were to be 'cohesive agents' in such circumstances, they should themselves be apolitical and ideologically naive, and if the strictly controlled life of the nineteenth century training college was not in itself sufficient to achieve this end, then the curriculum and learning experiences provided pointed thereto. Students were not by and large offered the means for theoretical engagement with issues connected with their future role, nor was there much opportunity for intellectual (or indeed any other) reflection. The narrow curriculum (particularly after the Revised Code of 1861), learning by rote, and a strict routine to occupy students from early rising to 'lights out', were to characterise training college life until well into the twentieth century.[12]

The college that Kay-Shuttleworth had established left its mark upon the character of the forty or so colleges started by 1870 (Rich, 1933, p. 64), and despite various improvements, life in the late nineteenth century colleges continued to be 'narrow, strenuous and rather drab' (ibid., p. 207). Indeed, even the practical elements of learning to teach seem to have been neglected, and particularly so in the case of preparing to teach in urban schools. The early tendency to establish colleges outside urban centres, or indeed, to move from cities,[13] increased their physical and social isolation, fostered the idea of a seminary, and rendered unlikely the possibility of contact with the realities of urban life. The experience of a consequent 'reality shock', on appointment to urban schools, is vividly recalled in the accounts of former students of the colleges (Ballard, 1937; Spencer, 1938). Furthermore,

> The attention of the teachers of the people continued to be fixed firmly upon *ameliorating* activity, upon a social pathology view of the working class, and away from any serious analysis of the structural conditions which required such amelioration. (Grace, 1978, p. 13)

This tendency was to continue until well into the twentieth century. In a sense, teacher training as established in the nineteenth century was to confer a legacy upon the teaching profession that put the urban problem out of sight and out of mind.

To some degree this state of affairs was improved by the establishment of day colleges in the 1890s, later to develop into the university departments of education.[14] However, this development did not signal the end of the residential training college system. Early in the twentieth century local education authorities established a new wave of residential colleges on more or less the same pattern as before and which, in turn, came to predominate over the older denominational sector. The religiously inspired crusade gave way to a desire to create the disinterested vocational dedication of professionalism. This, likewise, pointed away from serious engagement with political and economic questions and served to set teachers apart from making common cause with working class movements.

The embryonic study of education in the colleges, much of it based upon educational psychology, probably had similar effects. Taylor discerns in this period a rejection of pluralism, rationality and intellect, together with lack of interest in the political and structural, a stress upon the intuitive, creativity, personal autonomy through artistic expression and the value of a community life. For him, the dominant value orientation of teacher education in the first six decades of the twentieth century was 'social and literary romanticism' (1969, p. 12). The urban context did not seem to have been a major concern, except in so far as occasional contacts and references provided support for vocational commitment and the professionally useful experience of contact with the urban working classes.

This latter theme surfaced from time to time over a period of about forty years.[15] Instances of 'good practice' are referred to in a series of commentaries and official reports culminating in specific recommendations for action in both the Newsom and Plowden Reports. Teachers in training should 'know' about the social and cultural backgrounds of their future pupils so that they might 'understand' individual and group behaviour: an improvement in these matters would benefit pupils and teachers and nowhere might this be more true than in the 'worst' urban areas. Thus Newsom suggested a lengthened school day and approved of extra-curricular work in youth clubs, school societies, school journeys and camps. By joining such activities the young teacher would be helped

> to recognize the significance of the social and recreational side
> of the school's life, and to participate more readily in it;
> secondly because those contacts with young people will provide
> a useful background to the sociological studies which we
> believe should be a part of any general training course. (Ministry
> of Education, 1963, p. 103)

Produced at a time of growing awareness of the differential educability of children in terms of their socio-economic origins, the Newsom

Report paid particular attention to 'Education in the slums' (the title of its Chapter 3), and observed that 'certain problems which are primarily educational have wider social implications . . . In the slums the need for reform is not confined to the schools' (ibid., p. 26). In some senses one could say that the wheel of educational ideology had taken 120 years to come full circle; Kay-Shuttleworth and his contemporaries would have responded to this conception. The urban context had been re-awarded its salience in education.

The rediscovery of the 'urban problem' was not simply confined to the field of education, nor were the remedies offered remarkable for their novelty, as has been suggested. Thus, if we consider Victorian conceptions of the 'urban problem' and responses to it, as, for example, revealed in Jones's (1971) study, there are noteworthy parallels with more recent approaches.

Jones shows that the social stability of urban society in the second half of the nineteenth century was threatened by large numbers of 'casual poor' who congregated in the metropolis, constituting 'Outcast London', an unregenerate 'residuum', and 'a disquieting alien presence in the midst of mid-Victorian plenty' (ibid., p. 14). Unless means of reform were found, 'the forces of progress might be swamped' (ibid., p. 16). Since the problem was conceived in the essentially moral terms of 'pauperism', rather than that of structurally and economically sustained poverty, the reforms were likewise: 'Social Bridges' were to reach into 'Town Swamps'.[16] Material improvements in the shape of better housing, transport and public utilities were the background to an ambitious attempt to re-establish 'proper', and more secure, relations between the urban social classes. Thus schooling, charitable activity of various types, and schemes of moral and cultural elevation and of 'civilization' were employed. Many of these remedies had been tried before. However, there were differences of scale, and the remedies became highly organised, bureaucratised, and were provided for the urban working classes, and, in some cases, enforced by legislation.

That these policies had become more urgently necessary was chiefly thought to lie in the geographical gulf which had opened up between the classes. 'At the most fundamental level, the separation of classes had led to a breakdown of social relationships and traditional methods of social control' (ibid., p. 251). 'The gift', that is, charitable giving, had become deformed: 'the hand that has given and the hand that has taken have never felt the warm electricity of each other's touch' (contemporary statement, quoted ibid., p. 253), and 'the elements of prestige, subordination and obligation' had been lost (ibid., p. 252). The root of the problem was seen to be the absence of a 'resident gentry' and 'the only real solution to the . . . separation of classes was for the rich to resume residence in the poorer areas' (ibid., p. 258).

Accordingly the cultural invasion of the East End of London commenced in the shape of the settlement movement. By these and other schemes of self-help forming part of those social policies which represent, above all, the assertion or re-assertion of 'class-cultural control' (Johnson, 1976, pp. 49—50), it was hoped that London 'would be turned into a gigantic village, and its poor would be led back to manliness and independence under the firm but benevolent aegis of a new urban squirearchy' (Jones, 1971, p. 261).

In due course it was realised that 'manliness' and 'independence' did not necessarily occur through moral polemic nor through new forms of social contact between the social classes. The organisation of the market for casual labour and attempts to prevent unemployment through government action indicate that the causes of poverty were regarded by some as economic or structural in origin. By the time of the First World War, all 'surplus' labour had been absorbed and the 'unemployables' proved impossible to find (ibid., p. 336). Obsession with the particular problem of 'Outcast London' came to an end, and the spectre which had haunted respectable society was temporarily laid to rest.

Since the 1960s, the re-emergence of the 'spectre' in the shape of notions of 'inner city crisis' has been coupled with a heightened public awareness of urban deprivation. This has led to various forms of remedial action many of which, in essence, were similar to those attempted in Victorian times. Ameliorative in intent, interventionist in character, and informed by a vocabulary of modern social science, new 'social bridges' have been erected by national and local activities.

In the training of teachers, emphasis was to be placed upon sociological studies, suitably supported by practical encounters of the sort recommended by the Newsom Report and endorsed by the subsequent Plowden Report, which states that all students in training

> need to understand the effect of home and community on
> children. Special emphasis should be placed on the problems
> of children who are, in one or another way, gravely deprived by
> the circumstances of their homes and districts, and on the
> help that teachers can give to these children, in collaboration with
> other social services. Contacts with parents and others in the

neighbourhood should be organised in a positive fashion and should introduce students to situations to which they themselves can make a positive contribution. (Department of Education and Science, 1967, p. 348)

These prescriptions seem to indicate a rather pressing desire, especially in the case of those urban areas inhabited by the 'gravely deprived', to extend the teacher's role beyond the traditional confines of the classroom, and for closer contact with the home and community life of his/her pupils to obtain a fuller understanding of why pupils act, feel and think as they do.

On the practical level, various institutions had already taken the initiative to provide their students with this sort of opportunity.[17] In due course, others were to follow. The best known is probably the Urban Studies Centre of the College of St Mark and St John which moved from London to Plymouth in 1973.

This centre was established in the East End of London in the same year as a residential base for students from that college, and elsewhere, to undertake practical work in an urban environment in order to prepare them for professional work as teachers. In terms of scale, although still relatively small, the centre is unique in Britain in that up to the time of writing, in excess of 600 students have passed through it, typically spending three months there, and undertaking both teaching practice (in primary and secondary schools) and community work (in a range of local organisations and projects). The centre thus represents an important contemporary initiative in the preparation of teachers for urban schools and some account of its origins and activities seems desirable.

The Urban Studies Centre was conceived as rather more than a convenient base for teaching practice purposes in an urban setting. From the point of view of its founder, Frank Coles, the centre was the culmination of a number of attempts to establish a means of 'enriching, or making more fruitful, a teaching-at-school experience'.[18] Previous attempts were short-lived but 'they did involve various programmes for involving students in the lives of the children inside and outside the schools in the way that the Urban Studies Centre attempts to do.' Indeed, at the time of the Newsom Report, Coles wished 'to attach all the students to schools to work the "Newsom" longer day', but was 'defeated by the system'. Thus one strand of thinking behind the Urban Studies Centre is directly linked to that report's support for an extended school day and the value of extra-curricular activities.

Coles's analysis of inner city schools began with the basic proposition that 'school has a capacity for inhibiting learning in a way that no other form of childhood experience seems to have'. In badly run schools 'most children's learning goes on outside school', and

> Many of the schools that were breaking down in the 60s . . . were places where children felt they didn't want to learn. That didn't mean they stopped learning, it meant that all their learning took place elsewhere. A teacher who is going to contribute to any improvement in the situation has got to observe and be in contact with children where they learn which is outside school.

In line with the official reports mentioned above, the thrust of Coles's thinking is that the teacher (and by implication, the student teacher), requires to experience out-of-school contact with children and their local community as a precondition of becoming a successful practitioner in the inner city school. Armed with the understanding that comes from such experience, the teacher is enabled to comprehend the unsatisfactory nature of schooling, of children's learning, and to contribute to the task of improvement. That the teacher's role should be redefined in this type of way, and should feature in preparation for teaching in urban areas, is by no means new, though relatively rarely practised, as suggested above. Nor is it entirely new that the boundaries between home, schools and community should be reduced or abolished. Indeed, perhaps the most celebrated exemplar of this approach is the system of Cambridgeshire Village Colleges established by Henry Morris almost fifty years ago, and this particular influence on the thinking behind the Urban Studies Centre is confirmed in the account provided by Raynor (1978, p. 2).[19]

The subsequent development of the idea of community schooling towards apparently more radical ends is also cited as being significant. The present director, Roger Tingle, mentioned the work of Midwinter in this context. Raynor, too, claims to discern some influence from 'the EPA action-research projects' (1978, p. 2), and the adoption of the practice of joint teaching activity community work as the basis for the centre's activity leads Raynor to observe that:

> (a) it lays challenge to a view of restricted professionality widening it out in ways not normally accepted;

(b) it helps to break down the old Victorian legacy of the professional-lay distinction;
(c) it holds out the hope that the student can enter school with that 'critical discontent' with the situation outside that the community involvement has engendered, so that what goes on in school, as part of its evolving policies, may become more sensitively tuned to community needs. (ibid., p. 9; also 1981, p. 41).

Expressed in these terms, the ideology of the Urban Studies Centre is close to that suggested by Halsey (1972) and Midwinter (1972) for a programme of community education. This approach is one which essentially seeks to initiate movements towards greater social justice through local educational and social action in the inner city, and contained within the framework of existing institutions. Raynor seems to be expressing the hope that this may occur through the activities of the Urban Studies Centre. However, there is a problem about the generation of 'critical discontent'. It should be noted that 'critical discontent' does not feature as a pedagogic aim of the centre. As the director pointed out,

In terms of a radical critique of the role of the teacher . . . or indeed the role of the education system, obviously that's something that students going on into teaching may develop, and it may, in fact, be something members of staff here would welcome. They would regard this as a positive way of thinking about the job, but *it's not something, necessarily, which is built in to the structure of the Urban Studies Centre as it stands*. (Cook, 1980, p. 60).

Thus the development of 'critical discontent' seems to be rather left to chance. There is reason to suppose that students may leave the centre without it, and the case for the centre to be regarded as a 'growth point for a new social consciousness' of the sort endorsed by Halsey (1972, p. 5) is thereby weakened.[20]

What is perhaps a more satisfactory assessment of the centre's understanding of communitarian thinking is that contained in the work of Anderson (1975). Appointed as principal of the College of St Mark and St John in 1972, apparently his support for Coles's project was crucial.[21] In an analysis of the problems of inner city schools, Anderson refers to 'deteriorating relationships' between pupils and teachers, 'clashes' over the purposes of school, and maintains that the 'empirical task' of learning to teach

> has to be centred on the practical experience of watching and working with children and other teachers. Of course, theoretical knowledge provided by the various social scientific disciplines can be helpful, but only when it is related to the practical tasks of building responsive relationships and communicating clearly with pupils and parents. The colleges are continually searching for the magic formula that relates theory to practice. (1975, p. 54).

In so far as this statement might be said to apply to the work of the Urban Studies Centre (and such a case could be made, given that it forms a prelude to an outline of the practices and purposes of the centre), it highlights two aspects. Firstly, that the centre's activities are essentially practical and experiential, and secondly, that there is a problematic relationship between the centre's work and academic and theoretical work in the preparation of teachers.

The director was emphatic on these points. The centre offered 'essentially a fieldwork experience', and

> No matter how imaginative members of staff [at Plymouth] may be . . . no matter how much hard work they put into trying to prepare students for the experience . . . *there is no preparation*. I mean *this is the whole point of the Centre*. You cannot theoretically and methodologically prepare people for something they haven't experienced. The experience has to be the starting point. (Cook, 1980, p. 64)

Thus experience is all, and the student's time is fully occupied with practical work in school and community placement, leaving little time for reflection or reading. In any case, Coles was critical of the academic preoccupations of the college, and the way that teacher education had developed in general. He noted 'a serious dereliction of duty . . . with respect to involving students with any of the processes connected with working with children' (ibid., p. 63).[22]

In some respects, then, the Urban Studies Centre can be seen as a reversal of major trends in teacher education. In particular, it can be seen as a deliberate attempt to move away from an increasing emphasis

Teachers for the inner city: change and continuity / 281

upon the theoretical study of education and other academic disciplines. The centre takes seriously the notion of both the problems of inner city schools and the likelihood that many newly qualified teachers will find their first appointments in such schools. Accordingly, it provides the possibility for obtaining the sustained direct experience of school and community that is seen to be relevant to the solution of such problems.

The key to this approach seems to lie more than that of any other in Coles's remarks on the position of contemporary urban teachers: a stubborn adherence to outmoded practices, their role and self-confidence diminished by the deleterious effects of social change. The practices and orientation of the Urban Studies Centre would improve this state of affairs and 'restore to the education of teachers its professional character' (1975, p. vii ff.) in the manner described above.

There seems little doubt that students value highly the experience that the Urban Studies Centre provides. Various accounts attest to this.[23] At one level, support for the centre is instrumental, in that some students feel that their employment prospects are enhanced. Indeed the college advertises the centre to intending students with precisely this appeal. At another level, Coles felt that some students regarded the centre as a 'crusade of rescue or mission to the slums . . . they come up with romantic ideas about it' (Cook, 1980, p. 70).[24] However, whatever the attitudes and motives of the students who choose to come to the centre, they are, by and large, unprepared for what happens to them. Neither school placement nor community work represents a soft option for the inexperienced. Taken together, they constitute a 'baptism by fire'. The student, like an anthropological stranger, suffers 'culture shock' through immersion in a largely unknown environment. In daily contact with an urban working class community, students begin to shed, and some of them to question, their own presuppositions. As one commentator put it, they 'upset some of the stereotypes gained from a mixture of watered-down deprivation theory and an atavistic view of poor children as barefoot illiterates' (Makins, 1974).

This new awareness and understanding apparently has beneficial effects. Quite clearly, 'getting to know the kids' was found to be a valuable asset. It led to greater confidence on the part of students in dealing with children either in school or outside, and served to allay some of the fears they might have had about classroom control. To some extent the 'formidable difficulties' noted by Kay-Shuttleworth could be overcome. Clearly this was intended by Coles, and in this sense the centre is successful. However, what should be emphasised is that this understanding is of a practical sort. Knowing *how* children behave and react in the different circumstances that students are likely to encounter in homes, schools and community work activities is seen as the basis on which to develop the skills of communication in schools and outside. The process of coming into close contact with an urban working class community, and experiencing something of its cultural life, facilitates rapport with pupils, through an empathetic understanding of their milieu. Rapport, on this basis, makes for better teaching: an enhanced relationship with pupils assists the communicative aspects of teaching. Seen in this limited sense, teaching seems to be reduced to an essentially technical matter, and by implication, the problems in inner city schools may be ascribed to failures at the level of communication.[25]

Given this emphasis, the role of the staff at the centre is largely supervisory and supportive. There are no seminars, lectures or reading lists, and students are not required to produce academic work. Because the time available for the experiential component was limited, Coles felt that academic activities were an undesirable elaboration in the context of the Urban Studies Centre, and, furthermore, were inappropriate as preparation for teaching in urban schools.[26] For him, the successful students were able 'to abandon presuppositions which they bring with them from home . . . the College . . . or perhaps from their own reading.' They turn their backs on 'academic frippery' and get down to the real business of acquiring practical knowledge (Cook, 1980, pp. 75–6).

There is also the pragmatic question of what might be an appropriate theoretical contexting of the students' experience at the centre, if this were thought desirable. A number of strands of thinking that have influenced the establishment and form of the centre have been mentioned in this paper, but it is difficult, if not impossible, to refer to any body of theoretical work or literature as being of overwhelming importance. As the director stated,

> I think it would be extremely tenuous to try and pin it [the Centre's approach] down to any particular theory . . . If anything, I suppose it reflects his [Coles's] experience, over a long period of time, of working in schools in this area.
> (ibid., p. 75)

These remarks give an indication of the centre's attitude to a problem, familiar in teacher education, of the nature of the relationship of 'theory' to 'practice'. Commonly manifested by assertions of the irrelevance of the former to the latter, 'theory' is conceived of as separated from 'practice'. In the present instance, the key to successful 'practice' in the urban context is thought to be 'relevant experience', as defined above, and the competent professional practitioner of teaching is indicated by the ability to communicate effectively with pupils of a different background to him/herself, and to develop and sustain relationships with them, both inside and outside the school.

However, this conception of the theory/practice relationship was rejected by one of the centre's staff. In his view, the centre's approach was best understood in the terms advanced by Wilson and Pring that: 'theory already exists in practice — and that it can be found there if one looks for it . . . . "Theory", in this sense would be the set of reflective, critical, thoughtful features of the practice of which it was the theory' (1975a, p. 3). Seeing the 'theory' in the 'practice' in this way might then be fruitful in that critical reflection on presuppositions, which Coles desires, and thus:

> The improvement of one's practice . . . would consist in the
> first instance of becoming aware of the theory which
> one's practice already embodies, so that at least one begins to
> understand something of what one was doing all the time . . . . One
> would learn to teach by teaching (or trying to) — but this 'trying
> to teach' would be reflective, thoughtful, critical (that is,
> would contain theorizing) from the first. (ibid.)

In the context of remarks about the nature of the urban comprehensive school, Wilson and Pring make comments most apposite to the Urban Studies Centre's work and situation:

> To ask what it is to educate *these* children — possibly
> disruptive, uninterested or openly hostile — or what makes
> educational sense out of *their* school experience is very often to
> challenge received assumptions about education . . . and to
> raise a host of questions about the influences upon, the current
> interests and anxieties of, the context provided for the pupils that
> are there to be taught (1975b, p. 53).

Whether consciously or not, some students seem to begin the process of questioning of this type, and it is not discouraged by the centre's staff. On the other hand, this approach does not seem to be one that is applied in a systematic or general way, but on the basis of necessarily limited investigation, it would be unreasonable to press this point too firmly.

However, there are certain difficulties with Wilson and Pring's approach that are germane to a consideration of the work of the Urban Studies Centre. In attempting to resolve the problem of the relationship of theory to practice in teaching in the terms stated above, they maintain that a 'theory' of this kind must exhibit, amongst other things, situatedness, relevance, and explanatory power (Wilson and Pring, 1975a, pp. 5–7). By their own definition, 'situatedness' is limited to the reflective consciousness of the practitioners concerned, and 'relevance' eliminates from further consideration any theoretical matter whose practical relevance the practitioners cannot 'see'. Thus the issue of the location of theoretical understanding of practice in a context wider than that in which the practice occurs is constrained by the necessarily arbitrary matter of whether any particular practitioners define such contexting as relevant. From a socio-historical point of view, this approach to social theory is inadequate in that it is potentially ahistorical, astructural and apolitical. Thus when applied to educational practice, such an approach may be conservative in that it may mask the real connections of schooling with the exercise of power in society and the exigencies of social control.[27] There is, accordingly, the possibility that this may be the case in the preparation of teachers for urban schools as exemplified by the work of the Urban Studies Centre.

Conclusions

In this paper, an attempt has been made to construct a thematic account of the preparation of teachers for urban schools from the beginning of organised training until the present day.

Conceived against the background of nineteenth century anxiety over the 'urban problem', attempts to contain a potentially disruptive urban working class were seen to require a series of 'Social Bridges' offering 'amelioration', 'civilization' and 'rescue'. Amongst these, a publicly provided and compulsory system of elementary schooling was to form a significant part, and 'teachers of the people' were to be appropriately prepared for the responsibilities they were to bear.

The pioneers of the system of organised teacher training arranged forms of occupational socialisation so as to create a body of teachers 'humble, industrious and instructed' (Kay-Shuttleworth, 1862, p. 405), ready 'to combat the difficulties, to submit to the monotony, and to move with quiet dignity in the humbleness of [their] vocation' (Coleridge, 1862, p. 37). Substantially under the aegis of religious bodies, the nineteenth century training colleges were often remote in spirit, if not physically as well, from the urban context. A 'missionary spirit' was encouraged and students were carefully selected and strictly supervised. Dedication to the task of teaching was regarded as more important than either academic work or even the development of practical skills of teaching in urban schools. Many of these characteristics were to endure and provide pointers to an understanding of problems which perennially beset teacher education.

The notions of 'inner city crisis' during the 1960s and early 1970s inspired new forms of urban analysis,[28] and new awareness of the effects of home and environment upon schools and pupils.[29] Various initiatives in the professional preparation of teachers gave special attention to teaching in urban schools. Of these the Urban Studies Centre described above exhibits a number of interesting features.

There is some evidence of institutional continuity in that the present College of St Mark and St John acknowledges the concern of its antecedent colleges for the education of disadvantaged urban children through the work of the Urban Studies Centre. From a residential base in the East End of London, students undertake practical work in local schools and community organisations. Students value the experience and understanding gained thereby, and this aspect of the centre's work is highly commendable. It represents a real and useful engagement with the day-to-day difficulties of teaching in urban schools, and serves to reduce many of the problems commonly encountered by inexperienced teachers.

Whilst there is no intention to denigrate the centre's work, there are nevertheless some questions to be raised over its almost exclusive preoccupation with the *experiential*. There is little evidence of a systematic attempt in the work of the Urban Studies Centre to appreciate the complex of phenomena which have constituted the urban school and community. The experiential supplants the theoretical, and the possibility of the wider contexting of experience seems unlikely.

The particular conception of professionality in teaching embodied in the centre's approach stresses the relational and communicative aspects of teaching above all others. This, it seems, is a direct result of the essentially technicist concerns of the centre's founder: good teaching is a matter of exercising the skills of communication based on familiarity with the local community and its values. Stated in this way, teaching is reduced to a technical matter. It is a craft to be acquired, and the Urban Studies Centre provides a means. This begs the question of the limits of 'professional' (as opposed to 'technical') knowledge and understanding. If 'professional' is taken to mean merely skilful and dedicated, who is to comprehend the 'wider design'?[30] As Gouldner (1976, p. 213) observes, 'to have a purely technical interest is tacitly to have an interest in maintaining the larger social system'.[31]

This state of affairs is somewhat ironic. Urban analysts, such as Pahl and Castells,[32] would surely point to the obvious social contradictions and massive social and spatial injustice with which the Urban Studies Centre is surrounded. The *enduring* character of such circumstances demands comment and analysis. The problems of urban schools are not due to failure *merely* at the level of communication and teaching skills.

In considering the nature of the process of the preparation of teachers for urban schools, this paper has sought to illuminate and to draw attention to ways in which that process may inhibit their ability to question the basis of the system in which they are to work. Certain notions of professionality underplay the question of the relationship between education and wider social and political structures.[33] As Grace remarks (1978, p. 218), 'Such controls may currently have no very clear, conscious or unitary origin, but their existence serves a conservative function.'

Under the present state of economic recession, of which the 'inner city crisis' might be said to be symptomatic, the education system is subject to severe retrenchment. There is increasing government intervention, not least in the education of teachers. Now, perhaps more urgently than ever, teachers in urban schools need to develop 'critical discontent', and to articulate their direct experience with those wider social, political and historical issues which impinge so directly on their professional work.

Notes

1 See, for example, Field (1977), Hall (1974), Bazalgette and Buchan (1975).
2 See, for British examples, Halsey (1972), Midwinter (1972), Craft, Raynor and Cohen (1967).

3 Much of the material on which this paper is based is contained in Cook (1980).

4 This institution later came under denominational control as St John's College, Battersea, and subsequently merged with St Mark's College, Chelsea, to become the present College of St Mark and St John, which moved to Plymouth in 1973. Accounts of aspects of this latter removal are given in Cook (1980) and Raynor (1981).

5 Interestingly, some work was done on 'domestic economy' and health, as well as 'some general lectures on the relations between labour and capital' (Kay-Shuttleworth, 1862, pp. 365–6).

6 The first trained teachers were men. Subsequently, large numbers of women entered teaching through the pupil-teacher system.

7 A conception similar to the Marxian one of 'rural idiocy'.

8 See, for example, the account of his investigations in Manchester in 1832 (Kay-Shuttleworth, 1862).

9 Pupil-teacher centres for aspiring pupils were first set up in the 1880s, and lasted for about forty years.

10 Coleridge seems to have had a rural parish school in mind as the typical destination of his students.

11 Presumably an implied criticism of Kay-Shuttleworth's more restrictive conception of the teacher's status.

12 See, for example, Sturt (1967), ch. 7; also the personal reminiscences of Ballard (1937) and Spencer (1938).

13 By the end of the century, very few residential colleges were in towns. An interesting exception was Westminster College. It seems the Wesleyan authorities deliberately placed this college 'amid the slums of Westminster' so that students might remain in proximity to the inhabitants (Rich, 1933, p. 149). Jones (1924) gives tabular details of the foundation of colleges. Some of this data and the question of the location of colleges are discussed in Cook (1980).

14 For an account of this period see Rich (1933, p. 222).

15 Details of the development of this theme are given by Cook (1980, pp. 32–38).

16 These terms are appropriated from the title of a book by Godwin (1859), a leading social reformer. Jones (1971) discusses the application and effects of various 'Social Bridges'.

17 Midwinter (1972) and Halsey (1972) provide details of work in connection with educational priority areas. The Polytechnic of

North London (as then, North-Western Polytechnic) established optional courses, as part of initial teacher training, entitled 'Under-Privileged Zone', in 1967, later to become 'Social Problems in the Inner City' and then, by 1975, 'Educational Problems in the Inner City,' all of which included placements in various social agencies; see Marks and Parfitt (1974). Mention should also be made of the work reported in Craft *et al.* (1967).

18 This, and other quotations not otherwise referenced, are taken from fieldwork interviews reported in Cook (1980).

19 Morris's work also finds favour in the Plowden Report (Ministry of Education, 1963, p. 48) to illustrate ways in which the idea of the 'community school' might be revivified 'in all areas but especially in educational priority areas', and that schools should have schemes for liaison with the homes of their pupils.

20 Some students develop a form of 'critical discontent' (Cook, 1980, p. 81; Makins, 1974; Raynor, 1981, p. 46 ff.), and some are critical of the centre for its lack of attention to this matter (Raynor, 1981, p. 55). However, Raynor's evaluation is muted on this point, somewhat surprisingly in view of his support of a need for 'critical discontent' (1981, p. 8, p. 46).

21 A fuller account of Anderson's role is given by Cook (1980) and by Raynor (1981).

22 There does seem to be an awareness on the part of the college of possible shortcomings of the centre's approach. For example, Anderson writes, 'It is arguable . . . that practical involvement in inner city life may do more to create stereotypes and reinforce deficit theories than give personal meaning to valid social scientific analysis' (Raynor, 1981, p. 33). Furthermore, since 1977, students have had the opportunity to pursue an elective course in Community Studies, prior to work at the Urban Studies Centre and subsequently to take part in 'School and Community' courses. Details are provided by Raynor (1981).

23 See Cook (1980) and Raynor (1978, 1981).

24 The college is an Anglican institution, and in so far as a religious connection might be said to operate, a visible instance is the centre's use of redundant vicarages as premises.

25 This approach is not unlike that of 'policy science' (Fay, 1975, p. 14): the selection of the most technically efficient solution to a given social problem on the basis of available social scientific knowledge. This may have conservative effects, compared with 'critical social science' which seeks 'to enlighten the social actors so that, coming to see themselves and their social situation in a new way, they themselves can decide to alter the conditions

which they find repressive' (ibid., p. 103).
26 See note 22.
27 This point is taken from Hall (1974).
28 See, for example, the work of Castells (1977) and Pahl (1975).
29 As, for example, contained in the Newsom and Plowden Reports mentioned above.
30 In his remarks on teacher training, Dale suggests that teachers become 'in effect educational technicians, expert in maintenance and repair jobs on their part of the system, but unable to develop an overall view of the system or how it might be changed' (1977, p. 25).
31 See note 25.
32 See note 28.
33 Grace's (1978) study suggests that few teachers in urban schools adopt radical positions. For many, 'what passes for professionalism is an avoidance of the controversial and a naive belief that "being political" is "being socialist" ' (ibid., p. 249).

Bibliography

Anderson, J. (1975), 'Teacher education for the urban community', *Secondary Education*, June 1975, vol. 5, no. 2.

Apple, M.W. (1982), *Education and Power*, London, Routledge & Kegan Paul.

Ballard, P.B. (1937), *Things I Cannot Forget*, University of London Press.

Bazalgette, C. and Buchan, M. (1975), 'London problems', *London Educational Review*, vol. 4, no. 1, Spring.

Castells, M. (1977), *The Urban Question*, London, Edward Arnold.

Coleridge, D. (1862), *The Teachers of the People*, London, Rivingtons.

Coles, F. (1975), 'Foreword' in Pluckrose, H. (1975), *Open School, Open Society*, London, Evans.

Cook, C.D. (1980), *Schooling the Teachers: a Study of the Ideology and Practice of the Preparation of Teachers for Urban Schools with Special Reference to some Recent Initiatives*, unpublished MA dissertation, King's College, London.

Craft, M., Raynor, J. and Cohen, L. (eds), (1967), *Linking Home and School*, London, Longmans Green.

Dale, R. (1977), *The Structural Context of Teaching*, (Educational Studies: A Second Level Course, E202, Schooling and Society, Unit 5), Milton Keynes, Open University Press.

Department of Education and Science (1967), *Children and their Primary Schools*, (The Plowden Report), vol. 1, London, HMSO
Fay, B. (1975), *Social Theory and Political Practice*, London, Allen & Unwin.
Field, F. (ed.), (1977), *Education and the Urban Crisis*, London, Routledge & Kegan Paul.
Godwin, G. (1859), *Town Swamps and Social Bridges*, London, Routledge, Warne & Routledge (reprinted 1972, Leicester University Press).
Gouldner, A.W. (1976), *The Dialectic of Ideology and Technology: The Origins, Grammar and Future of Ideology*, London, Macmillan.
Grace, G. (1978), *Teachers, Ideology and Control: a Study in Urban Education*, London, Routledge & Kegan Paul.
Hall, S. (1974), 'Education and the crisis of the urban school', in J. Raynor (ed.), *Issues in Urban Education*, Milton Keynes, Open University Press.
Halsey, A.H. (1972), *Education Priority: EPA Problems and Policies*, vol. 1, London, HMSO.
Johnson, R. (1970), 'Educational policy and social control in early Victorian England', *Past and Present*, vol. 49.
Johnson, R. (1976), 'Notes on the schooling of the English working class 1780–1850' in Dale *et al.* (eds), *Schooling and Capitalism*, London, Routledge & Kegan Paul.
Jones, G.S. (1971), *Outcast London*, Oxford University Press.
Jones, L.G.E. (1924), *The Training of Teachers in England and Wales: A Critical Survey*, Oxford University Press.
Kay-Shuttleworth, J. (1862), *Four Periods of Public Education*, London, Lowland Green (reprinted 1973, Brighton, Harvester Press).
Makins, V. (1974), 'Inner city training ground', *Times Educational Supplement*, 13 December 1974.
Marks, A.H. and Parfitt, C.A. (1974), 'Problems of the underprivileged', *London Educational Review*, vol. 3, no. 2, Summer 1974.
Midwinter, E. (1972), *Priority Education*, Harmondsworth, Penguin.
Ministry of Education (1963), *Half our Future* (The Newsom Report), London, HMSO.
Pahl, R.E. (1975), *Whose City?*, Harmondsworth, Penguin.
Raynor, J. (1978), *The Urban Studies Centre: An Experiment in Teacher Education 1973–78* (abridged by Jean Anderson), unpublished.
Raynor, J. (1981), *Teachers for the Inner City: the Work of the Urban Studies Centre*, London, Calouste Gulbenkian Foundation.
Rich, R.W. (1933), *The Training of Teachers in England and Wales during the Nineteenth Century*, Cambridge University Press.
Spencer, F.H. (1938), *An Inspector's Testament*, London, English Universities Press.
Sturt, M. (1967), *The Education of the People*, London, Routledge & Kegan Paul.

Taylor, W. (1969), *Society and the Education of Teachers*, London, Faber & Faber.
Tropp, A. (1957), *The School Teachers*, London, Heinemann.
Wilson, P.S. and Pring, R. (1975a), 'Introduction', *London Educational Review*, vol. 4, nos. 2/3, Autumn.
Wilson, P.S. and Pring, R. (1975b), 'In conclusion', *London Educational Review*, vol. 4, nos. 2/3, Autumn.

Index of names

Abel, E. K., 151, 157
Acorn, G., 153, 157
Addams, J., 143, 189n
Aitken, W. F., 146, 157
Alden, P., 149, 157
Alexander, S., 165, 167, 189
Alford, R. R., 137n
Anderson, J., 279, 288n, 289
Apple, M. W., 40, 46n, 51, 289
Aristotle, 118, 210
Arnold, M., 153
Ashbee, C. R., 151-2, 157
Ashcroft, B., 51n
Attlee, C. R., 152, 157
Augustine, St, 118
Aumeeruddy, A., 87n, 88
Ausubel, D. P., 13

Bachrach, P., 27, 51
Bailyn, B., 119, 135n
Ballard, P., 273, 287n, 289
Banks, J. A., 164, 166
Banks, O., 164, 166, 176, 185, 188n, 189
Bannister, H., 88n
Bantock, G. H., 40, 264n, 266
Baratz, M., 27, 51
Barnes, J., 3
Barnett, H. O., 144, 149, 150, 157
Barnett, S. A., 143-6, 148-9, 150, 154
Baron, S., 85, 86n, 88n
Barrett, M., 170, 189
Basini, A., 51
Bass, H. J., 115, 137n
Baylis, J., 82

Bazalgette, C., 286n, 289
Beale, D., 176
Beard, C., 116
Bell, D., 136n
Bennett, D., 88n
Bennett, N., 234, 266
Benton, T., 49n, 51
Berman, R., 135n
Bernstein, B., xi, xiii, 24, 28, 39, 40, 45-6n, 241, 248, 258, 266n
Besant, W., 146, 157
Beveridge, W. H., 152, 157
Bhaskar, B., 61
Bird, M., 208n
Bloch, E., 87n, 88
Bloch, M., 134
Booth, C., 142, 157
Booth, W., 142, 157
Bourdieu, P., 24, 28, 40, 46n, 52
Bowles, S., 28, 67, 73, 86n, 88n, 120, 241
Boyson, R., 50n, 264n
Braverman, H., 62, 89
Brezniak, M., 73, 89
Brickman, W. H., 135n
Brickman, W. W., 47n, 52
Bridge, R. G., 232n
Brinson, P., 30, 52
Broadhurst, H., 170
Brook, M., 52
Broughton, J., 82, 89
Buchan, M., 286n
Burgess, E., 6, 97, 111
Burnett, J., 164, 189
Buss, F., 175
Butler, J., 171, 173

Byrne, D., 23, 25, 31-2, 48n, 67, 88n, 100, 111

Callaghan, J., 234
Campbell, R., 38
Cartwright, W.H., 134n, 137n
Castells, M., x, 5, 6, 18, 22, 26, 33, 35, 38, 44n, 51n, 68, 73, 95, 98, 103, 105-9, 110n, 235, 286, 289n
Catalano, A., 70
Cately, R., 73, 89
Child, R., 70, 89
Cirincione-Coles, K., 88n, 89
Clifford, P., 51n
Clough, A., 176
Cockburn, C., 31, 38, 103, 111
Cohen, J., 86n, 87n, 89
Cohen, L., 287n
Cohen, R. D., 127, 136n, 137n
Cohen, S., 5, 21, 31, 134n
Coit, S., 143
Coleman, J. S., 217-18, 232n
Coleridge, D., 271-2, 285, 287n, 289
Coles, F., 277-83, 289
Collings, T. C., 155, 157
Collins, J., 73
Conant, J., 8-11, 52
Conzen, K. N., 138n
Cook, C. D., 279-82, 287n, 288n, 289
Coulter, A., 209n
Cox, C., 264n
Craft, M., 287n, 289
Cremin, L. A., 119, 124, 134n, 136n
Cronin, J. M., 86n, 137n
Crozier, M., 127, 137n
Cuban, L., 52
Cubberley, E. P., 118-19, 123-4, 134n
Cuff, D., 137n
Cutler, W. W., 136n

Dahl, R., 27, 52
Dale, R., 49n, 266n
Darwin, C., 96
David, M., 160, 174, 185, 189
Davidoff, L., 162, 164-5, 187n, 189
Davies, E., 175-7
Davin, A., 182, 184, 189

Davis, A. F., 143, 157
Davis, B., 123, 136n
Dear, M., 87n, 110n, 111
Delamont, S., 159, 160, 175, 177, 187n, 189
Deleon, D., 138n
Demos, J., 133
Denham, C., 231n
Dentler, R., 47n, 52
Deutsch, M., 13, 24, 44n
Dodson, D., 45n
Donajgrodzki, A. P., 140-1, 157
Donald, J., 87n, 88n, 89
Donzelot, J., 168-9, 187n, 188n, 189
Douglas, M., 162, 189
Duffin, L., 183, 189
Duncan, O., 6, 52
Dunleavy, P., 110n, 111
Durkheim, E., x, 33, 60, 95-6, 140
Dweck, C., 204, 208n
Dyhouse, C., 171-2, 176-7, 179, 181, 183-5, 190

Edmonds, R., 218-19, 232n
Ehrenreich, B., 188n, 190
Elliott, B., 110n, 111
Engels, F., 33, 53
English, D., 188n
Evans, M., 27
Evans, R. A., 143, 157

Fantini, M., 24, 53
Fay, B., 44-5n, 48n, 50n, 288, 289
Feinberg, W., 87n, 89
Field, F., 23, 30, 86-8n, 286n
Fiennes, G., 151, 157
Fine, B., 87n, 89
Finn, D., 249
Fletcher, B., 100
Folin, M., 68, 89
Fraser, D., 31
Fraser, S. E., 138n
Freeland, J., 66, 82-3, 87n, 88n, 89
Freire, P., 40, 50n, 53
Friedman, N., 24
Frith, S., 78, 83, 88n, 237, 267
Froebel, F., 118
Fuchs, E., 14, 53

Galambos, L., 137n
Gamble, A., 73, 90

294 / Index

Gans, H. J., 23
Gell, P. L., 146-7, 157
Geoffrey, W., 14
George, H., 147
Giddens, A., 48n, 53
Gintis, H., 28, 67, 73, 86n, 88n, 120, 241
Gittell, M., 15, 86n, 90
Glass, R., 23
Glyn, A., 73, 90
Godwin, G., 287n, 289
Golby, M., 53
Goldberg, M., 13, 45n
Goodenow, R., 21, 138n
Goodman, P., 120
Gordon, L., 70, 185, 190
Gorst, J., 147, 157
Gough, I., 86n, 90
Gouldner, A. W., 286, 289
Grace, G., 47n, 87n, 179, 180, 195, 241, 270, 273, 286, 289n
Graham, P., 136n
Gramsci, A., 28, 40
Grant, N., 249
Gray, F., 31, 100, 111
Green, A., 42, 253, 257, 264, 265n
Green, R. L., 47n
Green, T. H., 143
Greven, P., 133
Griffiths, D., 177, 190
Grinling, C. H., 154
Gumpert, E. B., 135n, 136n

Habermas, J., 103, 111
Hall, C., 161, 168, 190
Hall, S., 24, 28, 37, 47n, 67, 87n, 88n, 235, 286, 289n
Halsey, A. H., 25, 32, 50n, 53, 279, 287n, 288n, 290n
Hamnett, C., 28, 53
Hanson, R. A., 231n
Harden, J., 23, 87n
Hargreaves, A., 86n, 90, 263, 267
Hargreaves, D., 202, 259, 267
Harloe, M., 26, 87n, 103, 110n, 111
Harris, E., 23, 26-7, 47n
Harris, L., 87n
Harris, N., 136n
Harrison, J., 73
Haubrich, V., 45n
Hauser, P. M., 127

Harvey, D., x, 22, 26, 28-9, 30, 33, 38, 41, 69, 70, 95, 98, 101, 103-5, 110
Havighurst, R., 4, 5, 10, 11, 18, 44n, 54
Hawley, A., 6, 54
Heath, A., 51n, 54
Herbert, D., 23, 30, 111
Hess, R., 13
Hevesi, A.. 15, 86n
Higham, J., 120
Hill, O., 171
Hill, R. C., 50n, 110n
Hirst, P. 188n, 190
Hofstadter, R., 138n
Hollis, P., 166, 168-9, 170-2, 174, 180
Holloway, J., 60, 90
Holly, D., 50n, 260-1, 267
Holt, J., 120
Howdle, L., 240, 265n, 267
Hummel, R., 86n, 90

Illich, I., 120
Issel, W. H., 136n

Jackson, C., 152, 155, 157
Jackson, K., 51n
Janowitz, M., 123, 136n
Jenkin, P., 187
Jessop, R., 38, 88n, 90
Johnson, H. C. Jr, 134
Johnson, R., 23, 30, 36, 49n, 141, 237, 249, 269, 276
Johnston, K., 87n, 88n, 90
Jones, D., 51n
Jones, G. S., 140, 142, 161-2, 168, 171, 173, 182, 275-6, 287n
Jones, L. G. E., 287n
Judd, C. M., 232n

Kaestle, C. F., 19, 21, 128-9, 130, 136n, 137n
Kalko, G., 120
Kammen, M., 138n
Karier, C., 120, 135n, 254, 267
Karnes, M., 24
Katz, M. B., 21, 36, 46n, 120-4, 131, 134, 135n, 136n
Katzman, M., 16, 55
Kay-Shuttleworth, J., xi, 270, 272-3, 275, 281, 285, 287n
Keddie, N., 24, 266n, 267

King, B., 152
King, R., 248, 265n, 267
Kogan, M., 30
Kohl, H., 14
Kopan, A., 44n
Kornberg, L., 45n
Kozol, J., 14, 55, 120
Kraditor, A. S., 138n
Kysel, F., 208n

Lacey, C., 257, 267
Ladurie, E. Le Roy, 133
Lampard, E., 116, 134n
Land, H., 188n, 190
Lang, C. G., 148
Lansbury, G., 153-4, 158
Laqueur, T., 36, 55
Larrain, J., 68, 91
Lawson, J., 177, 180, 190
Lawton, D., 40, 55
Lazerson, M., 19, 21, 136n
Leacock, E., 14, 55
Lebas, E., 87n, 110n
Lee, J., 234, 241, 252, 257, 259, 264n, 265n, 267
Lee, R., 64, 84, 91
Lehrer, S., 47n
L'Esperance, J., 162
Levin, H., 16, 55
Lieberman, A., 232n
Litt, E., 88n, 91
Locke, J., 118
Lockridge, K., 133
Lukes, S., 27, 55
Luxemburg, R., 88n
Lynch, G., 236, 267

McCann, P., 140, 158
Macchiarola, F., 212, 215
McCrone, D., 110n
MacDonald, M., 49n, 55
McFarlane, B., 73
McIntosh, M., 170
McKenzie, R., 6
Macpherson, C. B., 70
McWilliams-Tullberg, R., 176-8, 190
Makins, V., 281, 288n
Malpass, O., 171, 190
Mandel, E., 71-2, 86n, 87n
Mann, D., 231, 232
Mann, T., 154-5
March, J. C., 233n
March, J. G., 233n

Marginson, S., 81, 88n
Marks, A. H., 288n, 290
Marks, P., 159, 190
Marland, M., 23, 30, 31, 48n, 86n, 87n, 88n
Marsden, W. E., 31
Martini, R., 208n
Marx, K., 33. 68, 86n, 87n, 99
Massey, D., 70, 91
Mayo, M., 51n
Mearns, A., 143
Medley, D. M., 232n
Mellor, R., 44n, 94-6, 98, 111
Merson, M., 38, 55
Midwinter, E., 279, 287n, 288n, 290
Miliband, R., 38, 55
Mill, J. S., 188n, 190
Miller, H., 10, 21, 44, 46n, 86n
Mills, C. W., 8, 9, 12, 17, 20, 41, 43, 56
Mohl, R. A., 134n, 137n
Moock, P. R., 232n
Moore, G., 14, 56
Moore, R., 24, 49n, 101, 110n
Morant, R., 152
Morrell, F., 189n
Morris, W., 151
Mortimore, P., 208n
Morton, D. C., 24
Morton, L., 132, 138n
Mouffe, C., 49n, 56
Mullard, C., 42, 56
Mullins, P., 70, 91
Musgrave, P., 66, 91

Nagle, J., 86n
Nairn, T., 73, 91
Nash, V., 152
Nelkin, D., 82, 88n, 91
Newby, H., 162
Newitt, J., 88n, 91
Newsam, P., 198
Nunn, T. H., 146

Oakley, A., 167, 190
Okey, T., 152-3, 158
O'Neill, J., 135n
Overbeck, H., 73
Ozolins, U., 88

Pahl, R., 3, 7, 23, 25-6, 32-4, 38, 94, 98-102, 109, 110n, 111, 286, 289n

Parfitt, C. A., 288n
Park, R., 6, 96-7, 112
Parkinson, M., 88n
Parsons, T., 27, 140
Passow, A. H., 4, 11-13, 45, 47, 56, 64, 91
Perry, D., 70, 91
Pestalozzi, J. H., 118
Peterson, A. D. C., 188n, 190
Peterson, P., 16
Picciotto, S., 60
Picht, W., 143, 148, 155, 158
Pickvance, C., 6, 26, 44n, 87n, 103, 108, 112
Pierce, C., 121
Pimlott, J. A. R., 143, 158
Pinch, S., 100, 112
Plato, 118
Poole, R., 87n, 92
Poulantzas, N., 27, 38, 57
Powers, T., 135n
Pring, R., 283-4
Pusey, M., 66, 88n

Raggatt, P., 27, 57
Ravitch, D., 16, 17, 21, 22, 36, 46n, 47n, 87n, 126, 136n, 137n, 138n
Rawls, J., 29, 104, 112
Raynor, J., 3, 23, 26-7, 47n, 57, 87n, 278-9, 287n, 288n, 290
Reeder, D., 23, 31-2, 57
Rex, J., 23-4, 49n, 94, 101, 110n, 112
Rich, R. W., 270, 287n, 290
Riessman, F., 13, 24, 57
Riles, W., 5, 58
Rist, R., 14, 46n, 58
Robinson, P., 87n, 92
Rogers, F., 153, 158
Rogers, R., 82, 92
Rose, N., 162, 190
Rosemont, H., 87n
Roszak, T., 120
Rousseau, J. J., 118
Rovere, R., 120
Rubinstein, D., 188n, 190
Ruskin, J., 151, 163, 190
Rutter, M., 30, 42, 58

Salter, B., 88n, 92
Saraga, E., 177

Sarup, M., 88n, 92
Saunders, P., 38, 44n, 48n, 49n, 68, 95, 102, 110n, 112
Sawers, L., 50n, 103, 110n, 112
Sawyer, M., 87n, 92
Schlesinger, A. M., 116, 134n
Schnor, L. F., 137n
Schultz, S. K., 21, 124, 128, 130-1, 137n
Schutz, R. E., 231n
Scott, A., 87n, 110n
Scott, D. M., 136n
Searle, C., 50
Selleck, R. J. W., 239, 240-1, 265n, 268
Sennet, R., 134n, 160, 163, 190
Shapiro, H. S., 86n, 92
Sharp, R., 40, 42, 83, 86n, 87n, 88n, 92, 253, 257, 264, 265n
Shipman, V. C., 13
Silberman, C., 44n
Silver, H., 49n, 139, 159, 177, 180, 237, 239
Simmel, G., 97, 112
Simon, B., 36, 178, 237
Simon, J., 82, 92
Sims, G., 142, 158
Smith, H. L., 152
Smith, L., 14, 58
Sohn-Rethel, A., 62, 92
Spencer, F. H., 273, 287n, 290
Spender, D., 175, 178, 188n, 191
Spring, J. H., 120, 135n
Stafford, A., 88n, 92
Stead, W., 143
Stewart, J., 100
Stone, L., 138n
Stone, M., 42, 58
Street-Porter, R., 28, 58
Strom, R. D., 14, 58
Stubbs, W., 198, 200
Sturt, M., 271, 287n, 290
Summers, A., 168-9, 191
Susman, I., 138n

Tabb, W., 50n, 103, 110n, 112
Tapper, T., 88n
Tawney, R. H., 152
Taylor, H., 188n
Taylor, W., 272, 274, 290
Thernstrom, S., 117, 132-3, 134n
Tierney, J., 51
Tillett, B., 154-5, 158

Tingle, R., 278
Tizard, B., 51n, 58
Tomlinson, S., 49n, 101
Toynbee, A., 143, 147, 155
Troen, S., 128, 131, 137n, 138n
Tropp, A., 272, 291
Tunley, P., 100, 112
Turner, F. J., 115
Tyack, D. B., 21, 46n, 47n, 120, 125-8, 135n, 137n
Tyler, W., 87n

Unger, I., 138n

Violas, P., 120, 135n
Vogel, M., 83, 88n, 92

Wade, R. C., 115, 133, 138n
Walberg, H., 44n, 86n, 92
Walkowitz, J., 162, 173, 176, 188n, 191
Wallace, J. B., 120, 136n
Walvin, J., 161, 191
Warren, D. R., 138n
Watkins, A. J., 70
Watson, D. R., 24
Watson, R. L. Jr, 134n, 137n
Wayland, S., 45n
Webb, B., 147, 154, 169
Weber, M., x, 33, 60, 94, 99, 109, 248, 268
Webster, B., 100, 112
Webster, M., 242
Weeks, J., 70, 170, 191
Weinstein, G., 24
Weinstein, J., 120
Weisskopf, T., 73, 86n, 87n

Wexler, P., 88n, 92
Whitbread, N., 240, 265n, 268
White, J., 50n, 66
Whitty, G., 51n, 82, 93
Widdowson, F., 180, 188n, 191
Widlake, P., 30
Wiebe, R., 137n
Williams, B., 87n
Williams, R., 28, 49n, 59, 162
Williamson, W., 23, 25, 31-2, 48n, 67, 88n, 100, 112
Willie, C. V., 46n, 47n, 59
Willis, P., 42, 59
Wilson, E., 171, 191
Wilson, H., 70, 93
Wilson, P. S., 283-4, 291
Winnington-Ingram, A. F., 144-5, 149, 158
Wirth, L., 6, 23, 97, 105, 112
Wise, A. E., 232n
Wohl, A. S., 143, 158
Wolfe, A., 87n, 93
Woock, R., 10, 21, 44, 46n, 86n
Wood, N., 188n, 191
Woods, R. A., 143, 155, 158
Woody, T., 119, 135n
Worby, H., 208n
Wright, E. O., 93
Wright, N., 71, 87n
Wrigley, J., 128, 131, 137n, 138n

Yarmolinsky, A., 16
Young, M. F. D., 8, 24, 40, 46n, 51n, 59

Zahaykevich, 82

Index of subjects

abstracted empiricism, 17, 20, 41
access courses, 201
accountability, 81, 207, 229
administrators, 45n, 223
affirmative action, 65, 83
Afro-Caribbean Resource Group, 206
alienation, 35, 41, 97
American hegemony, 61, 72
anti-racism, 205
anti-sexist initiatives, 204, 209
assessment, 203, 228-9
attempted cultural imposition, 156
Australia: economy, 73, 89; funding of education, 83; positive discrimination in education, 66; private schooling, 81

Battersea Normal School, 270
Black Power, in education, 126
blacks, 15, 66, 84, 138, 210-11, 244, 249-252
Black Studies, 24
Boston, public schools, 130
Bradford College, 47
bridging courses, 201
Britain: economic position, 73; international position, 183
British race, 182
bureaucracy, 16, 21, 34, 36, 98-100, 102, 121-2, 127, 129

Cambridge, 144, 152
Cambridgeshire Village Colleges, 278

capital accumulation, 60-1, 70, 73, 89
capitalism, 19, 33, 38, 60-1, 67, 76, 87, 104-5
capital restructuring, 71-4
catchment areas, 69, 242
Catholic power, 126
charity, 168-9
Chicago, public schools, 10, 131-2
Chicago School, 6-7, 18, 19, 23, 33, 44n, 95-101, 105-6
'child centredness', 256
childhood, 250
childhood innocence, 251
cities: as arenas, 3, 34; and capital accumulation, 68, 70-1; cultural problem of, 19; economic regeneration, 17; educational ecology of, 31; fiscal crisis, 50n, 107; growth of, 161; metropolitan, 3, 6; political and economic crisis of, 38; political power of, 16-17; and poverty, 64; socialist, 38
city: and conflict, 99; and degeneration, 182; history of, 116; middle class exodus from, 16; moral order of, 97, 149; as moral problem, 143, 162; sociology of, 97
Civil Rights Movement, 15, 64
class, 20-1, 24, 74, 140, 144, 147, 243-9
class-cultural transformation, 36
class differences: in learning, 202-4

class guilt, 147-8
classification and framing, 28
classism, 206
class relations, 35, 37, 62, 139, 144-5, 156
classroom: constraints of, 42; research, 236; observation, 254-6
class struggle, 62, 89, 99, 235
collective consumption, 22, 99, 107
community, 6, 16, 18, 97, 252, 263
community control, 15, 125
Community Development Projects, 66
community education, 24, 41, 278-80
community history, 133
comparative method, 60, 86n
comparative studies, 38, 101, 109
compensatory education, 13, 15, 19, 24, 30, 45n, 65
conflicts, 103
contextual rhetoric, 12, 25, 33
contradictions: of capitalism, x, 33, 35, 40, 70, 103, 107, 235; in schooling, 78-9, 237-8, 242, 260-4
counter-work culture, 79
crisis in capitalism, 71-4, 84-5
critical consciousness, 40, 259
'critical discontent', 279
critical revisionists, 120
critical scholarship, xii, 18, 32, 43, 48n
critical social science, 50n
cultural capital, 28
cultural deprivation, 13, 19, 24, 65
cultural reproduction, 19, 24, 39
cultural theory, 28
cultural transmission, 19, 28, 39
culture, 19, 145-6
culture industry, 63
culture problematic, 13
curriculum, 14, 28, 39-40, 50n, 82, 160, 176, 179

Dalton Plan, 240
deficit theory, 39
desegregation, 15, 70
disadvantage, 13, 34
disadvantaged child, 45n, 196
disadvantaged schools programme, 66, 83

discipline: in schools, 81, 83, 129, 261; of workforce, 77
distribution problematic, 25, 29
distributive justice, 65
division of labour, 69
domestic: as site of labour, 164-8; as symbol, 160-4
domestication, 40
domestic economy, 179
domesticity, 179
domestic service, 164-6
domestic-urban dualism, 180

economic decline, 26, 76
economic expansion, 63
economism, 60
Edgehill College, 47
education: autonomy of, 262; compulsory, 169-70, 178; elementary, 237; and inner city, 30-1; and politics, 37; and urban politics, 31
educational achievements: of inner London pupils, 197-200, 208; of New York City pupils, 211-13
educational expansion, 63
educational opportunity, 9, 11, 31, 38, 64, 66, 79, 195, 218
educational policy: in inner London, 200-8; in New York City, 215-31
educational priority area, 25, 30, 65, 234, 278
educational priority indices, 201
educational progressivism, 124, 239-41
educational research, 83
educational vouchers, 81, 231
Equal Opportunities Unit, 204, 206
ethnography, of inner city schools, 13-14, 42
eugenicism, 182-3, 184-5
Evangelicals, 168
examinations, 203, 211-12
'exceptional state', 84
exchange values, 72

family: and blacks, 46n; decline of, 76; as symbol, 163
family discourse, 187
fascism, 61, 85, 87n
femininity, 177
feminism, 161, 176, 182, 185
feminists, 173

functionalism, 61
gender differences, in learning, 204-5
ghetto formation, 105
girls: education of, 159-60, 174-8; education of middle class, 184-5; education of working class, 178-81
Girls Public Day School Trust, 184
Goldsmiths' College, 47
Gulbenkian Foundation, 30, 48n

Hackney Radical Club, 151
Head Start, 65
hegemonic consensus, 65
hegemony, 28, 35-6, 49n, 61, 69, 141
history: 'hidden', 236; of urban education, 120-37; and urban schooling, 21-2, 31; and urban studies, 139
history of education, in USA, 115, 117-19, 124, 132

IBM, 30, 48n
idealism, 128, 145, 148
ideological conflict, 40, 42
ideological themes, 80-1
ideology, 18, 35, 37, 69, 106, 122, 144, 258-9, 264
indices of deprivation, 196-7
individualism, 152, 251-2, 262-3
infant schooling, contradictions in, 242
infant schools: history of, 238-9; inner city, 234; and progressive pedagogy, 238-42
inner city: crisis, 276, 285; problems, 30-1; sociology of, 24
Inner London Education Authority, 195-209
interest groups, 15, 34
internationalization, of capital, 69
invisible pedagogy, 258

Jews, 138
justice, see social justice and distributive justice

Karmel Report, 66, 92
Keynesianism, 62-3, 72
King's College, London, 47n

Labour Party: in Australia, 66; in Britain, 150

Labour Representation Committee, 153
labour reserve army, 74
liberal formulations, of distributive justice, 29, 104
liberalism, 73, 101, 122
local state, 38, 102
London: East, 144, 146, 150-2; 'outcast', 142-3; and urban problem, 161 (see also Inner London Education Authority)
London Institute of Education, 47
'London Portfolio', 203
London School Board, 179
Long Boom, 63, 67

Manpower Services Commission, 83
Mansfield House, 149
Marxism, and the urban, 26, 29, 33, 35, 87, 102-9
metropolitanism, 10-11, 18
middle class, 16, 35, 62, 121, 147-8, 156
minority groups, 12-13
monetarism, 81, 86n
'moral density', 95
moral mission, 19, 35
motherhood, ideology of, 181-7
mother tongue teaching, 52, 205
multicultural education, 26, 41, 66, 84, 209
multi-ethnic education, 205, 209

National Advisory Committee on Civil Disorders, 5
nationalism, 77
natural areas, 6, 97
neo-Conservatism, 75, 218
neo-Liberalism, 75
neo-Weberian: approaches to the urban, 25-6, 33, 49n, 99-102
Newcastle Commission, 180
New Right, 75-7, 80, 83, 85
Newsom Report, 274, 276-7
New South Wales, 83
New York: politics of schooling, 126; public schools, 129-30, 210-31
non-decision making, 28

Open University, 23, 25, 29-30, 47n
oppositional inquiry, 42

'organisational factor', 128
Oxford, 148, 151-2, 154
Oxford House, 142, 144

parental conflict, 252-4
parental involvement, 201
parents, 81, 206, 243-7
Paris, 6
patriarchal authority, 170
pauperism, 162, 275
Peace Studies, 82, 92
pedagogy, 39-40
petite bourgeoisie, 77
philanthropy, 35, 168-74
Plowden Report, 65, 234, 239, 274, 276-7
pluralism, 27, 36
policy science, 7-8, 32, 34, 43, 45n
political consciousness, 50n, 262
political economy, of urban question, 38, 102-9
politics, 15-16, 22, 25, 27-8, 32, 107-8, 243-9
Polytechnic of North London, 288
positive discrimination, 66, 201
poverty, 12, 64, 169
power, 13, 17, 20, 22, 27, 37, 38, 98, 140, 156, 235
powerlessness, 13, 38, 41, 71, 76
power relations, 108
privatization, 81, 87n
problem families, 246
professionalism, 249, 253, 289
profit, rate of, 69, 72, 104
progressive pedagogy, 238-41, 254-8, 261
progressivism, 122
promotional gates, 215-17
pupils: 'good', 42; urban, 84; working class, 204
pupil profiles, 203

'quality control', 83
Queensland, 82

race: and the city, 22, 24, 70, 101, 249; and education, 26, 28, 249-52
race relations, in Britain, 26, 34, 49n
racism, 11, 15, 21, 26, 41, 71, 101, 127, 206, 250, 266

Radical Education Dossier, 88
redistributive theory, 29
reformism, 62, 66
religion, 35, 145
resistance, 35, 50n, 108
resources, 34, 37, 65, 99, 102, 105
revolutionary theory, 29, 105
riots, 64, 84, 187, 249
rural: as symbol, 162-3

St Louis, school system, 131
St Mark's College, 271, 287
School Improvement Project, 217-21
schooling: bourgeois, 80; mass, 237-8; restructuring of, 78-9; social relations of, 39
school management, 222-30
schools: central city, 10; community, 202; community control, 15-16, 125; desegregation, 15; disadvantaged, 83; 'good', 42; inner city, 13-14, 39; levels of expenditure, 10, 16-17, 65, 83, 213-14; and politics, 125; suburban, 10; urban working class, 39, 42
school site budgeting, 225-30
'servant problem', 165
sexism, 41, 206
slums, 9, 12, 275
'social bridges', 275
social control, 21, 36, 39, 49n, 121-3, 140-1, 156, 236
social democracy, 85, 88
social democratic settlement, 66-7
social engineering, 68
social harmony, 147
Socialism, 62, 88n, 152
Socialist formulations, of distributive justice, 29
Socialist societies, 100
social justice, 28-9, 38, 64, 104
social mobility, 63, 121
social reform, 122
social wage, 72, 74, 78
sociology of education, xii, 26, 60, 65, 91, 236
sociology of knowledge, 8, 24
sociology of race relations, 101
socio-spatial systems, 25, 34, 99
space, social structuring of, 106-7
spatial analysis, 30
special needs, 206

state, 38, 62, 68, 75-6, 89
state apparatus, 73
state expenditure, 74
state intervention, 62, 68, 108
state socialism, 102
suburbanization, 70
surplus value, 72, 74, 78
symbolic violence, 28

teachers: elementary, 179-81; ideology, 240-1; professional autonomy, 82; professional status, 248-9; progressive, 248, 254-7; traditional, 242, 245-6, 261; in urban schools, 14, 39, 42, 45-6n; views on class and politics, 243-9
Teachers College, 11
teacher training, 258, 266, 272-4, 289
teaching, and women, 178
technology, 62, 72, 78
tertiary education boards, 201
theoretical distancing, 27-8
theory/practice relationship, 283-4
Third World, 77
'town swamps', 275
Toynbee Hall, 142-56
Toxteth, 262, 265
Trent Polytechnic, 47
Tyndale School, 234

unemployment, 26, 74, 79, 89, 201, 246
unions, 62, 71, 75, 77, 154-5, 204, 228
United Federation of Teachers, 223-4
university settlements, 139, 143-4
urban: as symbol, 160-4; theorisation of, 18, 68, 94, 106
urban blacks: cultural deficiencies, 13-14, 19; unemployment of, 9, 11
urban bureaucrats, 25, 99
urban conflicts, 18, 33, 34, 94, 99
urban contradictions, 18, 33, 95, 235, 243
urban crisis, 6, 30, 64, 115, 120, 127, 235
urban education: cultural and pedagogic theory, 39-40; culturalist perspectives, 18-20, 28; empirical exploration, 41-2; as field of inquiry, 34-5; and history, 21-2, 31; mode of inquiry, 20-1; political and economic issues, 37-8, 71; politics of, 15-17, 126; present crisis perspective, 22-4; and race, 22, 24, 46n; 'real issues', 109-10; studies in Britain, 23-32; studies in USA, 5-23, 64; theoretical limitations, 18, 27-9, 68; and urban theory, 33-5; work conferences, 11-12
urban educationists: founding fathers, 9-11; professional ideology of, 8-9
Urban Education Task Force, 5
'urban gentry', 171, 276
urban history, 116-17
urban intervention programmes, 104
urbanism, 6-7, 18, 19, 28, 44n, 97, 105
urban land use, 69
urban politics, 27, 108
urban problems, 18, 33, 94
urban programme, 66
urban question, 26, 38, 102, 109
urban schooling, 21, 34-6, 126, 128
urban social movements, 41, 64, 108
urban sociology, 6-7, 94-102, 106
urban studies, 5-6, 8
Urban Studies Centre, 277-86
urban systems, 7-8
urban theory, 33, 94-5, 106
urban working class, 31, 35, 39, 84, 140-1, 156, 236, 269
USA: economic crisis in, 72-3; history of urban education, 115-37; urban social movements in, 64

vocational education, 82

Welfare State, 152, 246
women: and paid labour, 167; and philanthropy, 168-74; and urbanisation, 159-60
women's rights, 84
Woolwich, 154
working class, 35-6, 62, 65, 74, 77, 121, 146, 152, 170, 206, 236, 245
working class culture, 149